THE LETTERS OF
KING GEORGE III

UNIFORM WITH THIS VOLUME

THE LETTERS OF KING HENRY VIII
edited by M. St. Clare Byrne

THE LETTERS OF QUEEN ELIZABETH I
edited by G. B. Harrison

THE LETTERS OF KING CHARLES I
edited by Sir Charles Petrie

THE LETTERS OF KING CHARLES II
edited by Sir Arthur Bryant

THE LETTERS OF QUEEN ANNE
edited by Beatrice Curtis Brown

King George III
By Gainsborough

*(Reproduced by gracious permission of
Her Majesty The Queen)*

THE
LETTERS
OF
KING
GEORGE III

Edited by

BONAMY DOBRÉE
O.B.E., M.A., F.R.Hist.S.

FUNK & WAGNALLS
NEW YORK

First published 1935
This edition © Bonamy Dobrée 1968
This edition first published 1968

Library of Congress Catalog Card Number : 68-25024
Published by Funk & Wagnalls, A Division of Reader's Digest Books, Inc.,
by arrangement with Cassell & Co. Ltd.
Printed in Great Britain.

CONTENTS

	PAGE
INTRODUCTION	ix
CHRONOLOGICAL TABLE	xv

CHAPTER

I. PRINCE AND PRINCE OF WALES	1
II. CHAOS (1760-1770)	17
III. LORD NORTH (1770-1773)	63
IV. AMERICA (1774-1781)	97
V. THE GREAT CRISIS (1782-1783)	145
VI. CALMER YEARS (1784-1790)	189
VII. THE FRENCH REVOLUTION (1791-1801)	209
VIII. LAST YEARS	249

APPENDIX

I. AUTHORITIES	275
II. GENEALOGICAL TABLE	285
INDEX	287

INTRODUCTION TO THE FIRST EDITION

GEORGE III was an unwearied and voluminous letter-writer. As can be seen from the times at which he dated his letters, he was at it from morning till night, except for the needful hours of relaxation and exercise, for he was his own private secretary. Indeed he wrote more often and far more fully than he need have done, always regardless of punctuation, sometimes heedless of grammar, and usually he wrote each letter twice, in draft and in fair copy. Besides this, he was for ever making copious memoranda, of considerations of peace or war, of the state of the armed forces, or of the distribution of bishoprics, or of the political situation. There are no less than three drafts of his negotiations with Chatham. His particular form of insanity is often associated with great oratorical power (as it was, it may be, in the case of the elder Pitt), and it is possible, that since oratory was denied the King, he found satisfaction in eternal scribbling. Thus what is presented here is only a dip of the bucket in the oceanic correspondence of the most prolific of royal letter-writers. I have had to omit altogether several matters upon which he wrote: on important subjects I have made a rigorous selection, trying to illustrate as many events as possible, whenever convenient by two or three letters, sometimes by only one. Many of the letters he wrote are, naturally, routine letters, such as any civil servant might have written, but I have tried to select those most characteristic of his nature. Even if he often wrote ungrammatically, there is never any doubt as to his meaning, which is vigorously expressed, and you can feel a definite personality behind the writer.

The reign of King George III offers no single curve; a view of it in letters, apart from inevitable gaps, is bound to present a somewhat choppy aspect. Great events occurred in it: the loss of the American Colonies, the great French Wars, the Union with Ireland; smaller events of interest are not lacking, such as the Wilkes affairs, the Gordon Riots, the naval mutinies of 1797; but there is no main structure to the story. Yet during the long reign a profound change came over England: George III began his life in the period of Walpole; he ended it in that of Wellington; when he came to the throne, England was still a wheat-exporting country; long before he died it had become the leading industrial country in the world, depending largely on imported supplies. To give an historical view of such a time in a selection of letters, by their nature already specialized, would be impossible. Rather than attempt the unfeasible, I have preferred to choose the letters which present the King himself, to offer, shall I say, materials for a biography rather than for a history, though even for this much is lacking. It has not been possible to give a picture of the dull, respectable Court which broke Fanny Burney's spirit, nor to give more than a glimpse of 'Farmer George', nor of the irate, disappointed father : but still, since the King was first and foremost a public servant, these letters, with the inclusion of a few irrelevant to politics, do not perhaps yield an untrue portrait of the man.

It would be an admirable thing if, in considering the first years of the reign, indeed until the second phase of the younger Pitt's period of power, one could rid one's self of the notions of Whig and Tory which have so deeply coloured most accounts of the reign of King George III. At his accession the terms had become practically meaningless, though they were to recur later with some definite sense attachable to them. The country gentlemen were always there, and the collapse of Jacobitism had healed the rift between the extremists and the 'Hanoverian' Tories; but what was of more importance at the moment was the King's declaration that he gloried in the name of Britain, which showed that he was going to govern in the interests of Great Britain, and let Hanover sink into the second place. This fact may account for his curious indifference towards the elaborate game of foreign politics, in which he showed such a marked contrast with his two predecessors, who, especially George I, were Electors of Hanover first, Kings of England second, and therefore sensitive to every ruffling of Continental politics. All that George III cared about was that England should keep out of foreign entanglements as far as possible, and here indeed it may be said that both he and his earlier governments had a Tory background. Yet, as will be seen, he theoretically accepted the 'old system' of the Whigs, and at the end of his reign it was the Whigs who wished to make peace with France, and the Tories who were for war to the bitter end. From other than political motives, too, the King was determined to keep out of war to the utmost extent that the national honour permitted, until the French Revolution aroused his monarchical fears.

His prime task, as he conceived it, was to bring good administration to England : it was his great love of administration which made him above all things a party leader. The stage was ready set for such a king, since, in truth, the two parties were not Whig and Tory, but Court and Not-Court. There was no formed opposition (for which most of the statesmen professed a nervous abhorrence), only people whose sole way of getting a coveted place was to turn somebody else out. When he came to the throne the places were mainly in possession of the old gang, the Newcastle or Pelham connection, with Hardwicke and others of his age, while those hoping to take their places were equally advanced in years, except for the smaller fry. To the young King it seemed that the realm was torn between various Whig factions, the Pelhamites, the Rockinghams, 'the Bloomsbury Gang' under the Duke of Bedford, 'the Family' of Temple, Grenville, and Pitt. He saw the country being governed, or misgoverned as he thought, by groups of rivals who all belonged to the same clans of plutocratic 'oligarchs'. In his view, perfectly constitutional at the time, his business was to be the head of an administration which should govern for the good of all, and consist of the best brains (and hearts) selected regardless of connection, chosen by himself. He was out, not to 'dish the Whigs', but to fight the vested interests. It cannot really be said that he tried to oust progressive Whiggery in favour of reactionary Toryism. He could not have done so, since there was no clear distinction. Look even at the so-called Tory administration of North. North himself had served his apprenticeship as a Pelhamite : but for Yorke's death he would have had a Lord Chancellor drawn from the Rockingham group; his Secretaries of State remained the same as under Grafton, and Grafton himself became Privy Seal : Chatham's son had a minor Court appointment; two powerful members of the Bloomsbury

Gang, Gower and Sandwich, had important posts; in fact it was these last who wrecked the most liberal measure brought forward during North's tenure of office, Chatham's attempt at American conciliation. When a government fell, the King could not call in the opposition as we understand it, because this was invariably composed of groups torn by internecine strife. When Suffolk brought in the old Grenville party to join North, there was hardly any communication left between the two wings of the remaining anti-governmental block, the Chatham group and the Rockinghams.[1] What the King was fighting for was his right to choose his own ministers, provided they were agreeable to the people. He succeeded finally, when in 1783 he defeated the coalition, and brought in Pitt amid popular applause in spite of his being in a minority in the House. After the general election of the next year had confirmed his choice, he largely ceased to be the party leader that circumstances had forced him to be, and paid less attention to politics. The drama of the reign ends in 1784.

That he was himself innately and unalterably conservative there can be no doubt: he was rarely on the ' popular ' side; but he was not a die-hard, except on the question of Catholic emancipation. He was deeply patriotic, imperialistic even, but he was no chauvinist: he was an admirable, devoted, indefatigable civil servant, who expected the holder of any post to do the work demanded of him: he was at once too single-hearted and too simple-minded for the complicated world of politics. He was, it is true, apt to be stubborn from a mistaken sense of ' firmness '; he was in many ways narrow-minded, in some respects stupid, and, of course, he went mad, so it is easy to make him a ridiculous figure. But he was far from being that, and his unlucky aspects are for the most part due to an exaggeration of very real and serviceable qualities. He was a far better king than most have been willing to concede; he had determination and vigour, there was nothing ignoble about his ideals, and one cannot emerge from a study of his letters without feeling for him a considerable degree of sympathy, and perhaps even affection.

I have as far as possible placed the letters in the order which

---

[1] Again, towards the end of the reign, what was it that converted the ' old Whigs ', when they joined Pitt, into Tories?

makes a continuous narrative; so as not to interrupt this I have added at the end of most chapters a few letters which have no connection with politics, or where the political issue has no bearing on the main trend of events. I have tampered freely with the punctuation in the interests of ease of reading; I have modernized the spelling, only here and there retaining a form which reveals some idiosyncrasy of thought or pronunciation, and have usually supplied names in place of dashes. I have included hardly any documents which were not letters, since, the King's habits being what they were, the letters themselves provide all the necessary material.

A considerable number of the letters in this selection have never been printed before (namely most of those from British Museum manuscripts, and some of those from the Chatham Papers) and the great majority of these are in the King's own hand. I have refrained as far as possible from burdening the text with notes; subsidiary information can be found in the index. The most important sources which I have tapped for unpublished letters (and of which I have only included a fraction) are P.R.O., Chatham Papers, C. III, C. IV; Add. MSS. 37833-37835, letters to John Robinson; Add. MSS. 38564, letters to Charles Jenkinson, 1st Earl of Liverpool; Add. MSS. 38190, letters to the 2nd Earl of Liverpool; Add. MSS. 40100, letters to Henry Dundas, Lord Melville. These contain a large number of letters on India, a subject I have hardly been able to touch.

I have to state the profound obligation I feel towards His Majesty the King for his gracious permission to print these letters. I would like to express my sincere gratitude to Sir Richard Lodge, who was kind enough to read through my manuscript, to advise me on some points and correct me on others, and to whose patience I am in many ways greatly indebted. I also have pleasure in thanking Professor L. B. Namier and Messrs. Macmillan for permission to include the letters to Bute which were printed in Professor Namier's *England in the Age of the American Revolution*.

CHRONOLOGICAL TABLE

1738. Birth of George III.
1751. Death of Frederick, Prince of Wales.
1756. Beginning of Seven Years War.
1760. Accession of George III.
1761. Bute becomes Secretary of State.
Pitt resigns.
Marriage of the King.
Bute becomes First Lord of the Treasury.
1762. Birth of the Prince of Wales, afterwards George IV.
1763. Peace of Paris.
Bute resigns.
No. 45 of the *North Briton*.
Grenville becomes First Lord of the Treasury.
1765. The Stamp Act.
Birth of William Henry, afterwards William IV.
Rockingham Ministry.
1766. Repeal of the Stamp Act.
Pitt takes office as Earl of Chatham.
1767. Grafton Ministry.
1768. Wilkes riots.
Chatham resigns.
1769. Letters to Junius begin.
1770. North administration.
Boston Massacre.
1771. Struggle over reporting Parliamentary debates.
1773. Boston Tea-party.
1775. Lexington.
Bunker's Hill.
1776. Declaration of Independence.
1777. Brandywine.
Burgoyne surrenders at Saratoga.
1778. Death of Chatham.
War with France.
1779. War with Spain.
1780. Gordon riots.
War with Holland.
1781. Cornwallis surrenders at Yorktown.
1782. Rockingham administration.
Battle of the Saints.
Shelburne Ministry.

1783. General peace: American independence recognized.
      Fox-North coalition.
      Pitt becomes First Lord of the Treasury.
1784. General election seals the King's triumph.
1786. Impeachment of Warren Hastings begins.
1788. The King's first serious attack of insanity.
1789. The French Revolution.
1793. Execution of Louis XVI.
      War with France.
1794. Battle of the First of June.
1795. Acquittal of Warren Hastings.
1796. French successes.
1797. French fleet destroyed by Jervis at St. Vincent.
      Mutinies at Spithead and the Nore.
      Dutch fleet destroyed at Camperdown by Duncan.
1798. Irish rebellion.
      French fleet destroyed by Nelson at the Nile.
1800. Union with Ireland.
1801. Pitt resigns.
      Addington Ministry.
      The King's second attack of insanity.
1802. Peace of Amiens.
1803. War with France renewed.
1804. The King again insane.
      Pitt resumes Premiership.
1805. Trafalgar.
1806. Death of Pitt.
      Ministry of All the Talents.
      Death of Fox.
1807. Portland administration.
1809. Corunna.
      Walcheren expedition.
      Perceval becomes Premier.
1810. The King suffers fresh attacks of insanity.
1811. Final insanity of the King: Regency declared.
1820. Death of King George III.

CHAPTER I

PRINCE AND PRINCE OF WALES

George William Frederick, who came to the throne as George III, was born on June 4th, 1738. A seven months child, he was not expected to live, and was hastily baptized, but by July 2nd he was considered strong enough to undergo the public ceremony. Since his father, Frederick Prince of Wales, had finally quarrelled with the King less than a year before, hurriedly removing his wife from the palace precincts almost at the moment of giving birth to a daughter, the future monarch was brought up in an atmosphere of opposition to the government and hatred of the King. Yet though there was little communication between the monarch and Leicester House, the opposition headquarters, the young prince was not altogether unknown to his grandfather, and once at least was summoned to see him.

1.To King George II

Clifden, June 2, 1749.

SIR,

I hope you will forgive the liberty I take to thank your Majesty for the honour you did me yesterday. It is my utmost wish, and shall always be my study to deserve your paternal goodness and protection. I am with greatest respect and submission,

> Sir,
> Your Majesty's
> most humble and most
> dutiful subject, grandson and servant,
> GEORGE.

Such a letter, written at the age of eleven, gives us no glimpse into his character or attainments, but at least it disposes of the report that at so advanced an age he could not read English, for the handwriting is good for a child of that age. The covering letter was perhaps his own, and is curious for showing that his habit of stating the very hour of writing goes back almost to infancy.

3

11. To Baron von Münchhausen[1]

Clifden, 10 *o'clock*.

Herr von Münchhausen, please be so good as to hand on to the King the letter which I have taken the liberty to write to thank him most humbly. I would have written sooner, but I have only just this minute arrived here to bring my Papa this good news.

I remain, Yours affectionately,

GEORGE.

The family was evidently nervous as to the result of the visit.

Until his father's sudden death on March 20th, 1751, George had been treated as the household dunce, for ever being unfavourably compared with his brother Edward. But from the moment when, on April 25th, he kissed hands as Prince of Wales, the situation was changed. He became the focus of both polite and political attention. Yet he led a miserable life, hemmed about by governors and tutors, strictly watched by a jealous and ambitious mother, Augusta of Saxe-Gotha, always urging him to become a ruler: ' George, be King,' echoed too often in his ears.

The Dowager Princess had no faith in the tutors provided by a government anxious to see that the youth imbibed true Whig principles. ' She said (to Bubb Dodington) she really did not know what they taught him; but, to speak freely, she was afraid not much.' If one of his earlier teachers had found him lethargic, she in her turn found him backward and childish for his age. The sensible thing would have been to let him run about with other children, but she dared not do this owing to the profligate way in which they were brought up. ' The mother and the nursery always prevailed,' his governor, Lord Waldegrave, wrote. It is from Waldegrave that we get a most revealing account of the young prince, who considered his governor ' a depraved, worthless man '. We learn that though he had an honest strength of opinion, he was too liable to error, since the strength was the issue of a dull spirit ' not of the active kind ': he was, in fact, obstinate. He hated business, nor was he eager to amuse himself, a pity, according to Waldegrave, ' for the transition from pleasure to business is both shorter and easier than a total state

---

[1] Hanoverian Resident in London.

4

of inaction'. Most interesting of all in view of George III's later attacks of 'manic depressive insanity' is Waldegrave's shrewd observation of the Prince's sullen fits. He was not given to angry outbreaks, but he would retire to his closet, 'not to compose his mind by study or contemplation, but merely to indulge the melancholy enjoyment of his own ill-humour'.

Neither Waldegrave nor any other tutor was able to make much impression on the young man, who was formed in his early years entirely by his mother and her close friend John, Earl of Bute. With the political intrigues and factions of the day we have nothing to do here; they belong to the history of the previous reign. We need not be concerned with the tergiversations of Pitt and Henry Fox; we need only note that the Prince learnt to detest all the 'old gang' of politicians, Hardwicke, Newcastle, Temple, and to fear his uncle, the Duke of Cumberland, regarded as a possible usurper; he hated the King, he despised Hanover. The Court party loathed Bute, a mere Scotch representative peer, not in the councils of the Whigs. They feared, quite wrongly, that Bute was inculcating the Prince with Bolingbroke's dangerous notions of a patriot king, and they could not get at the young man, for his mother and Bute, according to Chesterfield, 'agreed to keep the Prince entirely to themselves. None but their immediate and lowest creatures were suffered to approach him. Except at his levées, where none are seen as they are, he saw nobody, and nobody saw him.' It is not surprising that in these circumstances the mind and affections of the Prince turned to Bute, whose pedantry and stiffness were just the qualities to appeal to the melancholy youth; Bute, who seemed so wise, who was always so helpful and charming, and in whom his mother had so much confidence.

When his grandson was in his eighteenth year, the King, hoping to detach him from his mother, proposed to marry him to a charming young princess, a daughter of the Duchess of Brunswick-Wolfenbüttel; but the watchful dowager (who had, to her rage, not been consulted) instilled into her son's mind so strong a dislike of the arrangement, that he 'declared violently against being bewofenbüttled'—so Horace Walpole reported—and the marriage fell through. But a more serious attempt was soon made to detach the Prince of Wales from his ill advisers. On June 4th, 1756, on entering his nineteenth year, he was to be declared of age. The King, with great hopes of the efficacy of his bait, settled on the Prince an income of £40,000 a year, and proposed that he should move into apartments in St. James's

5

Palace, and take over those that had once been his father's in Kensington Palace. Most young men would have jumped at such an offer of freedom from apron-strings and admonitions. Leicester House, however, was equal to the emergency, and the Prince, while accepting the income, wrote to Waldegrave (Add. MSS. 32684, f. 91) asking him to thank the King for his condescension in communicating to him the plan of the settlement before it was concluded, and for allowing his favourite brother, Prince Edward, to remain with him: but, he added, would Waldegrave transmit a request that he might be allowed to stay with his mother? It sounded innocent enough, but it was well known that the Prince did not live with his mother either in town or country (so Dodington supposed), and Waldegrave was instructed to tell the Prince and his mother that the King thought Bute too closely connected with Pitt and the opposition for it to be proper for him to be about the heir-apparent's person. The Prince was panic-stricken at the thought of a separation from Bute, for whom he had now developed a passionate adoration: he was so far under his influence as to seem hypnotized by him: Bute, the bewildered young man was sure, had been specially sent by God to help him. In actual fact, Bute was trying to make a man of him.

III. TO THE EARL OF BUTE

Kew, June 31 [sic], 1756.

MY DEAR LORD,

I have had the pleasure of your friendship during the space of a year, by which I have reaped great advantage, but not the improvement I should if I had followed your advice; but you shall find me make such progress in this summer, that shall give you hopes, that with the continuation of your advice, I may turn out as you wish.

It is very true that the Ministers have done everything they can to provoke me, that they have called me a harmless boy, and have not even deigned to give me an answer when I so earnestly wish to see my friend about me. They have also treated my Mother in a cruel manner (which I shall neither forget nor forgive to the day of my death) because she is so good as to come forward and to preserve her son from the many snares that surround him. My Friend is also attacked in the most cruel and horrid manner, not for anything he has done against them, but because he is my Friend, and wants to see me come to the Throne with honour and not with disgrace and because he is a friend to the blessed liberties of his country and not to arbitrary notions. I look upon myself as engaged in honour and justice to defend these my two Friends as long as I draw breath.

I do therefore here in the presence of Our Almighty Lord promise, that I will ever remember the insults done to my Mother, and never will forgive any one who shall offer to spe disrespectfully of her.

I do in the same solemn manner declare, that I will defend my Friend and will never use evasive answers, but will always tell him whatever is said against him, and will more and more show to the world the great friendship I have for him, and all the malice that can be invented against him shall only bind me the stronger to him.

I do further promise, that all the allurements my enemies can think of, or the threats that they may make pour out upon me, shall never make me in the least change from what I do solemnly promise in this paper.

I will take upon me the man in every thing, and will not show that indifference which I have as yet too often done.

As I have chosen the vigorous part, I will throw off that indolence which if I don't soon get the better of will be my ruin, and will never grow weary of this, though —— [George II] should live many years.

I hope my dear Lord you will conduct me through this difficult road and will bring me to the goal. I will exactly follow your advice, without which I shall inevitably sink.

I am young and inexperienced and want advice. I trust in your friendship which will assist me in all difficulties.

I know few things I ought to be more thankful for to the Great Power above, than for its having pleased Him to send you to help and advise me in these difficult times.

I do hope you will from this instant banish all thoughts of leaving me, and will resolve, if not for my sake for the good of your country to remain with me. I have often heard you say,

7

that you don't think I shall have the same friendship for you when I am married as I now have. I shall never change in that, nor will I bear to be in the least deprived of your company. And I shall expect that all my relations shall show you that regard which is due to the Friend of the whole family.

I sign my name with the greatest pleasure to what I have here written which is my firm and unalterable resolution.

GEORGE P.

iv. To King George II

Kew, July 12, 1756.

SIR,

The great importance of your Majesty's message repeated to me by the Earl Waldegrave, makes me presume to address myself thus immediately to your Majesty.

I hope that I shall not be thought wanting in the duty I owe your Majesty, if I humbly continue to entreat your Majesty's permission to remain with the Princess my mother; this point is of too great consequence to my happiness for me not to wish ardently your Majesty's favour and indulgence in it.

I have not ventured hitherto myself to represent to your Majesty, my earnest wish that the Earl of Bute might be placed in some principal situation about my person; but being now commanded by your Majesty to explain myself upon that subject, I presume most humbly to lay before your Majesty this my most ardent request, and my only one with regard to an establishment your Majesty most graciously intends for me; nothing can make me happier, or fill my mind with warmer gratitude, than your Majesty's gracious condescension, in favour of a person, whom early and long acquaintance has so naturally pointed out for my preference, and of whose duty and zeal for your Majesty I have the most certain knowledge.

I humbly hope that this request will appear so reasonable to your Majesty, that I shall on this occasion experience the same paternal tenderness which has hitherto so much contributed to my happiness and the continuance of which I shall ever think my greatest comfort; penetrated with these sentiments, I beg to subscribe myself,

>Sir,
>
>Your Majesty's
>
>Most dutiful grandson, subject and humble servant,
>
>GEORGE P.

v. TO THE EARL OF BUTE

July 14, 1756.

. . . The K—— and those he has consulted have treated [me] with less regard than they would have dared to have done any Member of Parliament; I hope you will agree with me in thinking that if this just request is refused, that for my honour, dignity, and character, I may keep no measures with these counsellors who have not prevented the K—— treating me with such unheard of contempt, the longer I live the more I shall see how little any trust can be placed in most men except yourself.

In the end, the King was forced to make ' that puppy, Bute,' Groom of the Stole. Newcastle and Fox, well aware that the King could not live for ever, and that soon their destinies would lie in the hands of the young King and his Mayor of the Palace, persuaded the reluctant monarch to concede the point. He delayed as long as possible, but the ministers insisted that the establishment should be settled before they had to meet Parliament.

vi. TO KING GEORGE II

Kew, October 5, 1756.

SIR,

I humbly beg with a heart full of duty and gratitude, to lay myself at your Majesty's feet; and to return my most humble thanks, for the great tenderness your Majesty has been pleased to show me, in so graciously permitting me to remain with the Princess my mother; and for condescending to inform me of your Majesty's favourable dispositions to my humble request concerning the Earl of Bute. It has been and always will continue the

desire of my life to merit your Majesty's gracious favour and protection : I dare affirm to your Majesty that I shall never be
wanting in the sincerest returns of duty and gratitude that I owe
your Majesty both as a son and a subject; I shall think myself
bound to promote as far as lies in my power the most perfect
union and harmony in the Royal Family and by every action
convince the world of my sincere love and unalterable attachment
to your Royal Person.   It is with these sentiments I presume to
subscribe myself, etc.

*With this letter the King professed himself thoroughly satis-
fied: but alas for the harmony in the Royal Family, when the
next year Bute communicated with Newcastle through Chesterfield, suggesting a rapprochement, the King told Newcastle to
do what he could, but added, 'I very much doubt by what I
know of them, that you will meet any reason with those impracticable people'.   (Add. MSS. 32684, f. 102.)*

*Meanwhile Bute continued the Prince's education, instructing
him, not in arbitrary principles, as is so often assumed, but in
constitutional ones: George III always considered the Crown as
part of a delicate structure, and it is by no means certain that
he over-estimated its importance in the affairs of his time.   But
Bute's main task was to make him fit for the burden he was to
take up as soon as his grandfather died: his pupil's responsiveness
was abnormal.*

vii. To the Earl of Bute

Savile House, March 25 [1757 ?].

My dear Lord,

I have had your conversation of Wednesday night ever since
in my mind; it greatly hurts me that I cannot make an excuse for
myself.   I am conscious of my own indolence which none but
so sincere a friend as you could so long have borne with.   I do
here in the most solemn manner declare that I will entirely
throw aside this my greatest enemy and that you shall instantly
find a change; my negligence, which I reckon as belonging to
indolence is very great, but shall absolutely be for ever laid away.

I will employ all my time upon business, and will be able for
the future to give you an account of everything I read.

As to what you mentioned in your note of last night concerning F——x [Fox][1] it has made me strictly examine myself; and I do now here tell you that I am resolved in myself to take the resolute part, to act the man in everything, to repeat whatever I am to say with spirit and not blushing and afraid as I have hitherto; I will also never show the least irresolution, and will not from being warm on any subject, by degrees grow quite indifferent about it, in short my conduct shall convince you that I am mortified at what I have done, and that I despise myself as every body else must, that knows how I have acted; I hope that by altering now, I shall be able to regain your opinion, which I value above everything in this world.

I beg you will be persuaded that I will constantly reflect whether what I am doing is worthy of one who is to mount the Throne, and who owes everything to his friend.

I will by my behaviour show that I know, if I in the least deviate from what I here promise and declare, I shall lose the greatest of stakes, my Crown, and what I esteem far beyond that, my friend : I hope this will persuade you not to leave me, when all is at stake, when nobody but you can steer me through this difficult though glorious path.

I am, my dear Lord, with very great sincerity, your most obliged friend,

GEORGE P.

VIII. TO THE EARL OF BUTE

½ past eight [1757 ?].

MY DEAREST FRIEND,

My heart was so full with the many truths you told me last night that I was not then able to express my thoughts to you; I therefore take this method of laying them before you; but at the same time what hopes can I have that you will credit any resolution that I make when you cannot help remembering that as many as I have made I have regularly broke; my dearest friend, the considering of how little effect my promises have as yet been will

[1] Fox, being of the Duke of Cumberland's faction, was not *persona grata* at Leicester House.

be one of the strongest motives to rouse me to act with the greatest minuteness up to what I now promise.

All I beg of you is that you would have a little patience and judge by my actions whether my words are not my firm and unalterable resolutions.

I mean from the present hour to apply with the greatest assiduity to attempt if it be possible to regain the many years I have fruitlessly spent; I will engage that you shall find a very visible alteration in me, the thoughts of what I ought to be shall ever be in my mind, and that added to my desire of making a good figure in the station it has pleased Almighty Providence to place me in, will make me spare no pains to accomplish this, though I own I am of such an unhappy nature that if I cannot in a good measure alter that, let me be ever so learned in what is necessary for a King to know, I shall make but a very poor and despicable figure. My dearest friend, the only small return I can make you for your unwearied pains for my future quiet and honour, and the happiness of this my dear country is the making it appear that the many things you have said in my favour are not entirely void of truth.

I therefore desire that we may regulate my studies, and that you would at least once a week examine what I have done.

The more I consider how I have thrown away my time, the more I am surprised at the greatness of your indulgence, that you have been able to prevail upon yourself to remain with me.

I might add various other things, but they shall remain till I see you alone, when we will please talk the matter thoroughly over.

IX. TO THE EARL OF BUTE

September 25, 1758.

(*Admitting the ' many truths' Bute had told him.*)

. . . they have set me in a most dreadful light before my own eyes; I see plainly that I have been my greatest enemy; for had I always acted according to your advice, I should now have been the direct opposite from what I am. . . .

If you should now resolve to set me adrift, I could not obraid you, but on the contrary look on it as a natural consequence of my faults, and not want of friendship in you.

I say if you ever think fit to take this step, my line of action is plain; for though I act wrong in most things, yet I have too much spirit to accept the Crown and be a cypher, and too much love for my countrymen to mount this Throne and be their detestation; I would therefore in such an unhappy case retire to some distant region where in solitude I might for the rest of my life remain, and think on the various faults I have committed that I might repent of them.

The picture of a young man, obsessed by a feeling of guilt, trying to fit himself for the station he was to occupy, is touching: his utter subjection to his mentor is perhaps painful. Nor were politics the only sphere in which Bute guided his charge, and in other matters, perhaps, tortured him worse than ever.

x. To the Earl of Bute

1759.

You have often accused me of growing grave and thoughtful, it is entirely owing to a daily increasing admiration of the fair sex, which I am attempting with all the philosophy and resolution I am capable of to keep under : I should be ashamed after having so long resisted the charms of those divine creatures now to become their prey; Princes when once in their hands make miserable figures, the annals of France and the present situation of Government in the Kingdom I the most love, are convincing proofs of;[1] when I have said this you will plainly feel how strong a struggle there is between the boiling youth of 21 years and prudence; the last I hope will ever keep the upper hand; indeed if I can weather it but a few years, marriage will put a stop to this combat in my breast. I believe you will agree that application is the only aid I can give to reason, that by keeping the mind constantly employed is a likely means of preserving those passions

---

[1] In reference to Lady Yarmouth : but it does not seem that ' the lady ', as she was known to the ministers, had much effect on the policy of George II, though she was often used as intermediary, or to hint delicate matters.

in due subordination to it; believe me, I will with the greatest assiduity attempt to make all that progress which your good counsels, if properly attended to, have reason to expect.

Bute's reply aroused the Prince to write another letter, which betrays signs of intense mental and nervous agitation.

XI. To the Earl of Bute

On receiving your note I find my dearest friend intimates something I did not mean in my letter this morning; you seem to think of the most important step to my happiness, but I can never agree to alter my situation whilst this old man [George II] lives; I will rather undergo anything ever so disagreeable than put my trust in him for a single moment in an affair of such delicacy; my dearest friend will, I am sure, entirely agree with me, I shall therefore, only add that I hope the dose you are taking to-night will have its desired effect.

The Prince, however, was not all humility, and sometimes exhibited considerable faith in his mission as God's emissary. (See a letter printed by Namier, 103.) And at this period, too, he made a gesture characteristic of the gallant, combative, one might almost say pugnacious spirit of the future monarch, characteristic, too, of the profound sense of his position, a sense which was one of the guiding principles of his life. In 1759, during the Seven Years War, there was an invasion scare, and the whole country- side, heartened by Pitt's genius, was eager to get into uniform.

XII. To King George II

Kew, July 20, 1759.

Sir,

I beg to lay myself at your Majesty's feet, humbly to offer up a petition, in the success of which I feel extremely interested. While this country remained in tranquillity, I thought my time best employed in acquiring a thorough knowledge of all matters peculiarly suited to my situation; but now that every part of the nation is arming for its defence, I cannot bear the thought of continuing in this inactive state. When your Majesty's kingdoms are threatened, a quiet retreat ill becomes my birth and station. Permit me therefore humbly to request your Majesty to give me an opportunity of convincing the world that I am neither unworthy of my high situation, nor of the blood that fills my veins. Your Majesty's known valour will diffuse its influence on my head, and make the presence of your grandson an encouragement to your people; a terror to the enemy; and joined to his own resolution may in some measure supply the want of experience in military affairs; and enable him to support, with dignity, the post of danger, which he esteems a post of honour.

I earnestly beseech your Majesty to receive this humble request, with your accustomed goodness. I intended to have made it in person, on Tuesday; but too great anxiety kept me silent; and the fear of that returning reduces me to the necessity of having recourse, in this manner, to your Majesty's favour and indulgence.

The King, however, remained deaf to this appeal; ' He wants to be rising, monter un pas,' the old hero of Dettingen grumbled. He took it to mean that the Prince was asking to be made commander-in-chief. The ministers agreed, but thought that the suggestion was put forward, not in the hope of a favourable answer, but to make it more difficult to appoint the Duke of Cumberland, should he emerge from the disfavour in which he had languished since the Convention of Klosterseven. The ministers prevailed upon the King to return a soft answer, but it did not satisfy the Prince.

XIII. To the Earl of Bute

July 27, 1759.

You will see by H.M. letter how shuffling it is and unworthy of a British Monarch; the conduct of this old K—— makes me ashamed of being his grandson; he treats me in the same manner, his knave and counsellor, the D. of N[ewcastle], does all people. For this answer by some may be looked upon as agreeing to my petition, by those who think further as an absolute refusal.

I am going to carry a copy of this unworthy letter to my mother.

Perhaps George III remembered this incident when, in 1803, he received a similar application from his own son. (See Chapter VIII, III.)

It was not long, however, before the Prince of Wales became master of his own destinies; for King George II died on October 25th, 1760, and his grandson was proclaimed King. George III had no doubt in his mind as to the sort of King he was to be. 'Let a good and great Prince born in a free country, fond of the cause of liberty,' he wrote in one of his exercises,

be but true to himself, true to religion, virtue, honour, freedom; such a Prince has a right to expect, and will most certainly have the support of that Almighty Power that decides the fate of kingdoms, and baffles all the black designs and wrecks the cunning of proud, ambitious, and deceitful men. (Namier, 105.)

The reign of virtue was about to begin, and the monarch would be supported by God.

CHAPTER II

CHAOS

1760-1770

*At the end of the month, indeed, the young King issued a
proclamation for the encouragement of piety, and the punishment
of vice, profaneness and immorality, but the effect was not notice-
able compared with that of two other utterances. The first was
when he (or rather Bute) antagonized Pitt by referring to the
war as ' bloody and expensive ' in his first speech to the council;
the second when he insisted on the insertion of the following
passage in the speech from the throne:*

I

Born and educated in this country I glory in the name of
Britain, and the peculiar happiness of my life will ever consist in
promoting the welfare of a people, whose loyalty and warm
affection to me, I consider as the greatest and most permanent
security of my throne.

*The purpose, presumably, was to show that in foreign policy the
government would never again be steered by ' the Hanoverian
rudder,' as the opposition had so often complained, and that ' the
horrible electorate,' as George III called it, need no longer be
taken into such grave consideration.*

*Pitt's antagonism to Bute dates from before this time, and it
was Pitt's actions now and for the next ten years that produced
the administrative chaos. According to the constitutional
practice of the time, the King chose his own ministers, and the
government managed the House of Commons. We need no
longer take the view that on his accession George III unconstitu-
tionally smashed the Whigs, and founded his reign on corruption.
All he tried to do was, as chief of the executive, to make the
administrative machine work, using for his purpose the man he
most trusted. He plunged boldly into battle as early as March
25th by making Bute Secretary of State. There is no space here
to enter into the intricacies of the time:[1] all that the meagre*

[1] The reader is referred to Professor Namier's *The Structure of Politics
at the Accession of George III*, and his *England in the Age of the American
Revolution*. A different point of view will be found in Yorke's *Life of
Hardwicke*.

correspondence of this period can show, is the dominance of Bute,[1] and the veering away of foreign policy from Germany, and ' the German war '.

II. TO THE EARL OF BUTE

November 11, 1761.

Nothing can be more false than what regards Smith. He has got Prevôt's Battalion of Americans. Boscawen's remains vacant for Col. Peirson, in case it is asked for him; as I understood from my Dearest Friend, the D. of N——e would apply for him, I did not order it till that happened. If, on the contrary, my Dearest Friend rather wishes Peirson should previously be appointed, I will order it before the D. of N——e comes to-morrow.

Pitt had resigned on October 5th, owing to the King's refusal to make war on Spain; nevertheless war had to be declared on January 4th. This provided an excuse for not continuing the subsidy to Frederick.

III. TO THE KING OF PRUSSIA

March 30, 1762.

MONSIEUR MON FRÈRE,

In thanking your Majesty for the two letters he was kind enough to write me on the 22nd January and the 22nd inst., I would congratulate you sincerely on the happy change which has come about in Russia, and particularly on the declaration made on the 23rd of last month by that Emperor to the Courts of Vienna, Versailles, and Stockholm.[2] The resolution this worthy prince took of telling every one his views on the present war, and his intention of making every effort to contribute to the re-

---

[1] It is understood that an edition of the letters of the King to Bute will shortly be produced by Mr. R. Sedgwick.

[2] The happy change was the death, on January 5th, of Frederick's inveterate enemy the Tsarina Elizabeth. She was succeeded by Peter III, a great admirer of Frederick's, who reversed Russian policy, and declared against the Court of Vienna. This course also brought Sweden out of the war. The throne was shortly afterwards usurped by the new Tsarina, Catherine. Peter was murdered, and Frederick lost his ally.

establishment of a general peace, was extremely agreeable to me.
And as my way of thinking on these great matters entirely
corresponds with his, I will not fail to co-operate in every way
open to me, in such a salutary design.

I pray your Majesty to be assured that I am as ready as ever
to come to your help. You will see, however, that my capacity
to do so lessens from day to day as a consequence of the new war
in which I find myself engaged to give indispensable support to
my good and ancient ally the King of Portugal. It is not that,
as soon as your Majesty has told me what means he proposes to
use to procure peace, I will not be resolute to do everything in my
power to forward your success.

I am, with the most perfect esteem and affection, etc.

*Newcastle, whose main idea of foreign politics was to grant
enormous subsidies, from now intimated his wish to resign. The
King had no regrets.*

IV. To the Earl of Bute

April, 1762.

The more I consider the Prussian subsidy, the more objections
arise in my mind against it, and as to the German War, I am
clear that if France is not willing for peace, we must instantly
knock it in the head; and if men will leave my service because I
love this country preferably to any other, it will be they that
will be run at and not me; the successor I have long had in my
eye to the D. of N. is a man void of his dirty arts who will think
of mine and his country's good, not of jobs; if my dearest friend
does not know of him by this character, I will add that he now
holds the Seals, and lives in S. Audley Street.

*The invitation to exchange the post of Secretary of State for that
of First Lord of the Treasury was soon made more clearly:*

V. To the Earl of Bute

May 7, 1762.

The D. of N. has been here and to my great astonishment
has waived his opinion but ended with resigning his office, that
is to say when I may have made proper arrangements; his

language was full of duty, and protesting he meant to support my measures with all his weight; the thing he most rested his opinion on was his Board's deserting him; this being the case I hope to see my dearest friend in a fortnight resign the Seals for the Treasury: then the government must be formed in a manner to continue, not a patch: believe G. Greenville is not right at present therefore cannot be too narrowly watched and sifted.

Grenville, or Greenville as the King insisted on calling him, became Secretary of State in Bute's room. Meanwhile the war went on, everywhere showing successes, but these seemed only to increase the Court's ardour for peace. Although the real negotiations appear to have proceeded privately between Bute and Choiseul, aided by Viry, the Sardinian minister, in the autumn the Duke of Bedford was sent over to Paris, but was not allowed a free hand, nor permitted to claim what the victories suggested. Public pressure, however, forced Bute to make certain demands in excess of what he originally intended, and on October 26th Bedford was told to demand either Florida or Porto Rico in return for Havanna. The King wrote a covering letter.

VI. TO THE DUKE OF BEDFORD

Whitehall, October 26, 1762.

MY LORD DUKE,

This is so critical a minute both for my own honour and the security of the nation, that I think it necessary to send you these few lines, not to exhort you, for I know your steady and affectionate adherence to my interests, but to declare to you with my own pen, that after weighing every consequence, I am determined to make the peace I now send you or to continue the war. I think if the French and Spaniards have not very bad intelligence, they will see the danger run by suffering this to hang till the meeting of my Parliament; the best despatch, therefore, I can receive from you, and the most essential to my service, will be the preliminaries signed. May Providence, in compassion to human misery, give you this means of executing this great and noble work, and be assured I will never forget the duty and attachment you show me in this important crisis.

In December the preliminaries were passed in the House of Commons by an enormous majority, and the Peace of Paris was signed on February 10th, 1763.

In the meantime the government had undergone strange vicissitudes. Grenville had been persuaded to resign the Seals and had taken over the Admiralty, and Henry Fox, afterwards Lord Holland, had seized the leadership of the House of Commons. Newcastle had induced several others to follow him into retirement, and a proscription of the Pelhamites had followed in December, those in power being determined to get rid of their opponents in foreign policy. There was no formed opposition, partly because the idea was repellent to most of the old statesmen, partly because there were no parties. The old division of Whig and Tory had to all intents and purposes broken down. George III's attempt to govern without party was in no way sinister; with the welter of factions it was the only possible thing to do. Unfortunately the personalities who were available made smooth working impossible, and apart from all other dislikes the growing hatred of Bute, fanned by Wilkes, which extended to the once popular King, made administration still more difficult. The King, however, in the autumn of 1762, welcomed resignations and dismissals.

VII. To the Earl of Bute

October 29.

After the Drawing Room Lord George Cavendish resigned his wand, but did not utter a syllable; taking it I told him I willingly let every one quit my service who have lost the zeal to serve me, and then turned on my heel; thus the two brothers are gone;[1] Lord Rockingham resigns on Wednesday, whether any of the Bedchamber will follow his example is entirely unknown to me.

When Rockingham resigned, the King wrote that if Rutland, Lincoln or Coventry were to do the same, he would be pleased.

VIII. To the Earl of Bute

November 3, 1762.

. . . I should think myself well rid of them; force and steadiness will undoubtedly overturn this faction and I can't help hinting

[1] The Duke of Devonshire had been dismissed.

again what I did last night that every officer who votes against Government at a time like this ought to be made an example of.

He egged on Fox in his attack on the Pelhamites.

IX. TO THE EARL OF BUTE

December ?, 1762.

. . . I am provoked that Mr. Fox should every moment cry out for mildness, that at this minute would be pusillanimity; the sword is drawn, vigour and violence are the only means of ending this audacious faction; indeed I have but one man about me, that is my dear friend, the others are to-day angry, to-morrow perhaps soft, but now they must go on with spirit or else are unfit to aid Government at this hour of faction.

Bute himself, however, felt the force of the storm, and suggested that he would shortly resign the Treasury.

X. TO THE EARL OF BUTE

December, 1762.

Now I come to the part of my dear friend's letter that gives me the greatest concern, as it overturns all the thoughts that have alone kept up my spirits in these bad times; I own I had flattered myself when Peace was once established that my dear friend would have assisted me in purging out corruption, and in those measures that no man but he that has the Prince's real affection can go through; then when we were both dead our memories would have been respected and esteemed to the end of time, now what shall we be able to say that Peace is concluded, and my dear friend becoming a Courtier, for I fear mankind will say so, the Ministry remains composed of the most abandoned men that ever held those offices; thus instead of reformation, the Ministers being vicious this country will grow if possible worse; let me attack the irreligious, the covetous &c. as much as I please, that will be of no effect, for the Ministers being of that stamp, men will with reason think they may advance to the highest pitch of their ambition through every infamous way that their own black hearts or the rascality of their superiors can point out.

Remember what Fox formerly said, we will give Lord B. a Garter and a Court employment and then we may do as we please.

The dream of an ideally virtuous state, ruled by the King and his angel of light, still persisted; but alas, Fox seemed to have been right, for Bute had his Garter, and on April 8th, 1763, resigned all his employments. Grenville succeeded to the Treasury, and Fox became Lord Holland, though to the King's disgust he insisted on retaining the place of Paymaster to the Forces. The King's view of Fox was clearly enough stated to his dear friend when th latter proposed him as his successor in the Treasury.

XI. TO LORD BUTE

[c. April, 1763.]

I have one principle firmly rooted in my mind from the many seasonable lessons I have received from my dear friend, never to trust a man void of principles; if any man ever deserved that character 'tis Mr. Fox; the seeing him at the head of the House of Commons was very unpleasant to me : but I consented to it, as that was the only means of getting my dear friend to proceed this winter in the Treasury. . . . His [Fox's] . . . bad character comes strongly into my thoughts whenever I hear him named; 'tis not prejudice but aversion to his whole mode of Government that causes my writing so openly my thoughts to my only friend.

The Grenville administration, which the King found intolerable from the first—a futile advance to Pitt was made early in its course—is marked by the passing of the Stamp Act, the effects of which were to be seen later, and the Wilkes affair. The famous No. 45 of the North Briton *appeared on April 23rd. Wilkes had been seized, but released on the ruling of Chief Justice Pratt, afterwards Lord Camden, that General Warrants were illegal. The question of the libel, against the King through Bute, and that of Parliamentary Privilege, formed much of the business of the next session, which began on November 15th.*

XII. To George Grenville

12 minutes past 11 [Tuesday, Nov. 15, 1763].

Mr. Greenville,

Your account of the meeting last night gives me well grounded hopes that everything in Parliament will go well; the continuation of Wilkes's impudence is amazing, when his ruin is so near. . . .

XIII. To George Grenville

40 min. past 7 [November 25, 1763].

By your coming early, Mr. Greenville, the Speaker presenting the address at half-past two will be very convenient. It rejoices me much that this great question should have been carried by so great a majority! The Duke of Bedford and many others pressed much for the dismissing some of those that have gone against us; that if we defer it longer we shall lose more people.

I don't differ much with them in this, therefore should propose dismissing General Conway both from his civil and military commissions; also Mr. Fitzherbert,[1] and any others who have equally with these gone steadily against us, and giving it out that the rest would have the same fate if they do not amend their conduct.

On the question of general warrants the results were not so favourable, the government majority dwindling to fourteen.

XIV. To George Grenville

10 min. past 10, February 18, 1764.

Mr. Greenville,

If you should be up in time, I should be glad if you could be at St. James's by twelve; the defection last night is undoubtedly very great, but my nature ever inclines me to be acquainted with who are my true, and who false friends; the latter I think worse than open enemies. Firmness and resolution must now be shown, and no one's friend saved who has dared to

---

[1] M.P. for Derby, and a Lord of the Board of Trade.

fly off; this alone can restore order, and save this country from anarchy; by dismissing, I mean not till the question is decided, but I hope in a fortnight that those who have deserted may feel that I am not to be neglected unpunished!

At the close of the session in April, General Henry Seymour Conway, Lord Hertford's brother, was dismissed from his post in the Bedchamber, and deprived of his regiment. Such dismissals did not increase the popularity of the government, in which Bute, though he held no office, was regarded as being ' that invidious thing, the minister behind the curtain '. The King was ever more harassed by his failure: he had already found that, as he was to tell General Irwin three years later, ' ce métier de politique c'est un très vilain métier; c'est le métier d'un faquin; ce n'est pas le métier d'un gentilhomme.' It is perhaps not surprising that early in 1765 he had his first attack of mental illness, though it was at the time not publicly, perhaps not even privately, recognized as such.

On his recovery he proposed measures for a Regency should he die, since the Prince of Wales was at that time only three years old. In deciding that he should be allowed to choose any member of the Royal Family usually resident in England, he gave his ministers an opportunity of gratuitously insulting his mother, whose connection with Bute made her most unpopular. It was decided that the Dowager Princess of Wales was not a member of the Royal Family: readers of Tristram Shandy *will remember that it is a debatable point whether a mother is of kin to her child. The insult determined the King to get rid of his ministers if he could, with, at their head, Grenville who was perpetually lecturing him. He had recourse to his uncle, the Duke of Cumberland, who went to see Pitt at Hayes, at the very moment when the riots of the silk-weavers broke out; these men were especially incensed against the Duke of Bedford, who had opposed a protective bill against foreign silks. Pitt could not agree with Temple, and the negotiations fell through. The King also induced the Earl of Egmont, First Lord of the Admiralty, to try to form a ministry, but this, too, proved a failure, and the King found the fetters of the Grenville-Bedford group more firmly riveted on him than ever, with Bute banished from London, and his brother, James Stuart Mackenzie, dismissed from the post of Privy Seal for Scotland, which had been promised him for life. The Duke of Cumberland began his work on 12th May:*

*the silk-weavers riots took place from the 15th to 17th, but, as
we shall see, there was still fear of them on the 20th.*

xv. To the Duke of Cumberland

Richmond, May 20, 1765.

Dear Uncle,

The very friendly and warm part you have taken, has given
me real satisfaction; but I little thought I should have been so
troublesome to you as the conduct of the men I have employed
forces me. I, in the whole course of the transaction, had proposed
consulting you in particular on all military affairs; but now I
must desire you to take the command to-morrow morning as
Captain General. I should think Lord Albemarle very proper
to put your orders in execution. I have sent this by one who has
my orders not to deliver this to any one but yourself, and to
bring an immediate answer, and also your opinion where and
how soon we can meet; for if any disturbance arises in the night,
I should think the hour proposed for to-morrow too late. I beg
you will show the enclosed abstract of their very extraordinary
paper to those whom you may think it may force to act a right
part.

I remain, dear Uncle,

Your most affectionate nephew,

George R.

xvi. To Lord Halifax[1]

[May 20, 1765.]

Lord Halifax,

I will be at St. James by twelve to-morrow, when I will
receive the address of the Lords through the White Staves.

As to the directions I shall think necessary to give for appointing any generals, I will talk of that when I shall see you at that
hour, at St. James.

---

[1] Secretary of State. Halifax had presented the King with a note
intimating that Granby was to be made Captain-General, and that on no
account must Cumberland be put forward. The King was fighting
gallantly, and ultimately won this point, owing, however, only to Granby's
withdrawal.

A Council must be ordered also for that hour.

The Regiment at Chatham must instantly be ordered to advance. You will therefore intimate this in my name, to the Secretary at War.

XVII. To Lord Egmont

[*May 20, 1765.*]

DEAR EGMONT—had I a few such men as you are, I should not be in the situation I now am; whatever happens believe me incapable of forgetting your handsome part yesterday. The D. of Cumberland says he shall honour you whilst you live, and wishes your example could prompt others to follow it; be at St. James by half hour past eleven at latest : I don't date this as I am unable to say when I can send it.

The King's gratitude for Egmont's willingness to play any part that might be assigned him is shown by the almost unique mode of address. Only once again, when parting from the younger Pitt, shall we find him employing it with one of his servants. Negotiations having failed, the monarch was extremely anxious to know the terms his conquerors were to impose on him, terms which were being debated at Bedford House.

XVIII. To George Grenville

15 *min. past* 9 *p.m.* [*Tuesday, May 21, 1765*].

MR. GREENVILLE,

I am surprised that you are not yet come, when you know it was my orders to be attended this evening. I expect you therefore to come the moment you receive this!

Grenville, therefore, returned in triumph, but the position could not last, especially as to Grenville's pedantic sermons was now added the insolence of Bedford, who went so far as to accuse the King of not keeping his word as to not receiving any advice from Bute. In June, the Duke of Cumberland wrote to tell his nephew that Bedford proposed to resign in favour of Temple, and suggested that they had better approach Pitt once more.

XIX. To the Duke of Cumberland

Richmond Lodge, June 12, 1765.

DEAR UNCLE,

Your friendly hint concerning the Duke of Bedford's intentions calls for my warmest thanks; I perfectly agree with you in thinking the receiving his resignation with temper [temperately], though rejecting the successor he will propose, the only eligible mode of acting at this moment; I shall rather be surprised if Mr. Pitt can be persuaded to accept office on terms not entirely to my dishonour and to that of those worthy men, Lord Rockingham, the Dukes of Grafton, Newcastle and others; for they are men who have principles and therefore cannot approve of seeing the Crown dictated to by low men; if Mr. Pitt should again decline, I hope the Parliament being prorogued they and their friends will join amicably the few persons that have zealously stood by me, and that the world will see that this country is not at that low ebb that no administration can be formed without the Grenville family;[1] as you sent your letter by a private hand I have followed the same method in sending my answer. I remain, dear Uncle, your most affectionate nephew,

GEORGE R.

XX. To the Duke of Cumberland

Richmond Lodge, June 12, 1765.

DEAR UNCLE,

Your very friendly concern for my situation will undoubtedly make you anxious to hear the fate of this day; the D. of Bedford came to ask leave to go to Wooburn, then he drew a paper out of his pocket and read it to the following effect that he found he and his colleagues had lost my favour, that they would not serve without it, that when he returned in the course of the next month if he did not find they were liked by me, and if those they looked upon as their personal enemies, and those who were in opposition to them were not frowned upon they would retire : many invectives against Ld Bute as his enemy and as wishing any others in their places; he even intimated that perhaps persons of more

[1] Temple was Grenville's brother, and Pitt their brother-in-law.

elevated stations might do them disservice, then he entered on the mode of his first accepting. In short I with difficulty kept my temper, but did master it, and let him retire without giving him that kind of answer that my own feelings dictated. Things being in this situation, I beg you will redouble your attention that something may be soon formed, for in this state of things no business is carried on; I know my ministers don't disguise to the foreigners that I dislike them; this will soon be known all over Europe, therefore no time ought to be lost in restoring order into government. I beg an answer may be sent by some means or other whether this has been safely delivered; as for the bearer of it, he will not wait for it to prevent suspicion. The Lord Cavendishes brought the D. of Devonshire to-day, who seems a pretty behaved young man.

On this occasion Pitt made every effort to form a ministry, but Temple's obduracy again prevented him. The King was extremely grateful for his efforts.

XXI. To William Pitt

Richmond, 20 min. past 6 p.m., June 25, 1765.

My Friend, for so the part you have acted deserves from me, think it not strange if in my present distress I wish to see you again and have your advice; many things have occurred since you left me I much want to have your opinion about, and I will answer for you, you will give it without hesitation. I wish to see you at ½ hour past eleven after I come from the review.

In spite of Pitt's failure, it was found that an administration could be formed without ' the family ' with the help of the New-castle faction. The Duke, that ' young, disinterested politician ' as Walpole called him, became Privy Seal: Rockingham became First Lord of the Treasury, the least satisfactory part of the business from the King's point of view being that Conway had to be re-employed, this time as Secretary of State, in company with the Duke of Grafton. But Mackenzie was restored to the Privy Seal of Scotland.

Although averse from foreign politics, George III could not altogether ignore them. At this time the eternal question of

*the Newfoundland fisheries arose again, and there was an attempt
to make an alliance with Russia and Prussia. In view of the
desertion of Frederick during the Seven Years War, the King of
Prussia's ' coyness ' is understandable.*

XXII. To LIEUTENANT-GENERAL CONWAY

August 11, 1765.

LIEUT. GEN. CONWAY,

The letter and enclosures from Captain Pallisser are of so
very serious a nature that I esteem it highly proper to give
you my ideas on their contents on paper as a more clear method
than any other. . . . I think it would be . . . expedient that
Mr. Hume[1] should with civility complain of the French ships
of war that have visited the coasts of Newfoundland, and of
the encroachments made by the French fishing vessels, as that
will greatly destroy the fallacious arguments they will probably
use in the Autumn as accusations against the Captain.

The only method that at present occurs to me by which the
French can be prevented settling on the coast of Newfoundland,
would be the having a greater military force in that island; but
the economical and I may say injudicious ideas of this country
in time of peace makes it not very practicable, for a corps ought
on purpose to be raised for that service, we having more places
to garrison than we have troops to supply. I wish you would
think over whether some other effectual method may not be
adopted that will prevent the like infraction of treaties for the
future; for my sole view in this and every other article of our
treaties, is with temper and firmness to make France observe them
strictly, and to do nothing that may hurt their honour, for that
is dearer to them than their interest, knowing how very unable
we are at this hour to make war, and that let their inability be
ever so great, we are undoubtedly less able to draw the sword.

---

[1] David Hume, the philosopher: he was at this time secretary to Lord
Hertford, ambassador at Paris: in 1767 he became under-secretary to
Conway.

XXIII. To Lieutenant-General Conway

30 *min. past* 1 *p.m.* [*September* 27, 1765].

Lt. Gen. Conway,

I have just received your packet but cannot help expressing some surprise at the great coyness of the K. of Prussia; I should have expected a different answer to the very friendly and I may say indulgent part I have on this occasion acted towards him; but I would feign hope this is owing to the fallacious accounts he has received from Baudouin; if he expects that I am to go all the way and that he is only to receive me if he pleases he is much mistaken, for I think the Crown of G. Britain a more useful ally to the K. of Prussia than he ever can be in return; and I here repeat what you heard me express to the D. of Grafton at the opening of this affair; that if the K. of Prussia means anew to live well with me I shall have no objection to do so with him; but if he expects I am to express any sorrow for what has passed betwixt us, that is impossible for I could not act otherwise than I have done if my sole object was the interest of my country, which I should not be an honest man if I at any time neglected for other concerns.

The most important event of the Rockingham administration was the repeal of the Stamp Act.

XXIV. To Lieutenant-General Conway

53 *min. past* 5 *p.m.* [*December* 5, 1765].

. . . I am more and more grieved at the accounts of America. Where this spirit will end is not to be said. It is, undoubtedly, the most serious matter that ever came before Parliament; it requires more deliberation, candour, and temper than I fear it will meet with.

XXV. To the Lord Chancellor[1]

Queen's House,[2] *February* 3, 1766.

My Lord,

According to your desire I saw Lord Rockingham yesterday, and very fully explained what you had said; but found by him

[1] Lord Northington. [2] The present Buckingham Palace.

33

D

that even the D. of Grafton is warmly of the opinion that they should meet the fate of this day;[1] I gave him every light I could as to the difficulties they will have to struggle with; he called on my promise at all times of not giving up administration whilst they thought they could act; by this you are fully apprised of the part they will take this day, which I believe will prove a fatal day to them; this hou? is perhaps one of the most critical ever known in this country; but I hope Providence will steer me through it with honour and at the same time in whatever manner may in the end be most to the advantage of this (from various factions) much injured country. You will I know be desirous of hearing how I find myself this morning; my headache is not abated, nor the feverish complaint.[2]

xxvi. Memorandum by the King

[*February* 10, 1766.]

Lord Rockingham this day came & complained to me as if he was accused of having wrong stated my opinion on the Stamp Act; I told him I had on *Friday* given him permission to say I preferred repealing to enforcing the Stamp Act; but that Modification I had ever thought both more consistent with the honour of this country, and all the Americans would with any degree of justice hope for.

The Duke of Bedford tried to seize the opportunity to ingratiate himself with the King, whom he approached through the Duke of York, only to be rebuffed.

xxvii. To the Duke of York

February 18, 1766.

I have carefully considered the Memorandum you this day delivered to me of what the D. of Bedford had drop'd to you; I have never refused any man of quality an audience who has desired it; but as all the D. of Bedford said can only be looked on

---

[1] The debate on the right of England to tax America.
[2] He had had a slight recurrence of his illness.

as an intimation that he is willing to attend me by way of offering his advice and assistance in regard to the Stamp Act, I cannot take notice of it, as I do not think it constitutional for the Crown personally to interfere in measures which it has thought proper to refer to the advice of Parliament.

From the beginning the Rockingham administration had been very feeble, and a flirtation with Pitt was very soon begun. The King, however, was anxious to avoid the humiliations of the previous summer.

XXVIII. To the Lord Chancellor

January 8, 1766.

My Ld. the D. of G[rafto]n appeared confused on coming to me this day, showed an inclination of speaking, yet remained silent; I thought it best therefore to mention the account I had received from Ld. R[ockingha]m & Mr. C[onwa]y of Mr. P[itt's] language to Mr. Th. T[ownshen]d on this. . . . The colour of what he said was that he saw a great prospect of Mr. P. being now ready to accept . . . therefore that he wished I would see him & form such an administration as that gentleman should think equal to the very great difficulties of the time; but if I thought this idea inadmissible, that to act consistent with his most private language as well as his public one, he should see himself in the unpleasant situation of desiring to resign the seals. . . .

Upon this I told him I had never showed any dislike to their drawing Mr. P. towards them, but that driving the P.S. [Privy Seal, Newcastle] out, insisting on an offer of the Treasury to Ld. T[emple] and new modelling the S[ecretarie]s of S[tate] was a total change of administration. . . . I next saw Ld. R[ockingham]. I cannot enough express how handsome and firm his language was; he seems willing to continue though the D. of G. should retire if he can see daylight for carrying on my business; the D. of N., who very properly offered to retire if that could assist my affairs; but showed manifestly a desire that things might go on.

I have now given you pretty nearly all the marrow of all their conversations, and now call on your advice at this very critical moment; my own opinion I confess is if possible to keep this administration on foot; if others thought as I do of both the Ss. of S. in point of abilities there would not be many long faces on their retiring : would it not be best to tell the D. of G. that I remain of the same opinion I did this day; and that I don't see the hurry of sending any message at all to Mr. Pitt. I must desire some answer this evening for every hour is of consequence. Lord R. dropped that Lord A[lbemarle] had said the best way would be the sending the D. of G. to Bath with such a message as G.A. proposed, and that perhaps Mr. P. would then talk so absurdly that it might open the D. of G. eyes; one reflection & I will conclude; the various unpleasant scenes teach me who act from principle & who not, & they rather increase my natural firmness; for as I have no one wish but what is for the advantage of my country, I have no temptation to submit to any of the humiliating steps that are recommended.

XXIX. TO THE MARQUESS OF ROCKINGHAM

January 9, 1766.

LORD ROCKINGHAM,

. . . I have revolved, most coolly and attentively, the business now before me, and am of opinion that so loose a conversation as that of Mr. Pitt and Mr. Townshend is not sufficient to risk either my dignity or the continuance of my administration by a fresh treaty with that gentleman; for if it should miscarry, all public opinion of this ministry would be destroyed by such an attempt. I shall therefore, undoubtedly, to-morrow decline authorizing the Duke of Grafton to say anything to Mr. Pitt, and don't doubt that when I set the example of steadiness, most of you will see the propriety of that conduct, and will follow it also. I wish therefore, you would be at St. James's by one to-morrow, that I may talk this affair over with you, previous to my seeing the two Secretaries of State. The Duke of Newcastle's conduct this day was very handsome and dignified.

xxx. To Lord Rockingham

Queen's House, January 10, 1766.

LORD ROCKINGHAM,

You have very properly put an end to the idea of writing to Mr. Pitt; if you continue firm I don't doubt of success, but if you in the least seem to hesitate the inferiors will fly off.

xxxi. To the Lord Chancellor

Queen's House, January 11, 1766.

MY LORD,

As I desire to inform Y.L. of every step of every [the very?] extraordinary affair before us; the D. of G. and Lt. G.C. wanted yesterday permission to write in my name to Mr. P. that I should have no objection to hear his opinion on the American affairs whenever he came to Town; on talking over this proposition with Ld. R. I authorized him to quash it; now I suppose the D. of G. will make one more attempt to get me to see him when he comes to Town. I hope you agree with me that after what has passed it would be very much below me to stoop to such a measure; Lord Al. came and spoke very respectfully and declared that there were no men of honour if I was to be given up for so audacious a proposal; he told me that the D. of G. conduct was solely bias'd by a resolution of retiring, for that he said that if Mr. P. proposal had come to anything, he would have retired! Your language to E[gmont] had perfectly satisfied him.

xxxii. To Lord Egmont

Queen's House, January 11, 1766.

MY DEAR LORD, I have entirely rejected the Duke of Grafton's plan of writing to Mr. Pitt, and am strongly of opinion that it would be *both below me and impolitic* to *see him alone when he* comes to Town; pray see Ld. Rockingham previous to his coming to me to-morrow, and *keep him steady*; for I fear lest the Secretaries should stagger him; all I desire is that they will act firmly till the arduous business of the American colonies is over, then I can stand upon my own feet.

Grafton, however, did see Pitt, and got a somewhat evasive answer. But still the game went on.

XXXIII. TO LORD ROCKINGHAM

10 min. past 9 a.m., January 16, 1766.

I think your sending a written answer to Mr. Pitt extremely dangerous, and, therefore, am clearly of opinion that your even seeing him alone is preferable. I at the same time confess that I think the Duke of Grafton has more delicacy than there appears cause for in declining accompanying you. I recommend it strongly to you to avoid a long conversation, by saying your business only permits you to call for a few minutes. Be extremely civil, but firm in what you say; and as the Duke of Grafton will not accompany you, I think the showing him the impracticability of his answer to my first question is necessary. Pray, as soon as you have seen him send me a line how things have passed. As to the full explanation, that may wait till I see you to-morrow. I am much pleased that Opposition has forced you to hear your own voice, which I hope will encourage you to stand forth in other debates.[1] . . .

On the 18th, however, the King authorized Grafton to take a message to Pitt: the King proved wiser than his Secretary, for Pitt was again evasive.

It must not be supposed that the King was especially attached to his ministers; and he became less so when they made a difficulty over granting his brothers' incomes out of the Civil List.

XXXIV. TO LORD EGMONT

Eight o'clock, Wednesday evening, May 28, 1766.

MY DEAR LORD,

I wished much to have seen you this day, but was so fatigued by the uneasiness I felt, that I could not when the Council was over send for you. The cause of it was the very extraordinary note I received this morning from Lord Rockingham, which I

---

[1] Rockingham hated speaking. In December he had written to the King: ' Lord Rockingham is ashamed to inform His Majesty that he did not attempt to speak upon this occasion.'

enclose for your information. So lately as Sunday last Lord Rockingham talked of obtaining the £40,000 per annum to be divided between my three brothers as.without fail to be moved this week, and now without one reason that has any solid foundation, he and his colleagues went to put it off after his having above six weeks ago desired me to promise my brothers it should be done this session : he wants now to make me break my word, which I cannot do; on my telling him this day that Opposition if they found the Ministry silent would propose it, he said that it must be withstood; I on that sharply replied that no man of honour could have advised a measure and then reject it because taken up by adversaries. I beg your thoughts on this if at home; my brothers have been with me, and are sensible I mean to stand by them : see what treatment I receive for [sic] every set of ministers; the rejecting General Warrants because their popularity was engaged, was to be firmly pushed though the most able of my servants were against the measure, but because a few weak boys are unwilling this session to pass the provision for my brothers, my word is to be set at naught; *my prudence is now exhausted I am inclined to take any step that will preserve my honour*; if you should be out when this arrives, pray send me a line by eleven to-morrow to the Queen's House.

Yet it would have required more than a private matter to cause the King to take the distasteful step of making yet another change.

Towards the end of May, however, the Duke of Grafton resigned, his fellow-Secretary, Conway, being with difficulty persuaded to remain. The government staggered on weakly till the end of the session in June, but very soon an internal disagreement on the civil government of Quebec showed even Northington that it was impossible to go on. Nothing could be done without Pitt.

xxxv. To William Pitt

Richmond Lodge, July 7, 1766.

Mr. Pitt,

Your very dutiful and handsome conduct the last summer makes me desirous of having your thoughts how an able and dignified ministry may be formed. I desire, therefore, you will come, for this salutary purpose, to town.

I cannot conclude without expressing how entirely my ideas concerning the basis on which a new administration should be erected, are consonant to the opinion you gave on that subject in Parliament a few days before you set out for Somersetshire.

I convey this through the channel of the Earl of Northington; as there is no man in my service on whom I so thoroughly rely, and who, I know, agrees with me so perfectly in the contents of this letter.

Temple was once more a serious difficulty.

XXXVI. TO WILLIAM PITT

Richmond Lodge, 15 min. past 7, July 15, 1766.

MR. PITT,

Lord Temple has been with me, and has desired me not to see you to-morrow, that he may have time fully to talk with you. I have, therefore, entrusted him to acquaint you I shall not expect you then; but, on recollection, I think it may be both of utility and not void of amazement, for you to know the substance of what has passed.

I opened to him a desire of seeing him in the Treasury, and, in conjunction with you, chalking out such an administration as can be formed, considering the unhappy divisions that subsist between men, yet taking the present administration for the basis to build on, with such alterations as might appear necessary.

I am sorry to see, though we only kept in generals, that he seems to incline to quarters very heterogeneous to my and your ideas, and almost a total exclusion to the present men—which is not your plan; but as we did not come to particulars, I hope I am not quite founded in my apprehensions.

I concluded with saying I should only agree to such a plan as you could with pleasure be a part of; but not to one wherein you had not a principal share.

I should wish to see you on Thursday at eleven, at the Queen's House; as that will give you time to consider the whole of this weighty matter. This letter remains a perfect secret betwixt me and you if you think it best that it should.

Temple was not at all attracted by the idea of having the place but not the power of the First Lord of the Treasury. He would only come in on perfectly level terms, at least, with Pitt. This was not at all Pitt's idea. He was prepared now to accept the King's notion of getting together the best administration possible regardless of faction and interest, but on condition only that he should be the undoubted leader. Finally it was arranged that Grafton should have the Treasury, Conway should remain Secretary of State, Camden should become Lord Chancellor, while Northington took the Presidency of the Council. Pitt himself would replace Newcastle as Privy Seal, be the head of the government, and go to the House of Lords.

XXXVII. To William Pitt

Richmond Lodge, 25 min. past 5, July 29, 1766.

Mr. Pitt,

I have signed this day the warrant for creating you an Earl, and shall with pleasure receive you in that capacity to-morrow, as well as entrust you with my privy seal; as I know the Earl of Chatham will zealously give his aid towards destroying all party distinctions, and restoring that subordination to Government which can alone preserve that inestimable blessing, Liberty, from degenerating into Licentiousness.

It was not long before the King had an opportunity of testing the mettle of his new administration.

XXXVIII. To Lieutenant-General Conway

Queen's House, 8 min. past 9 p.m., September 20, 1766.

Lieutenant General Conway,

I think the summoning a Committee of Council on Wednesday next to afresh consider the dearness of corn, and what means may be expedient to remove the evil at the present moment, is very proper; but as the Attorney General's opinion was so very strong even yesterday, when he was just returned from his visit to the Lord President, I very much doubt whether that Lord and the Chancellor as lawyers will venture to change their opinions; though great evils must require at times extraordinary measures to remove them, the present risings are only an additional proof to me of the great licentiousness that has infused itself into all orders of men; if a due obedience to the law, and the submitting to that as the only just method of having grievances removed does not once more become the characteristic of this nation, we shall soon be no better than the savages of America, then we shall be as much despised by all civilized nations as we are as yet revered for our excellent constitution. . . .

XXXIX. To Lieutenant-General Conway

Queen's House, 5 min. past 7 p.m., September 24, 1766.
Lieut. Gen. Conway,

As there seems to be so real a distress from the present excessive dearness of the corn, and a great probability that if a prohibition is not issued to prevent the further exportation of it the evil may greatly increase before the Parliament can possibly put a stop to it, I am glad the Council have unanimously thought it expedient that such a prohibition should be immediately ordered; I desire therefore the proclamation may be prepared for my signing on Friday. I think it would be but right you should acquaint the Lord President with the result of this day's Council.

The exportation of corn was prohibited by an Order in Council, which procedure was violently attacked by the opposition as being ' arbitrary ' as soon as Parliament met in November.

The government might be ' firm ' in George III's sense, but it by no means provided that haven he had hoped for, an administration of sensible men without allegiance to party, faction, or family, which would reasonably carry on the King's business. Chatham, as head of a weak government, soon found it advisable to make advances to ' the Bloomsbury Gang ', but their demands were more than he could stomach.

XL. TO THE EARL OF CHATHAM

35 min. past 8 a.m., November 28, 1766.

LORD CHATHAM,

I returned so late from the play, that I thought it unfair to acknowledge the receipt of your letter containing the issue of your conversation with Lord Gower till this morning. I augur from it that he will on his return from Woburn, accept; for he is too well versed in the manners of the world to have shown so good an inclination unless he had been certain the proposal would meet with the Duke of Bedford's concurrence; but should it prove otherwise, it will not lessen my confidence that my affairs will meet with success, whilst the advantage of my country is the sole end proposed by every measure, and that my administration follow strenuously my example in opposing factious bands, in whatever quarters they appear, though willing to receive able and good men, let their private friendships be where they will.

XLI. TO THE EARL OF CHATHAM

[November 29, 1766.]

LORD CHATHAM,

I am sensible of your attention in sending me the account of Lord Gower's return from Woburn, and that no answer will be made till Monday evening. I am so totally indifferent as to what it may prove that I can without the smallest share of impatience wait till then, though I think the answer might have been returned by this time as the Duke of Bedford was enough prepared by your conversations at Bath to have previously received the opinions of his friends; therefore I must think there is an air of more reserve than appears necessary.

XLII. TO THE EARL OF CHATHAM

St. James's, [1] min. past 11 p.m. [December 2, 1766].

LORD CHATHAM,

On my return from the ball-room, I found your letter containing the Duke of Bedford's extravagant proposal. Indeed I expected, from his choosing to deliver his answer in person, that he meant to attempt obtaining an office or two in addition to those offered; but could not imagine that even the rapaciousness of his friends could presume to think of more than that.

I know the uprightness of my cause, and that my principal ministers mean nothing but to aid in making my people happy; therefore I cannot exceed the bounds you acquainted Lord Gower were the utmost that would be granted. This hour demands a due firmness; 'tis that has already dismayed all the hopes of those just retired, and will, I am confident, show the Bedfords of what little consequence they also are.[1] A contrary conduct would at once overturn the very end proposed at the formation of the present administration; for to rout out the present method of parties banding together, can only be obtained by a withstanding their unjust demands, as well as the engaging able men, be their private connections what they will. I shall be ready to receive you to-morrow at two o'clock at the Queen's House.

At this time what Chatham called 'this transcendent object, India,' began to attract the King's attention: the subject was to loom big later in the reign, but George III was already wishing to take India out of the hands of a private company, and add it to his dominions. What was asked for now was an inquiry, and a statement of accounts.

XLIII. To Lieutenant-General Conway

Queen's House, 45 min. past 7 a.m., December 6, 1766.
Lieutenant-General Conway,

The debate of yesterday has ended very advantageously for Administration. The division on the motion for adjournment will undoubtedly show Mr. Grenville that he is not of the consequence he figures to himself. I am so sanguine with regard to the affair of the East India Company, that I trust Tuesday will convince the world that whilst Administration has no object but the procuring what may be of solid advantage to my people, it is not in the power of any men to prevent it. Indeed my great reliance on its success in the House of Commons is in your

[1] In the next year, however, Lord Gower became President of the Council.

abilities and character; and I am certain I can rely on your zeal at all times to carry on my affairs, as I have no one desire but what tends to the happiness of my people.[1]

One of the King's reasons for his eagerness is apparent.

XLIV. TO THE DUKE OF GRAFTON

Queen's house, [1] *min. past 7 a.m., December 9, 1766.*
DUKE OF GRAFTON,

On the issue of this day I think the real glory of this nation depends; the more I reflect on it, the more I am convinced that if zealously taken up by four or five of my ablest servants in the House of Commons, that there will be the greatest majority ever known in that House, and what is more agreeable that it will be from conviction that this is the only safe method of extracting this country out of its lamentable situation owing to the load of debt it labours under. I am therefore very desirous of being informed by you when Gen. Conway has taken his final opinion whether he will not support the calling for the state of the revenues of the E.I. Company, though Mr. Townshend[2] should unaccountably hang back. I am certain I need not press you to bring this about as I am thoroughly convinced by the conversations I have had with you on this subject that you view it in as strong a light as I do.

Though the motion resulted in a triumph for the government, it was not long before the administration received a severe set-back. The country gentlemen refused to continue the land tax at four shillings in the pound, bribing themselves, as Chesterfield put it, with a reduction of a shilling.

[1] On Tuesday, 9th, Alderman Beckford, at Chatham's instigation, moved for the production of papers relative to the revenue of Bengal. Grenville's motion for the adjournment was defeated by 164 to 54. The last sentence is directed at Conway's half-heartedness in the affair.
[2] Charles Townshend, Chancellor of the Exchequer.

xlv. To Lieutenant-General Conway

Queen's House, 5 min. past 11 p.m., February 27, 1767.

LIEUTENANT GENERAL CONWAY,

I am not less surprised than sorry that the Land Tax is to be reduced one shilling in the pound this year; those who have voted for it can have been guided only by the incitements that too frequently direct the conduct of politicians, the shadow of popularity (for the reality must consist alone in what is of real advantage to the country) and a desire of giving trouble; as the true interest of my people is the only object I wish to promote, and as I trust my ministers have no other view; though the fate of this day on that account is disagreeable, I doubt not on all other occasions a great majority will appear in their favour.

xlvi. To the Duke of Grafton

Queen's House, 45 min. past 11 p.m., February 27, 1767.

DUKE OF GRAFTON,

The zeal you show on all occasions for my service, makes me wish to open my mind to you on the strange conclusion of this day's debate. I feel sorrow not only as the continuing the four shillings tax was proposed by my ministers, but because I think it will greatly defeat the salutary measure of paying off the redeemable four percents within the year, and as it shows on what very sordid principles the majority must have acted, I recommend it to you at the same time not to let this check dismay you; in this world these things will happen, therefore rest assured that it will if possible stimulate me to act with greater vigour, and to show those who perhaps are rejoicing at this hour at their victory, that those who mean only what is right can show a degree of fortitude in reverses that their sordid minds are incapable of. I desire you will come in your morning dress at nine to-morrow morning.

The vote by itself would not have had much importance but for the fact that to help to make up the consequent gap in the revenue, the brilliant, mercurial Charles Townshend suggested, in May, certain excise duties in America, a point immediately

*taken up by Grenville. The administration was extremely averse
to the idea, but they could not disown their Chancellor of the
Exchequer, and dared not dismiss him in the absence of Chatham.*

*Chatham had been ill all the winter, but at last, in March, was
able to come to London, soon after the vote on the Land Tax.*

XLVII.TO THE EARL OF CHATHAM

Queen's House, 17 min. past 6 p.m., March 7, 1767.

LORD CHATHAM,

I cannot help taking up my pen to express how contented I
am at the favourable appearance of the House of Commons
yesterday. The not expressing any uneasiness at the division of
the last Friday has greatly contributed to this; which is chiefly
owing to that intrepidity which ever attends you.

Now you are arrived in town, every difficulty will daily
decrease; and though I confess that I do not think I have met
with that treatment I had reason to expect from many individuals
now strongly united in opposition, without any more honourable
reasons than because they are out of place, yet I can never believe
but the majority of the nation must feel themselves interested
to support my measures, while my ministers steadily assist me in
pursuing such as are calculated solely for the benefit of my
dominions.

I cannot conclude without desiring to learn how you continue,
and insisting on your not coming out till you can do it with
safety.

*Chatham's prestige was essential to the continuance of the
ministry: as the King had written to him on March 3rd, his
presence was necessary for the royal and the public services, and
he counted on him to ' withstand that coil called connection '.
But no sooner had Chatham come to London than he fell a
victim to the mental illness that prostrated him for two years.
It put Grafton in a very difficult position: he had accepted the
Treasury only on condition that Chatham should be the real
leader; but Chatham insisted upon staying in bed, invisible to
everybody, deaf to all appeals. Once more he was making the
King's government impossible. In May the situation became
critical: Chatham obdurately refused all Grafton's appeals for an*

interview, and on the 29th the Duke had to report a final refusal, after a letter to Chatham in which he had had to threaten resignation.

XLVIII. To the Duke of Grafton

Richmond Lodge, 18 min. past 11 a.m., May 30, 1767.

DUKE OF GRAFTON,

Though deeply concerned at the note you have wrote me, and in the most agitated state of mind, yet harbouring the most affectionate esteem for you, I think it necessary that you should come this evening at any time convenient to you.

In this agitated state of mind, the King in the meanwhile wrote to Chatham, then at Hampstead.

XLIX. To the Earl of Chatham

Richmond Lodge, 34 min. past 2 p.m., May 30, 1767.

LORD CHATHAM,

No one has more cautiously avoided writing to you than myself during your late indisposition; but the moment is so extremely critical, that I cannot possibly delay it any longer. By the letter you received from the Duke of Grafton, you must perceive the anxiety he and the President[1] at present labour under. The Chancellor[2] is very much in the same situation. This is equally owing to the majority in the House of Lords, amounting on the Friday only to six, and on the Tuesday to three, though I made two of my brothers vote on both those days; and to the great coldness shown those three ministers by Lord Shelburne,[3] whom they, as well as myself, imagine to be rather a secret enemy; the avowed enmity of Mr. Townshend;[4] and the resolution of Lieutenant-General Conway[5] to retire, though without any view of entering into faction.

My firmness is not dismayed by these unpleasant appearances; for from the hour you entered into office, I have uniformly

---

[1] Northington.
[2] Camden.
[3] Secretary of State.
[4] Charles Townshend, Chancellor of the Exchequer.
[5] Secretary of State.

relied on your firmness to act in defiance to that hydra faction, which has never appeared to the height it now does, till within these few weeks. Though your relations, the Bedfords and the Rockinghams are joined with the intention to storm my closet, yet if you was mean enough to submit, they own they would not join in forming an administration; therefore nothing but confusion could be obtained.

I am strongly of opinion with the answer you sent the Duke of Grafton;[1] but, by a note I have received from him, I fear I cannot keep him above a day, unless you would see him and give him encouragement. Your duty and affection for my person, your own honour, call on you to make an effort: five minutes' conversation with you would raise his spirits, for his heart is good; mine, I thank heaven, wants no rousing: my love to my country, as well as what I owe to my own character and to my family, prompt me not to yield to faction. Be firm, and you will find me amply ready to take as active a part as the hour seems to require. Though none of my ministers stand by me, I cannot truckle.

I wish a few lines in answer, as I am to have the Duke of Grafton with me this evening; and if you cannot come to me to-morrow, I am ready to call at North End on my return that evening to this place. Whilst I have sixty-five present and thirty proxies in the House of Lords ready to stand by me, besides a majority of 151 since that, in the House of Commons, against 84, though the Secretary of State[2] and the Chancellor of the Exchequer[3] were in the minority, I think the game easy if you either come out or will admit very few people.

The threat of a visit from the King for this once broke down Chatham's resistance, and he agreed to see Grafton, which at once gave strength to the ministry. But from then until his resignation in October 1768 he remained invisible at Hampstead, at Hayes, or at Burton Pynsent, merely answering the King's frequent and kindly letters by those servile protestations couched in the style he delighted to use when writing to his monarch. He threw himself at the King's feet, his heart was penetrated and

[1] That he should cling to his post.
[2] Lord Shelburne.
[3] Charles Townshend.

49

overcome by his royal master's goodness and condescension, but he would not budge. His mind, indeed, appears to have failed completely, but even so it was essential to government that he should be supposed to be working behind the scenes: his illness must be kept a secret.

L. To Lord Camden

St. James's, August 6, 1767.

Lord Camden,

The letter you have received from Mr. Nuthall concerning the very unhappy state in which he found the Earl of Chatham yesterday gives me great sorrow; the seeing a man that has appeared in so very great a light fall into such a situation is an abasement of human nature; I think it most prudent that this should not be communicated. . . .

The truth, however, could not be kept from leaking out; in September one of the earlier letters of Junius refers to Lord Chatham as ' a lunatic brandishing a crutch '.

Grafton, now Prime Minister, as we should say, in fact as well as in name, made an approach to the Rockingham faction during the summer, but was repulsed. The ministry therefore went on, but certain changes were made necessary by the death of Charles Townshend, then plotting a new administration with himself at the head. Lord North was induced to become Chancellor of the Exchequer; Conway, though he remained leader of the House of Commons, resigned his Secretaryship, which was taken over by Lord Weymouth; Northington's ill-health compelled him to resign, which gave an opening to the ' Bloomsbury gang '. Bedford himself, now failing, would take nothing, but Gower became Lord President. A new post, Secretary of State for the Colonies, was very properly founded, the post being filled by Lord Hillsborough. The general election of 1768 made no change in the political situation: party management went along the usual lines with the usual results.

One effect of the dissolution, however, was the return to England of Wilkes, and his candidature for Parliament. Though he failed in the City, he was successful for Middlesex. There were tumultuous scenes, even more riotous than there had been all over the country during the elections, and the troops had to be called out. On the 20th April he was due to appear at the Court of King's Bench to answer to his outlawry; he was released, but was expected to surrender again: otherwise he would be arrested. The Sheriff's officers, however, seem to have been afraid of the fury of the mob.

LI. TO VISCOUNT WEYMOUTH

Queen's House, 46 min. past 7 p.m., April 25, 1768.

LORD WEYMOUTH,

Your caution in renewing the former directions for the peace of the town is most seasonable, as the parties might otherwise have fallen into their usual state of negligence. The Attorney-General's letter makes me imagine that Mr. Wilkes will not surrender himself; therefore your having afresh insisted on the utmost being done to seize him, seems absolutely necessary. I cannot conclude without expressing my sorrow that so mean a set of men as the Sheriff's officers can, either from timidity or interestedness frustrate a due exertion of the law. If he is not soon secured, I wish you would inquire whether there is no legal method of quickening the zeal of the Sheriffs themselves.

In the meantime the question arose as to what was to be done about Wilkes qua member of Parliament.

LII. TO LORD NORTH

Queen's House, April 25, 1768.

LORD NORTH,

Though entirely confiding in your attachment to my person, as well as in your hatred of every lawless proceeding, yet I think it highly proper to apprise you that the expulsion of Mr. Wilkes appears to be very essential, and must be effected; and that I make no doubt, when you lay this affair with your usual precision before the meeting of the gentlemen of the House of Commons this evening, it will meet with the required unanimity and vigour. The case of Mr. Ward[1] in the reign of my great-grandfather seems to point out the best method of proceeding on this occasion, as it will equally answer whether the Court should by that time have given sentence, or should he be attempting to

---

[1] John Ward had been expelled the House in May 1728, on being convicted of forgery.

obtain a writ of error. If there is any man capable of forgetting his criminal writings, I think his speech in the Court of King's Bench on Wednesday last reason enough to go as far as possible to expel him; for he declared ' Number 45 ' a paper that the author ought to *glory in,* and the blasphemous poem a mere *ludicrous production.* . . .

When Wilkes was arrested, the mob rescued him, but he surrendered himself. When condemned to two years' imprisonment for libel on the King, and for blasphemy, the crowds attempted to rescue him on his way to the King's Bench prison. The King began to think that severe measures, shooting if necessary, would have to be resorted to to quell the disturbances.

LIII. TO VISCOUNT WEYMOUTH

Queen's House, 25 min. past 10 a.m., April 30, 1768.

LORD WEYMOUTH,

. . . If these tumultuous assemblies continue before the King's Bench Prison, it is worthy of consideration whether the Attorney-General ought not to move the Court that Mr. Wilkes be removed to the Tower, where the like illegal course will be effectually prevented without harassing the troops. If a due firmness is shown with regard to this audacious criminal, this affair will prove a fortunate one by restoring due obedience to the laws. But if this is not the case, I fear anarchy will continue till what every temperate man must dread, *I mean an effusion of blood,* has vanquished.

The King's views on riotous assemblies were not weakened by the actions of the sailors, who, on strike for higher wages, had paraded the town, rioted, called at Richmond Lodge, and fought with the coal-heavers.

LIV. TO VISCOUNT WEYMOUTH

Richmond Lodge, 10 min. past 6 p.m., May 7, 1768.

LORD WEYMOUTH,

The sailors have been here. The servants, according to my orders, acquainted them that I was out, at which they expressed

much concern.   On being asked their business, they said it was
for an increase of wages.   They were told that I had no power
to act in this affair, which they readily owned; said they were
fools for walking so far, and that they would go back to London;
but begged the petition might be given me when I came home,
as it was a proof that, though they were wrongly advised in
addressing themselves to me, they looked upon me as having the
welfare of the British sailors at heart.

LV. To Viscount Weymouth

Richmond Lodge, 16 min. past 6 p.m., May 9, 1768.

LORD WEYMOUTH,

Your indefatigable attention to preserving the peace of the
capital is highly praiseworthy.   Should it be thought advisable
on this occasion to issue any Proclamation, or any Order in
Council, I am ready to come at the shortest notice and at any
hour.   I cannot conclude without strongly recommending the
Justices, if they call the troops to their assistance, should show
that vigour which alone makes them respected.

*'This occasion' was the opening of Parliament on the next
day.   The mob, hoping to see their idol Wilkes on his way from
jail to Parliament, surged round his prison; when it was found he
was not coming out, a riot ensued; the Justices showed the vigour
which was to make them respected, and an effusion of blood
occurred, one man being killed.*

LVI. To Viscount Weymouth

Richmond Lodge, 50 min. past 6 p.m., May 10, 1768.

LORD WEYMOUTH,

This continuation of collections of the populace has a greater
appearance of plan than I ever remember before.   I therefore,
in the most earnest manner, require that Justices be told to show
the vigour in Westminster that has been this day at the King's
Bench Prison.   Bloodshed is not what I delight in, but it seems
to me the only way of restoring due obedience to the laws.   I
have just seen the paper that was distributed to-day, recommending the driving the Commons out of their House, which they for

their own sakes are bound to take notice of. I shall with pleasure sign any proclamation that can tend to restore order to this country, formerly looked upon as the seat of liberty, which has now degenerated into licentiousness. I mean to come instantly to town, and wish to see you about nine at the Queen's House.

For the moment matters remained quiet on the surface, but internal dissensions were rife in the cabinet.

LVII. TO THE DUKE OF GRAFTON

Richmond Lodge, September 15, 1768.

DUKE OF GRAFTON,

Having had a conversation of some consequence with the Lord Chancellor yesterday, I think it material to make you acquainted with it. . . . He asked me whether you and Lord Shelburne had in the least approached each other during his absence; I very frankly said that Lord Shelburne manifestly still attempted to thwart every measure that originated from you, and seemed to propose none himself, and that I believed he was lying by for some popular occasion to resign with some degree of éclat; that seeing this in a very strong light I had long declared to you that nothing could establish that harmony in the Cabinet which alone could give weight to measures taken either at home or abroad than the appointing a new Secretary to the Southern Department. He said he had long looked upon that measure as inevitable, but that as the Lord who held that employment had been recommended by Lord Chatham, he thought it best for himself to take a neuter part on this occasion, though privately he could not conceal his thoughts to me; and that he must add that Lord Shelburne had not only lost your good opinion, but that of every one of the other active members of the Cabinet; and was even shy with him, because he had not succeeded in raising doubts in his mind. I dropped the idea of Lord Rochford,[1] which seemed to please him, as he could neither be called of the Bedford connection nor adverse to the Earl of Chatham. He then concluded with telling me that the news from Hayes does

---

[1] Ambassador at Paris.

not mend, and that he himself entirely despairs of seeing that able man ever in a state of health to be of any farther use in public affairs. . . .

For a moment at this period there was a possibility of war. Genoa had sold Corsica to France, and the sympathies of this country were strongly with the island, then revolting. Arms were sent to their aid, but the King refused to countenance more active intervention; thus the sole result of the rebellion was the early addition to the amenities of English society in the form of Paoli, the Corsican leader.

LVIII. To the Duke of Grafton

St. James's, September 16, 1768.

Duke of Grafton,

On coming this instant to town, I have received your letter of yesterday, and entirely join in opinion with you that everything that can with any degree of propriety be done for the assistance of the Corsicans has been already ordered; for I am ready to declare it to the whole world that I cannot think under the present state of debt that it can be expedient for the sake alone of the Island of Corsica, to begin acts of hostilities against France; nor am I of opinion that we could now be in time to prevent her from succeeding in the conquest of that Island. Does it not appear very extraordinary that Paoli should have continued so long silent when by the account he sent through the channel of Sir Horace Mann,[1] M. de Choiseul[2] had interruptedly avowed in the correspondence that subsisted between them that the conquest of the island was intended, and now begin to call for our assistance? . . .

In October the internal crisis once more became acute. It had been found necessary, in view of the way matters were developing in America, to dismiss Sir Jeffrey Amherst from his post of Governor of Virginia, for the good enough reason that he refused ever to go there. A little later, the Cabinet found it

---

[1] Horace Walpole's friend, Envoy at Florence.
[2] The great French minister of foreign affairs.

intolerable to continue with Shelburne, and it was decided to dismiss him. Grafton was sent to Hayes to tell Lady Chatham, and ask her to break the news to her husband. Chatham at once wrote to Grafton to resign from the administration, implying that his reason was the dismissal of two of his friends. The King wrote to Grafton expressing his surprise and annoyance: he also wrote to Chatham.

LIX. To the Earl of Chatham

Queen's House, October 14, 1768.

Lord Chatham,

The Duke of Grafton communicated to me yesterday your desire of resigning the Privy Seal on account of the continuation of your ill state of health. As you entered upon that employment in August 1766 at my own requisition, I think I have a right *to insist* on your remaining in my service; for I with pleasure look forward to the time of your recovery, when I may have your assistance in resisting the torrent of factions this country so much labours under. This thought is the more frequent in my mind as the Lord Chancellor and the Duke of Grafton take every opportunity to declare warmly to me their desire of seeing that: therefore I again repeat it, you must not think of retiring, but of pursuing what may be most conducive to restore your health, and to my seeing you take a public share in my affairs.

Chatham, however, insisted on resigning, and even the King's fear of having once more to undergo the tyranny of Grenville could not bring him to make a further appeal.

In the spring of 1769 great excitement was caused by the action of the House of Commons in expelling Wilkes, who in January had been elected Alderman for the ward of Farringdon Without, and finally, though Wilkes was legally elected, declaring Colonel Luttrell Member for Middlesex. The populace made several violent demonstrations, one in particular directed against a procession which, on March 22nd, wished to present an address to the King. There was a tussle, the guards were called out, and fifteen men arrested. The Grand Jury of Middlesex refused to find a Bill of Indictment against them.

LX. TO LORD NORTH

Queen's House, 20 min. past 11 p.m., March 31, 1769.

LORD NORTH,

The short state of the bills preferred this day, which I have just received from you, manifests the factious and partial conduct of the Grand Jury. If there is no means by law to quell riots, and if juries forget they are on their oath to be guided by facts, not faction, this constitution must be overthrown, and anarchy (the most terrible of all evils) must ensue; it therefore behoves every honest man with vigour to stand forth, and by such methods as may seem most effectual to give elasticity to the springs of government. I am ready to take any forward path that the present crisis may require, and I trust that every man not absorbed in faction will now firmly unite to crush this party that aim at the very vitals of all government; as to your zeal and firmness I know I can thoroughly rely on them.

The King was delighted when on April 15th the House declared that Luttrell ' ought to have been returned': this, he told North, ' must greatly tend to destroy that outrageous licentiousness that has been so successfully raised by wicked and disappointed men': and he was still further pleased when on May 8th the House once more discussed the position following a petition from the freeholders of Middlesex.

LXI. TO LORD NORTH

Queen's House, 38 min. past 10 a.m., May 9, 1769.

LORD NORTH,

I received early this morning your account of the very honourable issue of yesterday's debate, and have this instant received the list of the speakers. The House of Commons has with becoming dignity supported their own privileges, without which they cannot subsist; it is now my duty with firmness to see the laws obeyed, which I trust will by degrees restore good order, without which no State can flourish.

In the summer, Chatham made an astonishing, one might say a miraculous recovery, and in July appeared at Court. At the opening of the next session, January 9th, 1770, he rose to reply to the King's speech. He referred unfavourably to foreign affairs, inveighed against the action of the House of Commons in the Wilkes affair, and passed strictures upon the dealings with America. It was true that in 1769 all the duties except that on tea had been taken off, and that only retained against Grafton's wish at North's instigation, but the growing discontent in the colonies was a serious matter. Camden at once resigned, and the ministry tottered. A desperate attempt was made to replace the Lord Chancellor, and Charles Yorke was induced to desert the Rockingham party to take the Great Seal: he died a few days later, by his own hand it was said at the time, overwhelmed by remorse at his own treachery. It was too much for Grafton. He had withstood popular abuse and the attacks of Junius, but he could not stand without Chatham. On the day that Rockingham was to move that the Lords should examine the causes of the present discontents, he resigned. The King was in a desperate position: he considered that Grafton had basely deserted him. Rockinghams, Bedfords, Grenvilles (to whom Chatham was now reconciled) were trying to take the closet by storm: a total change of administration would mean a dissolution, and the elections would be swayed by mob violence. Almost as a last venture he appealed to North, who was on the unpopular side in every question, and seemed willing to serve him.

LXII. TO LORD NORTH

Queen's House, 40 min. past 10 a.m., January 23, 1770.

LORD NORTH,

After seeing you last night, I saw Lord Weymouth, who, by my direction, will wait on you with Lord Gower this morning to press you in the strongest manner to accept the office of First Commissioner of the Treasury; my own mind is more and more strengthened with the rightness of the measure that would prevent every other desertion. You must easily see that if you do not accept I have no peer at present in my service that I would consent to place in the Duke of Grafton's employment. Whatever you may think, do not take any decision, unless it is the one of instantly accepting, without a farther conversation with me. And as to other arrangements, you may hear what others think, but keep your own opinion till I have seen you.

Reluctantly, Lord North accepted. The outlook was not very hopeful; the administration was even more rickety than Chatham's ' patchwork '; but he would do his best.

* * * * * *

Although at this time the King had no love for Hanover, it must not be thought that he neglected his duties with respect to that Electorate. He was continually writing to Baron Münchhausen, now his Minister at Hanover, or to the head of his army. A letter to each must suffice to illustrate this.

LXIII. To Baron Münchhausen
(French)

Queen's House, November 11, 1766.

MY FIRST MINISTER,

Having nothing so much at heart as the prosperity of my subjects, and looking upon the peasant as the most useful person in the State, I would like to have a statement of how much money such a man can earn a year if he has a wife and three children, and how much it will cost him to maintain them; then I can with certainty know the true situation of that useful sort of my subjects. I see that most of the sovereigns in Germany want to run after trade, but to my mind they are beginning at the wrong end; one must cherish agriculture; when one's production is greater than one's consumption in the country, then one can carry out an advantageous traffic with what is superfluous; linen, honey, wax, lumber, cloth are the branches of commerce which are natural in my Electorate, thus I recommend them to your particular care. For the rest, I pray God, my First Minister, to keep you in His holy and worthy Grace.

LXIV. To Field-Marshal von Spörcken
(French)

Queen's House, February, 1767.

MY FIELD MARSHAL,

I take great pleasure in occupying myself with everything which I think may help in perfecting my Electoral troops. I am quite convinced that the most essential point about cavalry is to be able to manage its horses properly. To attain this end, I would like to have your opinion if it would not be very useful for a Colonel or Lieutenant Colonel to come over here to study in detail the method of my British cavalry. I would wish Major General Freytag should accompany him, because he would be able to tell me from you about many minute points which cannot be made plain by letter, but which may influence the good of the service. I cannot conclude without expressing my contentment at the care which you take with the artillery in all its branches. So that you may meet with fewer difficulties, I have signed a rescript to the Ministry of War, in which I give the order that General Major Braun is to take any orders from you without their intervention.

He was not, however, unaware of Hanover as a factor in his life as King of Great Britain. The following letter is written to Grafton, his Secretaries of State, and Sir Joseph Yorke, Ambassador at The Hague.

LXV. To the Duke of Grafton, etc.

Queen's House, December 15, 1769.

The experience I have had of your zeal for my service, and of your knowledge of the sentiments of the principal persons in the Republic,[1] has occasioned my directing B. Bebr to enquire of you what conduct the United Provinces[1] are most likely to adopt in case the clouds that seem daily to thicken should produce a new war; for if I form a place of defence as Elector, it must in great measure arise from the hopes of assistance from so natural an ally as the Dutch; I shall be desirous of hearing from you in consequence of this, and of learning how far the influence of the Prince of Orange gains ground, and whether Prince Louis[2] still retains the influence he had with that Prince.

[1] Holland.
[2] Of Brunswick-Wolfenbüttel, who, called in to reorganize the Dutch army, came to prominence in the affairs of the United Provinces.

LXVI. To Sir Joseph Yorke

January 7, 1770.[1]

Sir Joseph Yorke,

Your letter has in the fullest manner satisfied the questions upon which I was desirous of information; and will be very material for my guidance whenever the calamity of war shall appear indispensably necessary; at present the firm though temperate language which has been held to the French Court has lowered her tone, and will I flatter myself shew that they cannot be less [so?] high in their future discussions; but great attention must be had to their conduct, as they can never be trusted, and whenever I see any cause of just suspicion, shall through your channel convey my ideas to the Prince of Orange.

I cannot help expressing my sorrow that the King of Prussia has any weight with that Prince, as I can never look upon him as a sincere friend to this country, or to the United Provinces, and as I know he has painted him [the Prince of Orange] to the Brunswick family in the most unfavourable colour.

I confess my political creed is formed on the system of King William; England in conjunction with the House of Austria and the Republic seems the most secure union against the Family Compact; and if Russia could be added to this, I think the Court of Versailles would not be in a hurry to commence hostilities. But this plan may be difficult to be effected, though I am sure it is the real interest of the four states.

Disinterested in foreign politics, it will be seen that here George III simply accepted the ' old system ' of the Whigs which had been the ruling scheme in foreign relations in the previous reign.

---

[1] Fortescue (II, 204) prints this letter under date 9 January, 1771.

CHAPTER III

LORD NORTH

1770-1773

The first ten years of the reign had been stormy. The young King, engaging and popular, had lost his initial advantage: instead of being successful in his efforts to unite, he had been buffeted more than ever his grandfather had been, by the blasts of faction. His pathetic belief in the general goodwill of men had been painfully disillusioned, as indeed had his touching faith in the efficacy of virtue. Compelled early in his reign to part with his virtuous support and mentor, for the last two years he had despairingly clung to a minister addicted to horse-racing, and given to publicly flaunting his mistress. Pitt had failed him, and he had never been within sight of that faithful minister who should help him in the difficult art of administering his realm for the good of his subjects: in the ten years he had had no less than six Prime Ministers, as we should call them. But now, instead of a very young man, dependent upon advice, afraid of himself, without any real knowledge of men and affairs, we have a monarch firm in his opinions to the point of stubbornness, able to hold his own, difficult to intimidate. If his virtues were the domestic rather than the public ones, he possessed at least one of the latter in a marked degree, namely moral courage; and at last, with North, he had his reward, a faithful servant willing to go the way he wished, able to manage his party. He had, in fact, as Professor Namier has said, found his Newcastle.

None of the big figures were of the new Court party, not Chatham, nor Grenville, nor Bedford; Burke was against it, and now Camden; the Rockingham faction would have nothing to do with it; and still Junius carried on his attacks. On the other hand, all the old commanding figures were, at long last, dead: Newcastle, the Duke of Cumberland, Hardwicke, Granville, Bath; Bedford was old, stricken by the death of his son; Grenville was ill; many of his old adherents were neutral, such as Conway and Grafton; though out of office they supported him in the two Houses. The stage was clear for a quiet administration, so long as it could hold its own, as it did for longer than all the previous administrations put together. It soon showed that it was not going to fall to pieces immediately, as at first seemed likely, though it was not without a certain art that it had to be held together.

1. To Lord North

Queen's House, 30 min. past 9 a.m., January 29, 1770.

LORD NORTH,

I hope you will either this morning or after the debate in the House of Commons see Lieutenant-General Conway, for I know how much he is pleased at little marks of attention, and that by placing some confidence in him you may rely on his warm support. . . .

11. To Lord North

Queen's House, February 1, 1770.

LORD NORTH,

I am greatly rejoiced at the conclusion of the debate.[1]   A majority of 40 at this particular crisis, considering that it is upon the old ground that has been at least ten times before the House, is a very favourable auspice on your taking the lead in administration.   Believe me, a little spirit will soon restore a degree of order in my service. . . .

and on February 28th he again wrote, 'The seeing that the majority constantly increases gives me great pleasure.'[2]

A historic occasion passes unnoticed in the available correspondence, except for a brief informatory letter from North to the King, in which he stated that he had moved for leave to bring in a Bill for repealing all the American duties except that on tea; an amendment by Governor Pownall to include tea had been rejected by 204 to 142.   It was on that very day that the Boston 'massacre' took place, which was not heard of in England for some time.   Growing irritation in the colonies had induced North to repeal Townshend's taxes, that on tea being retained as a matter of prestige.   What was of more concern to the government at the moment, was the number of petitions and remonstrances being brought forward.   The City of London, insisting upon its right to be received in state by the King, began with a petition that Parliament might be dissolved, since in the absence of Wilkes, none of the business transacted by the House of

[1] On the question of whether a resolution of the House could prevent a member taking his seat.
[2] On the Civil List debate.

Commons was legal. A cold answer was returned, the King saying in private that he would rather abdicate than dissolve Parliament, or even have recourse to the sword. In March, Wilkes was released from prison, and the City decided on a remonstrance. What was to be done caused some concern.

III. To Lord North

Queen's House, 20 min. past 4 p.m., March 11, 1770.

Lord North,

If you can call here between seven and eight previous to your going to Council, I shall be glad to hear what precedents you have got; but if you cannot come, I will briefly acquaint you that I continue of opinion that an answer must be given to the Remonstrance, and that, unless the instances are very similar of having directed a certain number to attend, it will be every way best to receive them on the Throne.

On the 19th, the House of Commons moved a very feeble resolution declaring that any attempt to prove the present Parliament illegal was highly unwarrantable, of such a nature as only to encourage ' the Catilinas of the City '. The King had more realistic views.

IV. To Lord North

Queen's House, 48 min. past 7 a.m., March 20, 1770.

Lord North,

The more I reflect on the present Remonstrance from the Livery, the more I am desirous it should receive an answer, otherwise this bone of contention will never end; I therefore am thoroughly of opinion that, as the Sheriffs (though falsely) have insinuated that it is properly authenticated, that the least inconvenience will be receiving them on the Throne, and that the sober party cannot be hurt with it when they find the answer is firm, which will draw on a joint Address from the two Houses of Parliament, and will enable the Aldermen and Common Councilmen who dissented from this strange libel, on my having received it, to write a letter to one of my principal Secretaries of State protesting against it, who may in answer say something civil from me in return. If this agrees with your ideas, I hope you will show the visitors you are to have this morning the necessity of thus ending the affair, which will be honourably for them and their worthy friends. As the Council meet at eight, I shall expect you at seven this evening. . . .

The ' libel' was the old Bute-cum-Dowager-Princess attack, asserting ' secret and malign influence' at Court: the Mayor, Beckford, and the Sheriffs, were hotly for it, but most of the Common Councillors against it. Nothing came of the Remonstrance, but the City returned to the charge in May.

v. To Lord North

Queen's House, 15 min. past 7 p.m., May 14, 1770.

Lord North,

If you are at liberty this evening, I wish you would call here at any time most convenient to you; the Sheriffs of London have just been here, whom I have again refused to see as coming at an improper place, and have said Wednesday is the time for them to bring their message. I suppose this is another Remonstrance; if so, I think it ought not to have any answer.

vi. To Lord North

Queen's House, 56 min. past 7 p.m., May 19, 1770.

Lord North,

The Remonstrance of the City of London is certainly less offensive than it had been reported . . . but I look on the whole performance of a nature to call for a short dry answer referring to the one I have already given. I should think on Monday evening you ought to communicate the Remonstrance and a sketch of an answer to the Cabinet.

When the Remonstrance was presented on the 23rd, the King read from the throne:

vii. To the Mayor and Sheriffs

I should have been wanting to the public, as well as to myself, if I had not expressed my dissatisfaction at the late address. My sentiments upon that subject continue the same; and I should ill deserve to be considered as the Father of my people, if, in the exercise of any of the powers with which I am entrusted, I should suffer myself to be prevailed upon by any importunity to adopt a measure inconsistent with the interests, and dangerous to the Constitution of, the Kingdom.

After which Beckford launched into his ' volunteer speech ', which though respectfully couched as an expression of loyalty, contained another attack upon the completely innocent Bute. The King returned no answer, but was determined such a thing should not occur again.

VIII. To Lord North

Queen's House, 40 min. past 2 p.m., May 29, 1770.

LORD NORTH,

I wish to see you about half-hour past nine this evening, and that you will bring the words proper for Lord Hertford[1] to give to-morrow to the Remembrancer expressing my expectation that the Lord Mayor's unexpected speech last Wednesday be not looked upon as a precedent.[2]

A further Remonstrance was prepared in November; this was obviously too much of a good thing.

IX. To Lord North

Queen's House, 5 min. past 11 p.m., November 15, 1770.

LORD NORTH,

The idea of a fresh Address Remonstrance and Petition is so extremely absurd, and considering the time I may add puerile, that it deserves contempt. I shall think Wednesday next a proper time for receiving it; the answer ought to refer to what I said the last year, and be dry and short; but more of this when we know the precise words of this performance. . . .

---

[1] Conway's brother. After filling various more important posts, he was made Lord Chamberlain in 1766, which post he retained till 1782.

[2] Beckford (the father of the author of *Vathek*) died about a month later, an event which was a great blow to the City party.

x. To Lord North

Queen's House, 5 min. past 8 a.m., November 16, 1770.

Lord North,

If you are not engaged this evening, I wish you would call here at any time most convenient, as I want to fix upon the answer to the Remonstrance of the City of London, and to hear your opinion on the answer arrived this day from the Court of Spain.

The King's reply was indeed dry and short, consisting only of the words: 'As I have seen no reason to alter the opinions expressed in my answer to your former address upon this subject, I cannot comply with the prayer of your petition.'

The conclusion of the last letter, referring to the answer received from the Court of Spain, is connected with the remark in the previous letter, 'considering the time'. England was during these months on the brink of war with Spain, and consequently with France, over the Falkland Islands. One of these islands had been in British occupation since 1763, but in June 1770, the Governor of Buenos Ayres appeared before Port Egmont with a large force, compelled the small garrison to surrender, and removed the rudder from the ship stationed there so as to delay the news. This was just the sort of action to call out all the King's 'firmness'. It was largely due to his vigour that measures were at once taken to prepare the fleet for war; press-warrants were put into operation, though they were opposed by the City led by Wilkes. Strong language was held towards the Court of Madrid, which was at first stubborn; but the fall of Choiseul on December 24th made it certain that France would not support Spain. It was, however, a very close-run affair, and in January the Chargé d'Affaires at Madrid, Harris (afterwards Lord Malmesbury), actually left the capital, though he was recalled after the first stage on his journey. When the question first arose, Lord Mansfield, acting as Speaker of the House of Lords while the Great Seal was in commission, advised against calling Parliament until the matter was clearer. The King's letters clearly show his attitude throughout the crisis.

XI. To Lord North

Queen's House, November 9, 1770.

LORD NORTH,

Though the more I reflect on what Lord Mansfield has suggested of the expediency of not assembling the two Houses of Parliament until the arrival of the Spanish Messenger, the more I am convinced that it would be improper, as that Court and that of Versailles would upon it augur that we are resolved at all events to accommodate the present dispute, and consequently would encourage them to raise perhaps so much in their demands as would make war absolutely necessary; yet I am desirous to hear by a line what he has said on that subject. . . .

XII. To Lord North

Queen's House, 2 min. past 5 p.m., November 23, 1770.

LORD NORTH,

I saw Lord Weymouth[1] on his coming from the Spanish Ambassador; the project produced this day differed but little from that of Wednesday. Lord Weymouth has renewed the demand of the Governor of Buenos Ayres being disavowed, and the island restored unattended by any discussion on the right. Prince Masserano[2] said he saw we meant war, but on going said he would draw up another project, which Lord Weymouth declared he would not accept unless agreeable to the demand. Lord Weymouth wished I would name an Admiral for the Mediterranean squadron, and give orders for augmenting the army; the former I thought ought to be proposed first at a Cabinet meeting, the latter I thought ought to be deferred until Monday, by which time we should know whether the Ambassador has powers to conclude in a manner suitable to our just demands.

XIII. To Lord North

Queen's House, 35 min. past 7 p.m., November 28, 1770.

LORD NORTH,

. . . Though I have but little hopes of any change in the conduct of the Court of Spain, yet I shall be very anxious to learn

---

[1] Secretary of State for the North.
[2] Spanish Ambassador.

what shall pass between you and Mr. Francès;[1] therefore, if he leaves you by ten, I wish you would call on me; if not, that you will send me a line, for every feeling of humanity, as well as the knowledge of the distress war must occasion, makes me desirous of preventing it if it can be accomplished, provided the honour of this country is preserved.

XIV. TO LORD ROCHFORD[2]

Queen's House, 44 min. past 10 a.m., December 6, 1770.

LORD ROCHFORD,

As I shall probably not see you alone this day and as the sending for you might occasion suspicion, I choose to take this method of opening my ideas to you on the very important subjects that will be this evening laid before the Cabinet. From the moment Lord Weymouth expressed yesterday a wish that Mr. Harris might be recalled and that I had from others heard he had at the meeting the night before avoided answering the proper question you had put whether all present were ready to advise the declaration if containing simply a disavowal of Mr. Buccarelli[3] and a restoration of the island; I have seen the above proposal as intended with a view to prevent any accommodation. I own I have no expectation the Spaniards will end this affair amicably, yet I do not wish they should have it to say that they would have complied provided we had not recalled the Secretary of the Embassy without giving them an opportunity to conform to our uniform demand. The opening anew the negotiation would be highly improper, the delaying his recall not less so; but the sending him an exact draft of such a Declaration as we can receive with orders to acquaint Mr. Grimaldi,[4] that if he does not receive the King of Spain's consent to it without the alteration of an iota, the next day he instantly quit Spain. Such a measure would enable the Spanish Ambassador to stay and obey any directions he may receive, whilst that proposed would immediately oblige

[1] Charge d'Affaires from the Court of Versailles.
[2] Secretary of State for the South.
[3] Governor of Buenos Ayres.
[4] The Marquis de Grimaldo, Prime Minister. He claimed to be of the princely Italian family of the Grimaldi.

him to quit the Kingdom, and consequently entirely shut the door against concluding this irksome affair as every honest and considerate man must wish.

As to the desire of the East India Company that they may be permitted to order Pondicherry and the French factory at Bengal to be attacked, this seems to me highly improper, as the ordering them to collect their forces; and that if a war should be commenced they will soon receive directions to attack those places, which we may within a month send by frigate, and for fear of accidents a messenger may also be sent by land. I should be desirous of having an answer to this that I may know your exact sentiments on these very important questions.

xv. To Lord Rochford

Queen's House, 5 min. past 10 p.m., December 6, 1770.

LORD ROCHFORD,

The enclosed paper[1] seems very judicious and ought to be attended to; I would therefore have you make that use of it that may best answer the putting the Naval preparations into a more expeditious as well as more certain state. . . . The East India warlike preparations cannot be otherways decided upon but in conformity to what I expressed myself to you this morning. I rely on your acquainting me with the minutest events that may regard this critical period.

xvi. To Lord North

Queen's House, 55 min. past 4 p.m., January 17, 1771.

LORD NORTH,

. . . I wish you would call here, either previous to seeing Mr. Francès, or that you would see him so early as to call here still within a reasonable hour; I mean by that, ten this evening.

By a note I have received from Lord Rochford, I know what Mr. Francès has to propose to you; it is that orders may be immediately sent to Mr. Harris to return to Madrid, upon which

[1] Reflections on the present state of the Navy and the reasons why the Fleet is not in greater forwardness than it is, and the evil consequences that may arise in case of war if the present management is not changed. . . .

the Spanish Ambassador will communicate his fresh instructions; if this is not complied with, he is to threaten war. I could not help answering Lord Rochford that I thought this a very absurd proposition; for that, as the Secretary is recalled, we ought to know whether we shall have such terms as we can accept, for otherways we shall to-morrow be ordering him to return, and in less than two days, perhaps anew directing him to come home.

The King's fears, however, were unfounded. Spain conceded all that was demanded of her.

We must return for a moment to an earlier date. For some time the King's second surviving brother, the Duke of Cumberland, had been leading a profligate life, and at this time Lord Grosvenor brought against him an action for criminal conversation with his wife, and won it, the damages accorded being £10,000. This was the first time a Prince of the Blood had appeared as a defendant.

XVII. To Lord North

Richmond Lodge, November 5, 1770.

LORD NORTH,

A subject of a most private and delicate kind obliges me to lose no time in acquainting you that my two brothers have this day applied to me on the difficulty that the folly of the youngest has drawn him into; the affair is too public for you to doubt but that it regards the lawsuit; the time when he must pay the damages and the other expenses attending it. He has taken no one step to raise the money, and now has applied to me as the only means by which he can obtain it, promising to repay it in a year and a half; I therefore promised to write to you, though I saw great difficulty in your finding so large a sum as thirteen thousand pounds in so short a time; but their pointing out to me that the prosecutor would certainly force the House, which would at this licentious time occasion disagreeable reflections on the rest of his family as well as on him. I shall speak more fully to you on this subject on Wednesday, but the time is so short that I did [not] choose to delay opening this affair till then; besides, I am not fond of taking persons on delicate affairs unprepared;

whatever can be done ought to be done; and I ought as little as possible to appear in so very improper a business.

XVIII. To Lord North

Richmond Lodge, November 5, 1770.

LORD NORTH,

I have just received your letter, by which you seem to think you shall be able to procure the sum required. After I have seen you on Wednesday, I will direct Mr. Legrand[1] to wait on you that the mode of repayment may also be settled. This takes a heavy load off of me, though I cannot enough express how much I feel at being in the least concerned in an affair that my way of thinking has ever taught me to behold as highly improper; but I flatter myself the truths I have thought it incumbent to utter may be of some use in his future conduct.

It is hardly necessary to say that the truths were of no use at all; in his next affair, however, the Duke chose a wife whose husband was as much flattered by his attentions to her as she was, so no disaster occurred.

It was in the spring of 1771 that Parliament made its last attempt to prevent debates being reported in the press. The House of Commons decided to summon the printers, and sent a messenger to the City to arrest one of them who had not appeared at the bar of the House; but this man pleaded membership of the Livery, and it was not he, but the messenger, who was arrested, and taken before the Lord Mayor and Aldermen. The Mayor, Brass Crosby, and Aldermen Oliver and Wilkes, were summoned to appear before the House: Wilkes, though called upon three times, refused: the only place he would occupy in the House, he declared, was his rightful seat as Member for Middlesex. No action was taken against him, but Crosby and Oliver were consigned to the Tower. The King was averse to taking any action against the printers, but since North had made the question a government one, and was largely supported by the opposition, George III felt it necessary to uphold the dignity of Parliament.

---

[1] Edward Legrand, ducal treasurer.

XIX. To Lord North

Queen's House, 40 min. past 8 a.m., February 21, 1771.
Lord North,

. . . I have very much considered the affair of the printers that is now coming before the House. I do in the strongest manner recommend that every caution may be used to prevent its becoming a serious affair. If you are of opinion that any alderman will take the unjustifiable part you hinted at yesterday, why may not the messenger be made to understand that on summoning them he could not find them? It is highly necessary that this strange and lawless method of publishing debates in the papers should be put a stop to; but is not the House of Lords, as a Court of Record, the best court to bring such miscreants before? as it can fine as well as imprison, and as the Lords have broader shoulders to support any odium that this salutary measure may occasion in the minds of the vulgar.

XX. To Lord North

Queen's House, March 17, 1771.
Lord North,

Though I sent Lord Hillsborough to you with my opinion, that, as the Lord Mayor has presumed to set the privilege of the House of Commons of ordering printers to be brought at nought, and even to issue a warrant for committing the messenger to the Counter for executing the duty of his office, the authority of the House of Commons is totally annihilated if it is not in an exemplary manner supported to-morrow by instantly committing the Lord Mayor and Alderman Oliver to the Tower; as to Wilkes, he is below the notice of the House; then a Secret Committee, or any other mode of examining farther into the affair, is open for the wisdom of the House. I wish you would send Jenkinson[1] to Lord Mansfield for his opinion as to the manner of enforcing the commitment, if these people should continue to disobey; a message of the same kind to the Chancellor[2] might also be right. You know very well I was averse to meddling with the printers,

---

[1] One of the Lords of the Treasury, afterwards Earl of Liverpool.
[2] Lord Apsley.

but now there is no retracting; the honour of the Commons must be supported.

XXI. To Lord North

Queen's House, 3 min. past 9 a.m., March 19, 1771.

Lord North,

The conduct of the majority seems to have been of that firm and dignified kind which becomes those who are on right ground. I am not surprised that the whole House . . . joined in condemning the conduct of the Lord Mayor, and in asserting the privilege of the House, which, if not in any exemplary manner supported on this occasion, must annihilate the House of Commons, and thus put an end to the most excellent form of government which has been established in this kingdom. Go on with resolution, and this affair will be happily concluded. It occurs to me that the mode of conducting the Lord Mayor ought to be well considered, that no rescue may ensue. Might not the conducting him by water be the most private manner?

The majority (267 to 80) may have conducted themselves in a dignified way, but it was the minority that talked sense, pointing out that the whole business was one of futile and petty irritation. The King's final suggestion was a wise one: the Lord Mayor was not taken by water, and his progress to the Tower was a popular triumph. Full of sense too, and not without humour, are some remarks in the King's letter to North of the next day.

XXII. To Lord North

. . . I own I could have wished that Wilkes had not been ordered before the House, for he must be in jail the next term if not given new life by some punishment inflicted on him, which will bring him new supplies; and I do not doubt he will hold such language that will oblige some notice to be taken of him.

The riots which accompanied the Lord Mayor's commitment were so violent (it was supposed they were encouraged by certain 'men of property') that North's coach was broken up, and he and Charles James Fox (a notorious anti-Wilkite), at that time in the administration, narrowly escaped injury. The following letter is characteristic of the King's courage.

XXIII.TO LORD NORTH

Queen's House, March 28, 1771.

LORD NORTH,

The conclusion of the debate and division has proved very honourable for the House of Commons, and I trust a due firmness will subdue the violence that has been encouraged by men of some property who dare not avow it. I rejoice much at your having got without farther insult home, and hope you will come to St. James's when I return from the House of Lords this day. I would upon no account pass the Bills otherwise than in person at a moment like this. Believe me the spirit you showed yesterday will prevent its being often called upon; they now know you are not alarmed, and therefore will not dare to again attempt what must revolt every man that has any regard to law, or even to humanity.

Since Parliamentary jurisdiction only extended during the session, Crosby and Oliver quietly emerged from the Tower after a few weeks of splendid entertainment offered by the City, enlivened by the visits of the opposition grandees. Since Parliament never again dared raise the question of reporting debates, it may be said that it was from this moment such reporting became legal by tacit consent.

By now the North administration was firmly in the saddle. Grenville had died: his faction virtually died with him: Lord Suffolk, regarded as his successor, became Secretary of State in place of Weymouth, who resigned on the Falkland Islands negotiations, thinking them not vigorous enough: Wedderburn, of the same group, if any, became Solicitor-General: Thurlow became Attorney-General, the two providing brilliant enough legal support for the weakest government. Sandwich, of the old Bedford connection, joined the government, and soon became First Lord of the Admiralty. One letter of the King's in connection with the negotiations for place which occupied so much of his mind, is of great interest, as foreshadowing a reform, long overdue, which did not, however, materialize for some ten years.

To us it seems absurd that there should have been two Foreign Secretaries, who also combined the office of Home Secretary; either there was constant friction, or one of them was a complaisant nonentity.

xxiv.To Lord North

Queen's House, 46 min. past 7 p.m., January 13, 1771.

Lord North,

Not having heard anything of Lord Suffolk since Friday, I am desirous of hearing whether you have not yet seen him. A thought has occurred to me, if he cannot speak French, which is an absolute requisite for one who's to treat with foreign Ministers, whether Lord Rochford could not transact the whole department of Foreign Affairs, which is the case in every other Court, and then Lord Suffolk might have the Home Department, which would be composed of all domestic affairs, with the addition of Scotland and Ireland.

A little later in the year, Grafton returned to administration as Privy Seal, though he refused a seat in the Cabinet: all was so tranquil, and seemed so unattackable with any profit, now that the Dowager Princess was dead, that even Junius gave up in despair. Thus at last the King, though Chatham, Burke, and Rockingham were in opposition, could feel secure.

It was family affairs which most concerned the King in the early part of 1772. Not only the death of his mother, but the arrest of his sister Caroline Matilda, by her husband, the King of Denmark, caused him a good deal of worry. The King of Denmark was half demented, and his Queen ultimately found a refuge at Zell.

xxv.To Lord North

Queen's House, 55 min. past 10 a.m., March 17, 1772.

Lord North,

As two o'clock is not convenient to you, a little before three will do just as well. I have dedicated this unpleasant morning to going through the whole of the Danish correspondence, which by the messenger's dispatches seem to be drawing to a conclusion.

Great rancour and an inclination to blacken the affair as much as possible is not wanting; therefore the decision must be now finally taken.

A further cause of perturbation was the matrimonial choices of his brothers. The Duke of Cumberland, turning moral, all at once announced his marriage with Mrs. Horton, the daughter of an obscure Irish peer, and sister to the Colonel Luttrell who occupied Wilkes's place in the Commons. At the same time, the Duke of Gloucester declared that he had for some years been married to the Dowager Countess Waldegrave, an illegitimate daughter of Sir Edward Walpole. This admixture of plebeian blood with the royal line outraged both the King and his Queen so strongly that the Dukes were banished from Court for some ten years. On January 16th, 1775, he wrote in a letter to Lord North (Donne, I, 222):

. . . My dear Lord, I cannot deny that on the subject of the Duke of Gloucester my heart is wounded. I have ever loved him more with the fondness one bears to a child than a brother; his whole conduct, from the time of his publishing what I must ever think a highly disgraceful step, has tended to make the breach wider; I cannot therefore bring myself, on a repetition of his application, to give him hopes of a future establishment for his children, which would only bring about a fresh altercation about his wife, whom I can never think of placing in a situation to answer her extreme pride and vanity. . . . I am certain you know my way of thinking too well to doubt that, should any accident happen to the Duke, I shall certainly take care of his children. . . .

The King insisted on the passing of a Royal Marriage Act, which should make the marriages of a King's sons a matter of State rather than of private desires. It was strenuously opposed by those of libertarian principles or republican tastes, and Charles Fox retired temporarily from administration so as to be able to attack it.

XXVI. TO LORD NORTH

Queen's House, 3 min. past 11 p.m., February 26, 1772.

LORD NORTH,

I cannot say that the management of the debate in the House of Lords this day has edified me. I hope there will be a meeting to-morrow to settle the mode of proceeding on Friday. I do expect every nerve be strained to carry the Bill through both Houses with a becoming firmness, for it is not a question that immediately relates to Administration, but personally to myself; therefore I have a right to expect a hearty support from every one in my service, and shall remember defaulters.

The King followed every phase of the debates with intense eagerness, determined that such a blow to family pride should never be allowed to occur again.

XXVII. TO LORD NORTH

Queen's House, 37 min. past 8 a.m., March 12, 1772.

LORD NORTH,

The turn of yesterday's debate is most favourable, as Opposition, or at least the greatest part of it, have been forced to change its ground and admit that there ought to be some regulations made with respect to the marriages of the Royal Family. It is a known maxim in all military operations that when the enemy changes positions that is the right moment to push them with vigour : the rule I look upon as not less good in Parliamentary operations : therefore a continuation of the zeal and activity you have shown in this Bill will carry it through with great éclat.

The only event of interest in domestic politics (apart from the annual motion on Wilkes, and the usual Remonstrances from the City) was the attempt made, first to free doctors and lawyers at the Universities from subscription of the Thirty-nine Articles, and second an attempt to repeal the Test Act. The King's innate conservatism (in which he was supported by Burke, and even, strangely enough, by Fox in so far as the first was concerned) is beautifully revealed by the letters he wrote on these subjects.

XXVIII. To Lord North

Queen's House, 20 min. past 10 p.m., February 23, 1772.[1]

LORD NORTH,

The account I have just received from you of the very handsome majority this day gives me infinite satisfaction. I own myself a sincere friend to our Constitution, both Ecclesiastical and Civil, and as such a great enemy to any innovations, for, in this mixed government it is highly necessary to avoid novelties. We know that all wise nations have stuck scrupulously to their ancient customs. Why are we therefore, in opposition to them, to seem to have no other object but to be altering every rule our ancestors have left us? Indeed, this arises from a general disinclination to every restraint; and I am sorry to say the present Presbyterians seem so much more resembling Socinians than Christians, that I think the test was never so necessary as at present for obliging them to prove themselves Christians. I think Mr. C. Fox would have acted more becomingly towards you and himself if he had absented himself from the House, for his conduct cannot be attributed to conscience, but to his aversion to all restraints.

The Bill passed the Commons easily, but the Bishops opposed it in the Lords, and brought about its rejection: in this they were helped by the King, who whipped up the Court, including the Queen's Groom of the Stole.

XXIX. To Lord Bristol

Queen's House, May 17, 1772.

LORD BRISTOL,

I write with the Queen's consent to desire you will not come on Tuesday evening till the debate is over in the House of Lords. I have authorized Lord Rochford to say to any others that are in the same situation, the injunction put on you, which will I trust make a good attendance at that debate; the question is a very short one; at the Revolution the Toleration Act was established, the Dissenters have not been molested, therefore why must now an alteration be made? This, I think, contains the sum of the argument.

---

[1] Fortescue wrongly dates this letter 1774.

xxx. To Lord North

Queen's House, April 2, 1772.

LORD NORTH,

As I understand the Petition of the Dissenters is to be presented to-morrow, I take this method of acquainting you that I think you ought not to press those gentlemen who are brought on that interest into Parliament to oppose this measure, as thus you [may?] be driving them out of those seats on a new Parliament; but I think you ought to oppose it personally through every stage, which will gain you the applause of the Established Church and every real friend of the Constitution. If you should be beat, it will be in doing your duty, and the House of Lords will prevent any evil; indeed it is the duty of Ministers as much as possible to prevent any alterations in so essential a part of the Constitution as everything that relates to religion, and there is no shadow for this Petition, as the Crown regularly grants a *noli prosequi* if any over-nice Justice of Peace encourages prosecutions.

Party management was not, however, always so easy, and the following letter is not unamusing as revealing the King keeping his team in a good temper with one another, and also as showing his opinion of some of his supporters.

xxxi. To Lord Suffolk

Kew, July 22, 1772.

LORD SUFFOLK,

The handsome manner in which you have unbosomed yourself to me by the letter I have just received gives me great pleasure, the more as I can perceive you take the affairs in the same light I do. I shall but briefly mention what has passed, that I may show what has been the cause of the present very unpleasant state of affairs. After your departure into the country, Lord North wrote to Lord Gower to desire the report on the Ohio business might be postponed, to which he received an answer that consented to it if the Cabinet, but particularly you and Lord Rochford, came into it; but the latter was certainly cold, the debating at Cabinet whether a report directed by the Privy Council should remain dormant was a new idea. Your brother Secretary, who, though possessed of many amiable qualities, is not very prudent, on receiving your letter (wherein you thought this unnecessary, but chose Lord North as he had got himself into the puzzle should extricate himself out of it) writes to the President that the two Secretaries were averse to the proposal, upon which Gower directs him to report it directly : this he has reported to Lord Hillsborough, who means to resign in a few days, but by the letter Lord Rochford sent me yesterday, I find Lord North takes the thing much to heart, and has certainly been actuated [sic] upon by Lord Hillsborough, whose natural suspicion is greatly increased by the whole of this transaction, and if care is not taken may be productive of some personal unpleasant thing between Rochford and him. By this short state of the affair you must see Lord North's natural good nature and love of indecision, added to too much precipitation in Lord Rochford, and suspicion in Lord Hillsborough, with want of confidence in all the parties, have brought this to the present strange situation which is rather difficult to be unravelled. I directed Lord Rochford yesterday to take no further step till he had seen Lord North and pave the way to his speaking openly to you : I know the share you have in his esteem, but while you show him an inclination to ease his mind, you must not forget that in trying to keep Lord Hillsborough, care must be taken of the danger of offending Lord Gower : this must be touched on very lightly in the first conversation.

A very pretty little Cabinet crisis about nothing at all.

More serious at the time was the situation which arose in respect of Sweden. That country had for a long time been a favourite intriguing ground for the English and French, the former supporting the Senate and its party, ' the caps,' the latter ' the hats' or Court, both of them with money. George III, not being interested in the game of foreign politics, had no wish to be very active.

XXXII. TO LORD NORTH

Queen's House, 42 min. past 7 p.m., February 28, 1771.

LORD NORTH,

Though I think you could not mistake my sentiments this day on the new scene that arises by the sudden death of the King of Sweden, I choose shortly again to sketch them. It has ever occurred to me that the gaining the Court of Sweden is no real object of this country, for if after a considerable expense that is effected, it will be impossible to keep her friendship unless a subsidy is granted, for that power cannot subsist without foreign money. Besides, as there is no public mode of obtaining the money that is expended in that corruption, it must be taken from my Civil List, consequently new debts incurred; and when I apply to Parliament for relieving me, an odium cast on myself and Ministry, as if the money had been expended in bribing Parliament. I therefore think we ought only to feed the opposition to France, that that Crown may carry no essential points, and may be drove to spend much greater sums to little purpose.

In July 1772, however, the Government got news, through intercepted letters from France, that the new King, Gustavus III, intended, with French aid, to upset the constitution by force. This occurred in August; but before then the King's suspicions of the French, never very sleepy, had been aroused by some work they were putting in hand at Dunkirk, a place which had been a tender point between the two countries ever since the Treaty of Utrecht. At the same time, his common sense, and his hatred of war, kept him in leash.

XXXIII. TO LORD NORTH

Kew, August 1, 1772.

LORD NORTH,

The dispatches that arrived last night from France are of so serious a nature that I am unwilling to be silent on the subject until Wednesday; I therefore mean by this method to convey my thoughts unto you, which will enable you to revolve it in your mind, and to suggest what has occurred to you when we meet next. Were the members of the French Ministry well settled in their employments,[1] and their King well instructed and able to weigh the consequences of the steps he may take, the language of intending to continue the quay begun the last year at Dunkirk would convince me that there was a hidden desire to enter into a war; but when I consider how unsettled everything is in France, and more so the character of the monarch, I am convinced they do not foresee the danger they are running of drawing themselves into discussion with us, which if not conducted with the greatest temper may draw both nations into that which they ought assiduously to avoid. I am glad to see that Lord Stormont[2] views it in this light also. Lord Rochford (whose zeal makes him rather in a hurry), by a note I received with the dispatches, wanted to write him an answer with strength to oppose the steps that are proposed to be taken. I wrote him in answer that with [what] the Lord Stormont represents to be a principal feature in the character of the King, too much fire might bring things to what no honest man can wish; that therefore I thought the matter too delicate to give any directions until I had received the opinion of such ministers as shall be in town this week. I do not mean that I am inclined to yield, but I am as averse to make a point of honour of such a trifle as the quay of Dunkirk. I would order Lord Stormont, with temper, politeness, and candour, to prove that what is proposed is contrary to the strict letter of treaties; but I would at the same time consider whether he might not grant a part, if not very material, to put an end to this tiresome correspondence. Lord Stormont's private letter to Lord Rochford seems to state a mode of doing it. You may think me prolix, but it is not from desiring that the heat of a boy[3] may throw me so much off my guard as to draw this country into another addition of 50 millions to the National Debt; we must get the colonies into order before we engage with our neighbours.

Thus when the coup de main *was successfully carried out in Sweden, it stirred very little emotion in the King's breast, until it*

---

[1] Having been in office only since the fall of Choiseul.
[2] Ambassador at the Court of Versailles.
[3] ' The *boy* I suppose to be the Duc d'Aiguillon, Madame du Barry's First Minister of France.' Donne's note.

seemed likely that the French would act; then he was inclined to hold very different language to the Court of Versailles, though still he would not be drawn in.

XXXIV. TO LORD SUFFOLK

Kew, 26 min. past 9 p.m., August 30, 1772.

LORD SUFFOLK,

Your letter to Lord North and his answer are so agreeable to the ideas I expressed in the letter I wrote yesterday to you, that I can only express my approbation of them. Therefore if by to-morrow's post we hear from Sweden that the States and Senate seem firm, it will be proper to empower Sir John Goodricke[1] to draw to the extent of £15,000, provided that sum can defeat the attempts of the King of Sweden; but otherwise that the Caps cannot expect any assistance from hence after having so little counteracted the intrigues of the Court, though so timely warned from hence : my reason for only naming the lesser sum is to keep something in hand, as Sir John is but too ready to go to the utmost extent of his credit.

XXXV. TO LORD SUFFOLK

Queen's House, November 5, 1772.

LORD SUFFOLK,

The draft to Lord Stormont meets with my thorough approbation, as it consists only [of] general reasoning well adapted to the present state of things, and what will probably be the issue of the Swedish business. I am clear we cannot appear too cold, and too strongly point out to Mr. Gunning the little real advantage that can accrue to Russia from new broils till recovered from the weak state to which she is now reduced by the waste of men and treasure; besides as we are not bound by any treaty of alliance, I cannot see any reason for joining with Russia in a declaration against the changes of the Swedish constitution; though if Russia is attacked by France, views of general policy [will] not permit our remaining idle spectators. The language to Baron Diede ought to be civil but clear of any engagement;

---

[1] British envoy at Stockholm.

whilst great firmness must be shown at Paris, and that if France sends a fleet into the Baltic the English ships cannot remain at home; indeed I wish to keep off a war as long as possible; we are vulnerable in so many parts that we cannot escape losses, and from the cause of the war it [will] be a Continental one, and from the little faith held in liquidating the demands of the last, I fear a much more expensive one than as yet we may imagine.

The danger of war grew much more acute in the next spring, when France and Spain threatened to fit out navies to attack Russia in the Mediterranean in reprisal for her depradations on their trade, and to show force in the Baltic. The King's vigorous initiative put a stop to this, though in the City the fear of war was so great as to cause stocks to fall from six to twenty per cent.

XXXVI. To Lord North

Queen's House, 15 min. past 8 a.m., April 20, 1773.

Lord North,

I received yesterday the dispatch from Lord Stormont, which convinces me, when the Duc d'Aiguillon finds we make preparations, that he will give up his *promenade*; which opinion I am the more confirmed in from a German interception I received also yesterday of a letter from Creutz, the Swedish Minister at Paris, to the King of Sweden, wherein he declares that M. d'Aiguillon has told that, as England would certainly take umbrage if he sent a fleet to the assistance of Sweden, that he therefore could not think of that mode of succour, for that, at *all events he would avoid a war with England.*

I instantly wrote to Lord Suffolk to summon a Cabinet this evening; Lord Rochford will, by that time, be also in town. The measure to be taken seems clearly pointed out: let all the guard-ships be ordered to Spithead; let them be completely manned, and twenty ships of equal strength be ordered to replace them; and let the Ambassador's conduct be approved of, and ordered to remain silent till the French Court renew the conversation; and I trust that, in less than three weeks the whole of this armament may be countermanded. I cannot conclude without expressing my approbation of Lord Sandwich's plan of having the guard-ships always ready for immediate service; that will, I am persuaded, prevent many wars; for by that means we have ever twenty large ships ready before the enemy can equip one; consequently, about the start of three months, which is an immense advantage in all military operations.

XXXVII. To LORD NORTH

Queen's House, 12 min. past 7 p.m., April 25, 1773.

LORD NORTH,

The letters arrived from Paris this day have proved agreeable to what I have uniformly declared, that on the return of M. de Mortanges, the fleet would be countermanded. I have, in consequence of the Duc d'Aiguillon's saying that the fleet is postponed, directed the two Secretaries to say publicly *that the letters arrived from France this day give reason to think the fleet will be countermanded, that, therefore, it is hoped we may do the same in a few days*—and I have ordered Lord Sandwich not to commission any ships, but merely fit out the fifteen, for that I hope by this day seven-night even they may be countermanded. We must see what effect our arming has had on Versailles before we can properly give counter-orders, and within that time we shall receive the messenger.

XXXVIII. To LORD NORTH

Queen's House, 55 min. past 12, May 21, 1773.

LORD NORTH,

I cannot refrain having the pleasure of acquainting you that there is just arrived from Paris a letter from Lord Stormont dated May 18th, that on saying to the Duc d'Aiguillon that our fleet is *suspended*, he had instantly answered, Ours is *countermanded, les matelots sont renvoyés; ce n'est pas une suspension, mais une cessation totale;*[1] there is to be no fleet of evolution this year : this so very decided that no farther doubt can be had, and the Admiralty must now restore things to a state of peace, but the ships had better remain at Spithead.

[1] The sailors have been sent home; this is not a postponement, but a complete stop.

In the autumn of 1772 the partition of Poland had taken place, Russia, Prussia, and Austria each taking a slice of that defenceless country by an arrangement which had long been maturing among themselves. George III's views are perhaps worth giving: his letter to the unfortunate Stanislaus Augustus Poniatowsky, in answer to his appeal for help, might, from another monarch, read satirically, but coming from him it reads rather as the issue of a guilty conscience: it does not seem to be an office letter. At all events, England, anxious to keep on good terms with Russia, and it being unthinkable that she should be allied with France, could do nothing.

XXXIX. MEMORANDUM ON THE PARTITION OF POLAND

The very extraordinary phenomenon of a coalition of the Courts of Vienna, Petersburgh, and Berlin, to take what may suit their separate conveniences of the Kingdom of Poland, is so subversive of every idea of their mutual jealousies, and of the balance of Europe, that it of necessity must give rise to very extraordinary alliances amongst the other powers.

Poland carries on a considerable trade with Great Britain for stuffs and cloth; this must inevitably be greatly diminished as the above powers have manufactures, and therefore will at least lay heavy duties on the importations of these manufactures if not entirely prohibit them.

The Dutch received a considerable quantity of corn, which they retailed to great advantage : this must also cease.

France will also find a diminution of its trade, but more particularly in the Levant, if Russia obtains the navigation of the Black Sea.

These three powers will certainly sooner or later be induced to unite, and when opportunities arise which the jealousies of Austria and Prussia cannot fail, perhaps within a short time, to give birth to, then an alliance may be formed which may extricate Poland from the tyranny that now seems impending.

This plan may perhaps seem chimerical, but if Britain and France would with temper examine their respective situations, the ancient animosity would appear absurd, and that they have by it aggrandized other powers and weakened themselves. Commerce, the foundation of a marine, can never flourish in an absolute monarchy; therefore that branch of grandeur ought to be left to England, whilst the great army kept by France gives her a natural pre-eminence on the Continent.

Some of the reasoning is curious, but in contradistinction with the ' old system ', shows a certain amount of realistic common sense.

XL. TO STANISLAUS AUGUSTUS, KING OF POLAND

St. James's, November 17, 1772.

MONSIEUR MON FRÈRE,

Your Majesty justly expresses my sentiments in his letter of the 18th September, with respect to his misfortunes, and those of his country. I have for long regarded with the deepest sorrow the evils which surround your Majesty, and which have destroyed Poland. I fear that these unhappy events have gone so far that they can only be set right (*redressés*) by the Hand of the Most High, and I can see no other intervention that could be of use. I would willingly exercise mine if I could see a moment at which it would have any effect.

Justice must ever be the pride of sovereigns; I would heartily wish that these would never disregard her. But if, unfortunately, temporal interests sometimes brush her aside, one must hope that she will always in the end take her rightful place in more favourable circumstances.

Your Majesty's steadfastness and magnanimity cannot but command universal admiration and esteem.

Two coming events cast their shadows before in the year 1773: securer settlements of the Irish and Indian questions. Ireland, as nearly always, was causing anxiety, and as early as the year before, the King had written:

XLI. TO LORD NORTH

Queen's House, 10 min. past 10 a.m., January 2, 1772.

. . . Mr. Allen's is only additional proof of that aversion to English government, and of that avowed profligacy that the gentlemen of that country seem to despise masking with the name of conscience, and must sooner or later oblige this country seriously to consider whether the uniting it to this Crown would not be the only means of making both islands flourish.

An aversion to English government is hardly surprising, seeing how strongly it opposed the passing of an Absentee Tax, though proposed by the Lord Lieutenant. The King, contrary to his usual custom, here supported the vested interests.

XLII. To Lord North

Kew, 28 min. past 8 a.m., November 24, 1773

LORD NORTH,

It is impossible to have wrote more candidly and ably than your letter to the Lord-Lieutenant; it perfectly conveys the point in which I view the Absentee Tax; I do not think the first commissioner to the Treasury can lose this political question in the Privy Council; for if the regulation of the bounty on corn does not accompany it, or the Absentee Tax be a separate Bill from the old additional duties, and thus postponed till after Christmas, you must yourself oppose this tax and risk even the additional duties being passed rather than consent to this measure, which without its proper accompaniment cannot be supported, nay, ought not.

It is unnecessary to follow the debates on India which filled up much Parliamentary time during 1773. The East India Company had grossly mismanaged its affairs, and declared high dividends when on the verge of bankruptcy. Feeling against the nabobs was also high. The House, while judging that Clive had been over-greedy, at the same time admitted that he had rendered great services to his country.

XLIII. To Lord North

Queen's House, 5 min. past 8 a.m., May 22, 1773.

LORD NORTH,

The vote carried this morning is a very strong proof of the propriety of your leaving to private gentlemen the punishing of servants of the East India Company; and by that wise conduct you as an individual have been in a minority that with every man of honour must do you credit, at the same time that the Minister had nothing to do with it. I own I am amazed that private interest could make so many forget what they owe to their country, and come to a resolution that seems to approve of Lord Clive's rapine. No one thinks his services greater than I do, but that can never be a reason to commend him in what certainly opened the door to the fortunes we see daily made in that country. . . .

An East India Regulation Act was passed in June.

XLIV. TO LORD NORTH

Kew, 33 min. past 7 a.m., June 11, 1773.

LORD NORTH,

I am much pleased at hearing that the East India Bill has passed this morning by so great a majority, and trust that it will prove a remedy to some of the many evils, that, if not corrected, must soon totally prevent any possibility of preserving that great branch of commerce; besides, it lays a foundation for a constant inspection from Parliament into the affairs of the Company, which must require a succession of regulations every year; for new abuses will naturally be now daily coming to light, which, in the end, Parliament alone can in any degree check; for the directors, from views of self-interest, must court their servants who make rapid fortunes, from the desire of remaining at the head of the Company. . . .

Unfortunately the laudable desire to regulate the Company was to have its repercussions in America.

Before passing on to those, it is to be noticed that self-interest and lack of patriotism were to be found nearer home. There were the usual Middlesex election troubles in the House, and outside there were further demonstrations by the weavers. In the autumn the City elections caused the King some anxiety.

XLV. To Lord Suffolk

Queen's House, 48 min. past 5 p.m., April 24, 1773.

LORD SUFFOLK,

I am much pleased that the wicked attempt of collecting different bodies of men with an intent of disturbing the peace of this town has through the becoming vigilance of the magistrates been prevented; nothing can be more proper than your seeing this evening the Attorney and Solicitor General, that it may be thoroughly ascertained what punishment can be inflicted on the author of hand bills to encourage tumultuous assemblies; it is impossible that in any society which deserves the appellation of civilized, such a crime shall not meet with a very exemplary one : the more I reflect on your proposal of writing to the Lord Mayor and one of the Sheriffs, the more I think it proper.

XLVI. To Lord North

Queen's House, 40 min. past 5 p.m., April 26, 1773.

LORD NORTH,

I am sensible of your attention in sending to me two accounts concerning the conduct of the weavers; it seems to me as if they would have remained quiet after the care taken on Friday last, if the same framer of mischief had not afresh exhorted them; and I am sorry to find the Crown lawyers do not well know that attempting to assemble riotous meetings is criminal. It is no great credit to the laws of this island if they do not provide against what is so detrimental to civil society.

XLVII. To Lord North

Queen's House, 46 min. past 10 a.m., November 4, 1773.

LORD NORTH,

It is melancholy to find so little public virtue remaining in this country; it is to the want of that, not to the strength of faction, that I forebode no hopes of restoring that order which alone can preserve this constitution; but men seem to think, provided they do not join in tumult, that they do their duty, and that an indolent indifference is not worthy of blame. . . .

These letters may be remembered in connection with the part the King was later to play during the Gordon Riots.
Two non-political letters may end this chapter.

XLVIII. TO LORD COWPER

Queen's House, March 16, 1773.

LORD COWPER,

The very curious and well executed copies of the painters' portraits in the Florentine Gallery which you have sent me are much enhanced by the very genteel epistle that accompanied them; the remaining part of the collection will be more agreeable as you promise to be yourself the bearer of it. I remember with great pleasure the moments I passed formerly with you, and have been much disappointed at your making so long absence from your native country.

It appears from subsequent correspondence that Lord Cowper's object in making these and further handsome presents to the King, was to obtain either the Garter or a Dukedom.

XLIX. TO LORD BRISTOL

Kew, July 8, 1773.

LORD BRISTOL,

I have heard that my laundress, Mary Smith, died on Monday. She suckled me, and to her great attention my having been reared is greatly owing; this ought to make me anxious for the welfare of her children, who by her great imprudence are left destitute of support. I therefore desire you will appoint her youngest daughter, Augusta Hicks, to succeed as laundress, who has frequently managed the business during different illnesses with which she has been afflicted.

I saw your brother yesterday, who seems more shattered than after any former confinement, and even more mortified at his not being able to appear at Portsmouth than I expected; he seems to attribute his state of relaxation to the continually taking

James's Powder, which he has now abandoned. I hope his example will deter you from medicines, and that you will attempt exercises as the best preservative against gout, and change your abstemiousness, which if it succeeds in keeping off that horrid complaint will do it at the expense of your health, and perhaps be productive of greater evils.

CHAPTER IV

AMERICA

1774-1781

Although nothing of critical importance had happened in the American colonies for the last two or three years, which were outwardly a period of quiescence, only some small spark was needed to set the blaze alight. There had been enough movement, Corresponding Committees and so forth, to show that some steps might have to be taken. At this time General Gage, who had succeeded Amherst as Commander-in-Chief of the American forces in 1763, was in England, and was among those who gave the King such fatally bad advice as to the temper of the colonists.

1.TO LORD NORTH

Queen's House, 46 min. past 6 p.m., February 4, 1774.

LORD NORTH,

Since you left me this day, I have seen Lieutenant General Gage, who came to express his readiness, though so lately come from America, to return at a day's notice, if the conduct of the Colonies should induce the directing coercive measures. His language was very consonant to his character of an honest determined man. He says they will be lions, whilst we are lambs; but if we take the resolute part they will undoubtedly prove very meek. He thinks the four regiments intended to relieve as many regiments in America, if sent to Boston, are sufficient to prevent any disturbance. I wish you would see him, and hear his ideas as to the mode of compelling Boston to submit to whatever may be thought necessary; indeed all men now seem to feel that the fatal compliance in 1766[1] has encouraged the Americans annually to increase their pretensions to that thorough independency which one state has of another, but which is quite subversive of the obedience which a colony owes to its mother country.

The disturbance, however, had already taken place. In order to help the affairs of the East India Company, this was

[1] The repeal of the Stamp Act.

99

permitted to export tea to the colonies without the tax of one shilling demanded by England: the American excise of three pence was, however, to remain. Seeing that the Americans would now get their tea cheaper than before, the Company sent a tea fleet to America. On its arrival at Boston, however, a number of colonists, disguised as Mohawks, boarded the ships, and threw the tea into the harbour. This famous ' Boston tea-party' had taken place on 16 December, 1773. It is not certain at what date the news arrived in England. At all events, Gage was sent out as Governor of Massachusetts, and on March 7th, Lord Dartmouth, who had replaced the somewhat too tactless Hillsborough as Secretary of State for the Colonies, presented to Parliament a message from the King commending American affairs to its attention.

II. To Lord North

Queen's House, 11 min. past 7 p.m., March 7, 1774.

Lord North,

It is carrying a very material point the ordering the Address without a division, and gives a degree of weight to the subsequent steps that will be taken on this business in the House of Commons.

The immediate step was the Port of Boston Bill, which virtually closed Boston as a port, and transferred the business to New Salem.

III. To Lord North

Queen's House, 55 min. past 8 p.m., March 14, 1774.

Lord North,

It could not be expected that any proposal on American affairs would pass without any opposition, but the Bill being ordered without a division is a material point gained; and I trust if the different propositions are brought forward as soon as possible, that this arduous business will be gone through with much [less] trouble than was supposed.

I have seen Lord Dartmouth this day very firm as to the alteration of the Council of Massachusetts Bay, but averse to the

Bill for trying future offenders in Britain, wanting in lieu of that, that offenders of that particular province should be amenable to the courts of justice of Nova Scotia, and particularly anxious that the present offenders should be somehow or other punished, and much taken with a proposition of Lord Buckinghamshire to disable them at least by Act of Parliament from holding any office in the province, or being members of the Assembly.

By the Massachusetts Bill, judges and sheriffs were to be appointed by the Governor and not by the Council: it was also decreed that offenders might be tried in any other colony, or even in England. The Massachusetts Bill, far more than the Boston Port Bill, alarmed the other colonies, as being a flagrant violation of a charter. The Bills passed easily.

IV. TO LORD NORTH

Queen's House, 35 min. past 8 p.m., March 23, 1774.

LORD NORTH,

The feebleness and futility of the opposition to the Boston Port Bill shews the rectitude of the measure, and want of matter, not of good will, has been the cause of its having met with so little trouble.

V. TO LORD NORTH

Kew, 51 min. past 8 p.m., May 6, 1774.

LORD NORTH,

The Bill for the better Administration of Justice in the Massachusetts Bay having been read the third time and passed the House of Commons this day, after a short debate, with a great majority, gives me infinite satisfaction; perseverance and the meeting difficulties as they arise with firmness seem the only means of either with credit or success terminating public affairs. Your conduct on the American disturbance is a very clear proof of the justness of that proposition.

The majority was not a very handsome one, only 24 (127—103), although more tea had been thrown into Boston harbour at the end of February; but the opposition was now reinforced by Fox, who had left the government owing to a growing discontent with North, to whom he had given trouble in the House by taking an independent line over the relations of Parliament and the Press.

.

vi. To Lord North[1]

Queen's House, 1 min. past 7 p.m., February 16, 1774.

LORD NORTH,

The House of Commons could not do less than order Mr. Horne to be taken into the custody of the Serjeant-at-Arms for his contempt in not appearing this day, agreeable to the summons of that House. . . . By what I heard this day of the transaction on Monday, I am greatly incensed at the presumption of Charles Fox in obliging you to vote with him that night, but approve much of your making your friends vote in the majority; indeed that young man has so thoroughly cast off every principle of common honour and honesty that he must become as contemptible as he is odious; and I hope you will let him know that you are not insensible of his conduct towards you.

North did indeed let him know: within a week Fox, then a Junior Lord of the Treasury, received a missive from his chief: 'Sir,—His Majesty has thought proper to order a new commission of Treasury to be made out, in which I do not see your name. North.' Fox forthwith attached himself to the Rockingham group, though he did not formally join it for some five years.

Individual opinion must decide whether the further Bill passed that session was reactionary or liberal: the Quebec Bill certainly deprived the Canadians of trial by jury, but it did assure the vast majority, who were French, that they were free to worship according to the Roman Catholic faith. The Canadians seemed to have approved, but the Bill was howled at in New England, and provoked the usual Remonstrance from the City of London. Of these the King was by now frankly contemptuous.

---

[1] See also letter LVII.

VII. To Lord North

June 18, 1774.

Lord North,

The Sheriffs of London have been here this evening with a message as I understand from the Lord Mayor : I ordered them to be acquainted that I did not receive messages from the City but on Court-days at St. James's. I understand they will therefore come to-morrow after the drawing room. I take it for granted it is to know when the Lord Mayor may bring the petition against the Quebec Bill. Quere whether it is to be called also an Address, and in either case I think it scarcely decent to receive them; if in the latter mode there must be an answer, which certainly ought to teach them that they are not proper advisers on political questions. I desire to hear what you have heard on the subject, that I may know what message they are to bring; upon the whole I suppose it is just to make a noise on Thursday at their Common Hall.

The answer finally given was that there was no answer, since the Bill was one agreed on by both Houses, and the King could not take cognizance of it until it was presented to him for his consent. The phrasing of this had, however, demanded a certain delicate caution.

VIII. To Lord North

Kew, June 19, 1774.

Lord North,

I very much approve of the proposed answer to the City Address against the giving my assent to the Quebec Bill . . . but [I] am clear, though I hope the Crown will ever be able to prevent a Bill it thinks detrimental to be thrown out of one or other Houses of Parliament, without making use of its right of refusing the assent; yet I shall never consent to using any expression that tends to establish that at no time the making use of that power is necessary.

The right of veto was a precious prerogative; but how much better to employ guile, and to show one's skill as a party manager!
The King continued to receive further bad advice.

IX. To Lord North

Kew, 2 min. past 9 p.m., July 1, 1774.

LORD NORTH,

. . . Lord Dartmouth brought Mr. Hutchinson, late Governor of Massachusetts Bay, to be presented at my levee, but I desired he would introduce [him] in my closet, as I was desirous of hearing his account how matters were when he left his government, and am now well convinced they will soon submit; he owns the Boston Port Bill was the only wise and effectual method that could have been suggested for bringing them to a speedy submission, and that the change in the legislature will be a means of establishing some government in that province, which till now has been one of anarchy. One of the regiments arrived the 1st of June, the day he sailed, and the people of Boston seemed much dispirited.

When, however, a Congress was called in America, the situation seemed so serious that the King decided on a general election.

X. To Lord North

Kew, August 24, 1774.

LORD NORTH,

I cannot let [go] the letter I have wrote in answer to the one that you sent me last week accompanying the Irish arrangements without just adding on a separate paper a few lines on the calling of a new Parliament. The general Congress now assembling in America, the peace of Russia with the Turks, the unsettled state of the French Ministry,[1] are very additional reasons to show the propriety of the measure; besides I trust it will fill the House with more gentlemen of landed property, as the Nabobs, Planters, and other Volunteers are not ready for the battle. As soon as you can fix on a proper day for the dissolution, I desire you will write to the Chancellor and Lord President, but not above a week before the measure is to be [put] into execution.

[1] At the beginning of the reign of Louis XVI.

Whether it was that the nabobs were taken by surprise, or for some other reason, the government was supported by far larger majorities in the next Parliament, in spite of the presence of Wilkes, who found no opponent at the polls, although the King had furiously striven to provide one. The increased majorities confirmed the King in his belief that the spirit in the country was hardening against America, and with this assurance his own spirit became more valiant. Certainly American opinion was hardening against England.

XI. TO LORD NORTH

Kew, September 11, 1774.

LORD NORTH,

The letter from the Quakers of Pennsylvania to some of [the] chiefs of that persuasion in London shows they retain that coolness which is a very strong characteristic of that body of people: but I was in hopes it would have contained some declaration of their submission to the mother country; whilst by the whole tenor they seem to wish for England giving in some degree way to the opinions of North America: the die is now cast, the colonies must either submit or triumph. I do not wish to come to severer measures, but we must not retreat; by coolness and an unremitted pursuit of the measures that have been adopted I trust they will come to submit; I have no objection afterwards to their seeing that there is no inclination for the present to lay fresh taxes on them, but I am clear there must be always one tax to keep up the right, and as such I approve of the tea duty. . . .

When Congress approved of the behaviour of the Bostonians, declaring that anybody who should accept any tampering with a charter as worthy of detestation, and when the people of Maryland burnt not only a load of tea but the whole ship as well, the King's ' firmness ' was weakened by no doubts.

XII. TO LORD NORTH

Queen's House, 48 min. past M., November 18, 1774.

LORD NORTH,

I am not sorry that the line of conduct seems now chalked out . . . the New England governments are in a state of rebellion, blows must decide whether they are to be subject to this country or independent. . . .

When Gage, who was having trouble in Massachusetts, finding all his attempts to build barracks successfully sabotaged, suggested that it might be wise to call a retreat, the King's contempt amounted almost to indignation.

XIII. TO LORD NORTH

Queen's House, 17 min. past 3 p.m., November 19, 1774.

LORD NORTH,

I return the private letters received from Lieut.-General Gage; his idea of suspending the Acts appears to me the most absurd that can be suggested. The people are ripe for mischief, upon which the mother country adopts suspending the measures she has thought necessary : this must suggest to the colonies a fear that alone prompts them to their present violence; we must either master them or totally leave them to themselves and treat them as aliens. I do not by this mean to insinuate that I am for advice [advising?] new measures; but I am for supporting those already undertaken.

Yet he did not altogether forget his role as Father of his People.

XIV. TO LORD NORTH

Queen's House, 33 min. past 6 p.m., December 15, 1774.

LORD NORTH,

I am much pleased at hearing that the Army and Ordnance estimates passed the Committee of Supply this day without any division.

I was much pleased with your ideas concerning the suspension of bounties and other regulations that may be effected this session towards bringing the Americans to their duty, but am not so fond of sending commissioners to examine into the disputes, this looks so like the mother country being more afraid of the continuance of the dispute than the colonies, and I cannot think it likely to make them reasonable; I do not want to drive them to despair but to submission, which nothing but feeling the inconvenience of their situation can bring their pride to submit to.

xv. To Lord Dartmouth

Queen's House, December 15, 1774.

Lord Dartmouth,

Nothing can be more provoking than the conduct of the inhabitants of Massachusetts Bay; some measures must undoubtedly be adopted after Christmas to curb them, and by degrees bring them to a due obedience to the mother country; but reason not passion must point out the proper measures.

But need any measures be necessary? Was it not possible that the naughty children might of themselves turn to the mother country for help and wise guidance? One wonders how it was he came to have such fantastic thoughts. Were they due to his hatred of war, which even he could hardly disguise from himself was impending?

xvi. Memorandum

[1774.][1]

There is no denying the serious crisis to which the disputes between the Mother Country and its North American Colonies are growing, and that the greatest temper and firmness are necessary to bring matters to a good issue; time is undoubtedly also an ingredient as indispensable on this occasion. Had the Americans in prosecuting their ill-grounded claims put on an appearance of mildness it might have been very difficult to chalk out the right path to be pursued; but they have boldly thrown off the mask, and avowed that nothing less than a total independence of the British Legislature will satisfy them. This indeed decides the proper plan to be followed, which is to stop the trade of all those colonies who obey the mandate of the Congress for non importation, non exportation, and non consumption, to assist them no further with presents to the Indians, and give every kind of assistance to those that conduct themselves otherways, which will make them quarrel among themselves:

[1] Fortescue dates this [? 1773], but Congress had not met!

their separate interests must soon effect this, and experience will then show them that the interference of the Mother Country is essentially necessary to prevent their becoming rivals.

Nevertheless, the path chalked out was so clearly the right one, that he could not conceive how any person of sense or honour could refuse to tread it.

XVII. MEMORANDUM

Perhaps no one in our history can produce so strange a circumstance as the gentlemen who pretend to be patriots, instead of acting agreeable to such sentiments, avowing the unnatural doctrine of encouraging the American Colonies in their disputes with their Mother Country; this so plainly shows that men not measures decide their opinions, that it is not necessary to deduce the total want of principle which this motley tribe by their conduct . . . [*unfinished*].

The motley tribe contained Chatham and Camden, Shelburne, Burke and Fox; in short, though the majority in the country was with the government, nearly every distinguished man was against it. This, in the King's eyes, made them little short of traitors: Chatham was ' a trumpet of sedition ', but since he was ill once more during 1775 and 1776, opposition languished, and to the King's delight, debates on the subject resulted in huge majorities in his favour.

XVIII. TO LORD NORTH

Queen's House, 50 min. past 11 a.m., February 8, 1775.
LORD NORTH,

The proposed answer to the Address is highly proper, as it conveys the sentiments that must be harboured by every candid and rational mind. This language ought to open the eyes of the deluded Americans; but if it does not, it must set every delicate man at liberty to avow the propriety of the most coercive measures.

Objections, however, continued to come from the City.

XIX. To Lord North

Queen's House, 5 min. past 9 a.m., April 7, 1775.

Lord North,

In revolving what you dropped yesterday of its being desirable by some mode or other to avoid receiving the new dish of insolence from the Livery of London in the Council Chamber, it has occurred to me that if the Sheriffs come this day to know when I will receive the Lord Mayor, &c., I may say that I will consider of the application they have been directed to make, and will transmit them my resolution through the channel of the Lord Chamberlain; then Lord Hertford may be directed to write to the Sheriffs that the Address, &c., may be presented on Monday, but that I shall not receive it on the Throne, nor deliver any answer; this will bring the affair into its proper order, and at least make a distinction between the Livery and the Common Council, and prevent my sitting in future to hear myself insulted. I wish to hear your opinion as to this mode. . . .

But the time of talking about deluded Americans, of writing memoranda, of arranging to be insulted standing rather than sitting, was passing, and matters soon took a definite turn. On 19 April, 1775, Gage sent a force out from Boston to destroy the military stores at Concord: the raid was opposed, and the skirmish known as ' the battle of Lexington ' took place. Gage accomplished his object, but with a loss of some 273 men, killed, wounded, and prisoners, the American losses being 90. Dartmouth sent the King the news as soon as it arrived, in two messages. The King desperately did his best to minimize the affair.

XX. To Lord Dartmouth

Kew, 40 min. past 4 p.m., May 29, 1775.

Lord Dartmouth,

It is not improbable but some detachment sent by Lieutenant-General Gage may not have been strong enough to disperse the Provincials assembled at Concord; but no great reliance can be given to the manner in which it will undoubtedly be exaggerated in American newspapers, or when related by an American trader.

XXI. To Lord Dartmouth

Kew, 37 min. past 8 p.m., May 29, 1775.

Lord Dartmouth,

By the newspaper you have transmitted, which undoubtedly was drawn up with the intention of painting the skirmish at Concord in as favourable a light as possible for the insurgents, I am far from thinking the general has reason to be displeased; the object of sending the detachment was to spike cannons and destroy military stores; this has been effected, but with the loss of an equal number of men on both sides; the die is cast. I therefore hope you will not see this in a stronger light than it deserves. As to Mr. Pownall's expression of *bad news* it shows he is more fit for expediting the directions of others than he would have been for a military department or giving advice where firmness is required.

Pownall, of course, was the ex-Colonial governor, who, unlike Hutchinson, really knew what the spirit and feeling of the Americans were; but he was not listened to.

At this stage it was necessary to raise forces to bring the colonists to a proper state of mind: recruiting was begun in the British Isles, and Hanoverian troops were mustered.

XXII. To Lord North

Kew, August 1, 1775.

Lord North,

I received an answer to the orders I had wrote to Hanover last night, and have already given every necessary order that the five battalions will be ready to embark at Stade early in September, consisting of 2355 effectives, officers included, provided money is sent from hence to put them in motion. The officers are poor, and are not able to prepare their equipage; many articles are wanting for the men to be able to go on this distant service. I suppose an advance of 10,000l. will effect it. Colonel

Faucitt[1] is the officer I propose to send to see they are complete when they embark. He ought to go within a week, for, though brave on shore, Continental forces fear the sea, and he must preach the little difficulties that will arise in their voyage. He would be the proper person to carry over any draft of money that may be necessary. I should not do justice to my Electoral troops if I did not express that they show the same zeal for my person they have ever shown for my ancestors. . . .

There was, however, some difficulty in getting men at home to enlist. Barrington, the Secretary at War, was inclined to abandon land operations, and let the campaign be carried on by sea. It became necessary to purchase foreign troops, who were bought and sold, as the King of Prussia remarked, like cattle.

XXIII. To Lord North

Kew, 2 min. past 5 p.m., August 26, 1775.

Lord North,

I have read Lord Barrington's two letters, which do not surprise me. He is diffident as to raising recruits, but that is as much occasioned by his wish to have the American war alone carried on by sea. I do not see the prospect so indifferent as he does; the best time for recruiting is yet to come, and the different arrangements now just set in motion must have a due time given them before any judgment can be formed whether the coming to the very disagreeable measure of raising new corps will be necessary; but in that case I shall never agree to the disobliging the whole army by giving them to every young man who pretends he can soon complete them. I know full well what little good arose from Charles Townshend's plan—when the corps were completed most of them were declared by the generals who received them to be composed of men totally unfit to carry muskets; besides, a new raised corps will from the time of being completed require at least a year before it can be properly trained for actual service; a regiment composed of good officers will bear a great augmentation, and three months fit them for service. The

[1] On a military mission to Hesse-Cassel and Brunswick.

misfortune is that at the beginning of this American business there has been an unwillingness to augment the army and navy. I proposed early in the summer sending beating orders to Ireland; this was objected to in the Cabinet; if it had been then adopted, the army would have been at least two or three thousand men stronger at this hour. There is now every means using to complete the old corps, and I cannot agree to putting additional irons into the fire.

As to the proposals transmitted by Mr. Römer, they all end in corps of officers, which cannot be done but by Act of Parliament; the only idea these Germans ought to adopt is the being contractors for raising recruits and fixing the prices they will deliver them at Hamburg, Rotterdam, and any other port they may propose. Mr. Römer seems alone to want to finger English money, but that I think should be prevented by giving no money in hand, but promising to pay 10 l. per man ready money on the recruits being approved by the officers sent to receive them in those ports.

Not a very pretty business: yet on certain points the King seems to have been tender, not to say delicate.

XXIV. To Lord North

Kew, 10 min. past 2 p.m., November 14, 1775.

Lord North,

I sent last week orders to the Regency and to Field-Mareshal Sporken that Scheither should be permitted to contract with Colonel Faucitt for raising 4,000 recruits for Great Britain, and that Stade and Nieuburgh should be the two garrisons where the recruits should be closely kept. These orders are certainly arrived this day; but to prevent any mistakes, I will have a fresh copy sent by the messenger this night. The laws of Germany are so clear against emigration, that I certainly in going thus far have done as much as I possibly can in my Electoral capacity; the giving commissions to officers, or any other of the proposals that have been made, I can by no means consent to, for they in plain English are turning me into a kidnapper, which I cannot think a very honourable occupation.

Still, none of this would be necessary if only people would recognize their duty: and was he not defending their constitution?

xxv. To Lord North

Kew, 46 min. past 9 a.m., September 10, 1775.

Lord North,

It is impossible to draw up a more dutiful and affectionate address than the one from the town of Manchester, which really gives me pleasure, as it comes unsolicited. As you seem desirous that this spirit should be encouraged, I will certainly not object to it, though by fatal experience I am aware that they will occasion counter-petitions. One from the merchants of London, if signed by a great majority of the most respectable names in the City, I should think highly proper, as that would show that the Corporation of London have not been actuated by the sense of the merchants who are the respectable part of the metropolis.

If the Opposition is powerful next session it will much surprise me, for I am fighting the battle of legislature, therefore have a right to expect an almost unanimous support. If there should arise difficulties they will not dismay me, for I know the uprightness of my intentions, and therefore am ready to stand every attack of ever so dangerous a kind with the firmness that honesty and an attachment to the constitution will support. If, in addition to the addresses you wish to encourage, the nobility and gentry of property would be persuaded separately in their parishes to give half of a guinea in addition to the levy-money for the encouragement of each of their parishioners enlisting in the army, that would be doing a real service. . . .

But alas, the King was left to wonder how it was that the London merchants were so absorbed in their private interests as not to feel what they owed to the constitution that had enriched them, so deeply absorbed that they would not show their willingness either by an address nor by something even better, a subscription to furnish comforts to the troops in America.[1] *(To North, 25 September.)*

[1] The City was against American taxation, since this amounted to taxing their foreign investments: the country gentlemen were in favour of it— till the war became so expensive as to make an increase in the land tax inevitable.

I

During the summer, Generals Burgoyne, Howe, and Clinton joined Gage, with 10,000 men, and on 17th September the expensive victory of Bunker's Hill was gained. It was decided, however, that the main attack should be in the south, the King being ready to consider this, since ' every means of distressing America must meet with my concurrence, as it tends to bringing them to feel the necessity of returning to their duty '. (To North, October 15.)

XXVI. To Lord North

Kew, 11 o'clock, October 16, 1775.

Lord North,

I have very maturely weighed the advantages of a winter expedition against the four southern colonies of North America, and the great difficulties of assembling 2,000 men for that service; but the former is so very material that I am ready to give direction for the 15th and 37th regiments of infantry being ordered to embark in the second week in December; they are not part of the 12,000 to remain in Ireland, and would probably have embarked in February for America : weak as we are in regiments of infantry in Britain, two regiments shall at that time be sent to Ireland to replace the 53rd and 54th regiments, which shall also go on this expedition, being next regiments for foreign service. . . .

I am clear the next attempt should be made on North Carolina, as the Highland settlers are said to be well inclined; they ought to be offered grants of land in the same manner as those raised by Maclean, to be looked on as provincial corps, whilst employed to have the same pay as the regular troops, one corps to remain in the province when the regiments go to the other colonies : Virginia may also be thus defended. . . .

As to the raising a corps of Highlanders, I will fully weigh the measure, and on Wednesday give you my sentiments on that subject.

PS.—When the two regiments are sent in December to Ireland there will remain in Britain but four battalions; though I have a great respect for the militia, I think nothing but the present moment could defend the weakening of the country so much, and I greatly prefer the calling out the militia to raising new corps.

The refusal of Russia to supply mercenaries caused the King some pain.

XXVII. To Lord North

Queen's House, 2 min. past 8 p.m., November 3, 1775.

. . . The letter of the Empress is a clear refusal, and not in so genteel a manner as I should have thought might have been expected from her. She has not had the civility to answer in her own hand, and has thrown out some expressions that may be civil to a Russian ear, but certainly not to more civilized ones.

The army votes passed by a large majority; but the proposal that the troops removed from Ireland should be replaced by Germans, was tactlessly handled in Ireland by the Lord Lieutenant, Lord Harcourt, and caused animadversions in the House of Commons.

XXVIII. To Lord North

Queen's House, 46 min. past 2 p.m., November 28, 1775.

LORD NORTH,

I can scarcely find words expressive enough at my astonishment at the presumption and imprudence of bringing forward in Ireland a matter of such great delicacy without having had the fullest directions from hence, and the very mode and words of the message, if that had been judged right, approved from hence. If this kind of conduct is continued in Ireland, one can scarcely sleep in quiet from apprehension of being daily drawn into difficulties. I honour[1] men that will act boldly when authorized, but I highly disapprove of those who, like quacks, engage in all matters from not knowing the magnitude of the undertaking.

At this time certain changes took place in the administration. The Duke of Grafton went into opposition: Lord George Germain (who as Lord George Sackville had earned so unenviable a reputation at Minden) became Secretary for the Colonies, and Weymouth once more became Secretary of State.

[1] Donne prints ' know ': emendation from Fortescue.

Nothing of importance occurred for some time. Gage was recalled, leaving in command Howe, who transferred his forces to Halifax with a view of occupying New York. The Americans failed before Quebec. During the summer Canada was cleared of them, but the English attempt on South Carolina failed. Howe was dilatory, and North became depressed. From now on we get the picture of the King prodding North on through the agency of John Robinson, who was to North what Stone had been to Newcastle. Robinson was a Treasury official from 1770-1782, and a man of substance in his county; as a side interest it may be noted that his aunt's husband was Wordsworth's grandfather.

xxix. To John Robinson

Windsor, 9 min. past 2 p.m., September 16, 1776.

. . . I am sorry to find Lord North by his letter so uneasy at the victualling ships being not yet sailed for Canada, as I attribute part of it to his not being in good spirits. I differ widely with him as to bad news being likely from New York, as we have had no account as yet; I reason just contrary, that Howe by delay has so much the better concerted his manœuvres, and having collected the greatest part of his forces will strike the more decisive blow.

In fact in that month Howe occupied New York, and Washington's forces seemed to be crumbling.

The period was critical, since Howe, with his brother, Admiral Lord Howe, had been appointed commissioners to try to conciliate the Americans: unluckily they had arrived a few days after the Declaration of Independence on July 4th. So little did they accomplish, that in November Franklin and Silas Deane went to Paris to obtain help there. A good deal of business was got through that session, especially during the absence of Fox in Paris, an opportunity the King urged North to seize: it was decided that Burgoyne should attack Albany in the next year. Severe measures were taken against Americans on the high seas, the Habeas Corpus Act was partly suspended, and John the Painter who had caused fires at the dockyards was hanged. The King was so confident, that the sudden and shocking defeat at Trenton hardly ruffled him.

XXX. To Lord North

Queen's House, 50 min. past 5 p.m., February 24, 1777.

LORD NORTH,

I am sorry to find your cold is increased, and strongly recommend ABSTINENCE and WATER as the ablest and safest physicians.

The accounts from America are most comfortable. The surprise and want of spirit of the Hessian officers as well as soldiers at Trenton is not much to their credit, and will undoubtedly rather elate the rebels, who till then were in a state of the greatest despondency. I wish Sir W. Howe had placed none but British troops in the outposts; but I am certain by a letter I have seen from Lord Cornwallis that the rebels will soon have sufficient reason to fall into the former dejection. . . .

It was to Robinson that the King addressed his letters while ' the old fat fellow ', as North's enemies called him, got so thin as to feel, as he told his doctor, what he had not felt for a long time, his ribs: and these letters are less formal than those he addressed his First Lord of the Treasury. He would refer to ' that babbler Skene ', suggest of one of his agents abroad that ' writing was not his fort ', or doubt of another ' whether any trust could be reposed in him '. The pessimistic reports of spies in France he was especially contemptuous of. ' I am quite convinced that Hynson as well as every other spy from N. America is encouraged by Deane and Franklin and only gives evidence to deceive '. Sometimes he was more his royal self.

XXXI. To John Robinson

Queen's House, 24 min. past m., March 5, 1777.

. . . I am sorry to find any one adopts the idea of there being any reason in Sir W. Howe's application for 20,000 additional troops; I know the thing is impracticable, and if he and his brother will act with a little less lenity (which I really think cruelty as it keeps up the contest) the next campaign will bring the Americans in a temper to accept of such terms as may enable the Mother Country to keep them in order; for we must never come into such as may patch for a year or two, and then bring on new broils; the regaining their affection is an idle idea : it must be the convincing them that it is their interest to submit, and then they will dread farther broils.

In May, Chatham made another miraculous recovery, and on the 30th made an attack on the administration which it was hard to answer. The King was not much disturbed, though he was angry.

XXXII. To Lord North

Kew, 25 min. past 6 a.m., May 31, 1777.

LORD NORTH,

. . . I have as yet not heard from Lord Weymouth concerning the debate in the House of Lords, and consequently am much pleased with your attention in sending unto me a copy of Lord Chatham's highly unseasonable motion, which can have no other use but to convey some fresh fuel if attended to by the rebels. Like most of the other productions of that extraordinary brain, it contains nothing but specious words and malevolence, for no one that reads it, if unacquainted with the conduct of the mother country and its colonies, [but] must suppose the Americans poor mild persons, who after unheard-of and repeated grievances had no choice but slavery or the sword; whilst the truth is that the too great lenity of this country increased their pride and encouraged them to rebel. But, thank God! the nation does not see the unhappy contest through his mirror; if his sentiments were adopted, I should not esteem my situation in this country as a very dignified one, for the Islands would soon cast off their obedience.

The summer was depressing for North: the French were now openly helping the Americans, and no successes were reported by Howe. The King relied on Robinson to imbue his Prime Minister with courage. ' I am sorry,' he wrote to the secretary, ' Lord North seems rather out of spirits, but I am certain when he has seen Mr. Robinson he will be more cheerful.' But it is likely that the victory at Brandywine in September, and the capture of Philadelphia, were more efficacious.

It was not long, however, before the news of Burgoyne's surrender at Saratoga was received; North hinted that he was

ready to resign, but the King, remaining calm, soothed him with
a letter which began informally, ' My dear Lord '.

XXXIII. To Lord North

Queen's House, 30 min. past 10 a.m., December 4, 1777.

My dear Lord,

I cannot help just taking up your time for a few minutes to
thank you in the most cordial manner for your speech; the manly,
firm and dignified part you took brought the House to see the
present misfortune in true light, as very serious, but not without
remedy; it may probably on due consideration, which I trust all
in my service will be willing to give, in the end prove the wisest
step in our present situation to act only on the defensive with the
army, and with great activity as to the troops. Canada, Nova
Scotia, the Floridas, New York and Rhode Island must probably
be the stations, but those who have served in those parts, particularly Lord Amherst,[1] must be consulted, and will be able to
point out what is best. I shall only add that I can never forget
the friendship as well as zeal you have shown to me by your
conduct yesterday.

During the next month it became increasingly clear that
France would before long declare war, though the King persisted
in belittling the news he got from his agents, since in his view
they were all ' stockjobbers '. Amherst declared that large forces
would be necessary to subdue the rebels, and though recruiting
was vastly improved, North became convinced that some means
of conciliation should be tried, and also that, given his past, he
was not the man to try it. On January 29th he wrote to the
King, putting his views forward.

XXXIV. To Lord North

Queen's House, 25 min. past 1 p.m., January 31, 1778.

Lord North,

The letter I received from you the last evening was of so
serious a nature that you cannot be surprised that I chose to defer
answering it until this day.

---

[1] Sir Jeffrey Amherst, now raised to the peerage, had served in America
under Pitt, and with great distinction.

I should have been greatly hurt at the inclination expressed by you to retire, had I not known that, however you may now and then be inclined to despond, yet that you have too much personal affection for me, and sense of honour, to allow such a thought to take any hold on your mind.

You must feel how very entirely I have confided in you since you have presided at the Treasury, how fairly you have been supported by your colleagues in the Administration, how sincerely you are loved and admired by the House of Commons, and how universally esteemed by the public; indeed, these reflections must rouse your mind, and enable you to withstand situations still more embarrassing than the present.

You will remember that before the recess I strongly advised you not to bind yourself to bring forward a proposition for restoring tranquillity to North America, not from any absurd ideas of unconditional submission my mind never harboured, but from perceiving that whatever can be proposed will be liable not to bring America back to a sense of attachment to the mother country, yet to dissatisfy this country, which has in the most handsome manner cheerfully carried on the contest, and therefore has a right to have the struggle continued until convinced that it is in vain. . . .

North, then, remained, and his Conciliatory Bills were passed in March: the late obnoxious measures, such as the Boston Port Bill and the Massachusetts Bill, were repealed, and commissioners were to be sent out to come to an understanding. The Howes were recalled. Soon afterwards, however, the French ambassador delivered an insulting paper which virtually amounted to a declaration of war. North felt the situation too much for him, especially since Germain had recently resigned, a 'defection' the King regarded as 'a most favourable event': only one man could carry on, and that was Chatham. The King was appalled; anything, anybody, rather than that monster, so great, so bitter, had his dislike become. Yet Chatham was obviously the man: he hated France, and though he would do all he could to conciliate the Americans, he was, unlike the Rockingham group, as stoutly, as desperately against independence as the King himself. For weeks North tried to resign, but all the while the King was obdurate: he would himself rather abdicate than fall once more into the hands of Chatham.

xxxv. To Lord North

Probably March 15, 1778.

Lord North,

On a subject which has for many months engrossed my thoughts, I cannot have the smallest difficulty instantly to answer the letter I have received from you. My sole wish is to keep you at the head of the Treasury, and as my confidential Minister. That end obtained, I am willing, through your channel, to accept any description of persons that will come avowedly to the support of your administration, and as such do not object to Lord Shelburne and Mr. Barré,[1] whom personally perhaps I dislike as much as Alderman Wilkes; and I cannot give you a stronger proof of my desire to forward your wishes than taking this unpleasant step. But I declare in the strongest and most solemn manner that though I do not object to your addressing yourself to Lord Chatham, yet that you must acquaint him that I shall never address myself to him but through you; and on a clear explanation that he is to step forth to support an administration wherein you are First Lord of the Treasury; and that I cannot consent to have any conversation with him till the ministry is formed; that if he comes into this, I will, as he supports you, receive him with open arms. I leave the whole arrangements to you, provided Lord Suffolk, Lord Weymouth and my two able lawyers are satisfied as to their situations;[2] but choose Ellis[3] for Secretary at War in preference to Barré, who in that event will get a more lucrative employment, but will not be so near my person.

Having said this, I will only add, to put before your eye my inmost thoughts, that no advantage to this country, nor personal danger to myself, can ever make me address myself to Lord Chatham, or to any other branch of opposition. Honestly, I would rather lose the Crown I now wear than bear the ignominy

[1] A brilliant and prominent member of the opposition.
[2] His Secretaries of State, and his law officers, Thurlow and Wedderburn.
[3] Welbore Ellis, a 'King's friend', then occupying a minor post.

of possessing it under their shackles. I might write volumes if I would state the feelings of my mind; but I have honestly, fairly, and affectionately told you the whole of my mind, and what I will never depart from. Should Lord Chatham wish to see me before he gives an answer, I shall most certainly refuse it. I have had enough of personal negotiation; and neither my dignity nor my feelings will ever let me again submit to it.

Men of less principles and honesty than I pretend to may look on public measures and opinions as a game. I always act from conviction; but I am shocked at the base arts all these men have used, therefore cannot go toward them : if they come to your assistance I will accept them.

You have full power to act, but I do not expect Lord Chatham and his crew will come to your assistance; but if they do not, I trust the rest of the arrangement will greatly strengthen, and will give efficacy to, administration. . . .

The notion of Chatham, with or without his crew, serving under North, is slightly ludicrous: he would, of course, have full power or none at all. The negotiations were undertaken by William Eden (afterwards first Lord Auckland), Under-Secretary of State.

XXXVI.TO LORD NORTH

Queen's House, 28 min. past 8 a.m., March 16, 1778.

MY DEAR LORD,

As you are now thoroughly apprised of the whole of my thoughts and feelings, you cannot want any explanation of my opinion of the language held to Mr. Eden the last evening; it is so totally contrary to the only ground upon which I could have accepted the services of that perfidious man that I need not enter more fully upon [it]. Lord Chatham as Dictator, as planning a new administration, I appeal to my letter of yesterday if I did not clearly speak out upon. If Lord Chatham agrees to support your administration, or (if you like the expression better) the fundamentals of the present administration, and Lord N. the head of the Treasury, Lords Suffolk, Gower, and Weymouth in great offices to their own inclinations, Lord Sandwich in the

Admiralty, Thurlow Chancellor, and Wedderburne a Chief Justice, I will not object to see that great man when Lord Shelburne and Dunning,[1] with Barré, are placed already in offices; but I solemnly declare nothing shall bring me to treat personally with Lord Chatham. What the D. of Northumberland told you yesterday is the old game over again; if I saw Lord Chatham, he would insist on as total a change as Lord Shelburne has yesterday thrown out. Therefore, my dear Lord, you will now understand that I entirely stick to what I wrote to you yesterday, from which I will not change one jot.

The next letter is almost plaintive.

XXXVII. To Lord North

Queen's House, 10 min. past 11 p.m., March 16, 1778.

Lord North,

I am fully convinced that you are actuated alone from a wish not to conceal the most private corners of your breast in writing the letter you have just sent unto me; but, my dear Lord, it is not private pique, but an opinion formed on an experience of a reign of now seventeen years, that makes me resolve to run any personal risk rather than submit to Opposition, which every plan deviating from strengthening the present administration is more or less tending to; therefore I refer you to the genuine dictates of my heart which I put yesterday on paper and transmitted to you; and I am certain, whilst I have no one object but to be of use to this country, it is impossible I can be deserted, and the road opened to a set of men who certainly would make me a slave for the remainder of my days; and whatever they may pretend, would go to the most unjustifiable lengths of cruelty and destruction of those who have stood forth in public office, of which you would be the first victim.

But still North, sure that he was right, hammered away at the point: but the more persistent he was, the more inflexible was the King's determination.

[1] A supporter of Shelburne, afterwards first Lord Ashburton.

XXXVIII. To Lord North

Queen's House, 25 min. past 11 a.m., March 17, 1778.

Lord North,

I am grieved at you continually recurring to a subject on which we can never agree. Your letter is certainly personally affectionate to me, and shows no sign of personal fear; but, my dear Lord, no consideration in life shall make me stoop to Opposition. I am still ready to accept any part of them that will come to the assistance of my present efficient Ministers; but whilst any ten men in the kingdom will stand by me, I will not give myself up into bondage. My dear Lord, I will rather risk my crown than do what I think personally disgraceful; and whilst I have no wish but for the good and prosperity of my country, it is impossible that the nation will not stand by me; if they will not, they shall have another king, for I will never put my hand to what would make me miserable to the last hour of my life. . . .

It became a question of personal loyalty: if this were lacking, abdication (not the last time it was threatened) would follow.

XXXIX. To Lord North

Queen's House, [1] min. past 8 a.m., March 22, 1778.

. . . My dear Lord, your now always recurring to a total change of Administration obliges me to ask you one clear question, which in my own mind I am almost certain cannot be your intention : If I will not by your advice take the step I look on as disgraceful to myself and destruction to my country and family, are you resolved, agreeable to the example of the D. of Grafton, at the hour of danger to desert me?

North consented to go on until the end of the session, hoping that Chatham would somehow come in: but on April 7th that great man was overtaken by a fit when making a speech in the House of Lords: it was clear that he was doomed, and the King was able to refer to it coldly as ' the political exit of Lord Chatham '. He died on May 11th. North was persuaded to go on. The King was relieved, and was able to turn his attention to naval affairs: he was ready to mark time in America, for

*the sake of beating the French, especially since North's con-
ciliators had failed, and Philadelphia and the Jerseys lost.*

XL. TO LORD NORTH

Windsor, August 12, 1778.

LORD NORTH,

The present accounts from America seem to put a final stop
to all negotiation. Farther concession is a joke; all that can now
be done is steadily to pursue the plan very wisely adopted in the
spring, the providing Nova Scotia, the Floridas, and Canada,
with troops; and should that not leave enough for New York,
which may in the end be the case, we must then abandon that
place; then we must content ourselves with distressing the rebels,
and not think of any other conduct till the end of the French
[war], which, if successful, will oblige the rebels to submit to
more reasonable [terms] than can at this hour be obtained.

*The French war roused the King's most combatant spirits, as
indeed it did that of the whole nation.*

XLI. TO JOHN ROBINSON

Kew, 35 min. past 8 a.m., August 29, 1778.

I shall be highly anxious until I hear the ships now collecting
for the defence of Jersey and Guernsey are got to their station :
if the French have acted with judgement, they would not have
sent out the Brest fleet until ready for the attack on those islands,
as the moment our fleet is off Ushant the coast would be clear
for their enterprise : but perhaps this may not be the case, and
that we may still be in time though I rather doubt it. I know
very well our situation is not very pleasant, but it behoves every
one the more to exert every nerf to bravely stand forth at this
hour of danger; Britain had better be totally destroyed than
crouch; I trust this firmness of mind which will never depart
from me while I live will encourage Mr. Robinson (of whose
good intentions I am ever certain) to rouse all he can approach
in their several situations, to see that spirit, not prudence, alone
can save a nation when surrounded with evils.

The King was hoping, as he told Robinson in another letter, that Admiral Keppel would gain a decisive victory, ' to rouse the nation from a lethargy that may prove very fatal '. Lethargy! That was the danger. Why, after Easter, attendance even at Parliament had been ' very sluggish ': and when he ordered North to draw up a plan to remedy this, the old fat fellow, too, was sluggish. This would indeed prove very fatal; North must be roused up, and Robinson roused up to rouse up North.

XLII. To Lord North

Kew, November 2, 1778.

Lord North cannot be surprised that, at an hour when this country is surrounded with impending evils, I should think myself highly culpable if I did not to the utmost of my ability prepare against them : on that account I the last week insisted on your forthwith preparing a plan for procuring a handsome attendance on the opening of the session, and a continuance of it during the sitting of Parliament. This you promised to draw up; yet the week has elapsed without your producing it, and your aversion to decide would lead you to postpone it till too late, unless forced by me to what I look upon not only as essential to the conducting public affairs with credit, but as necessary for your own ease of mind; I therefore must insist on your laying your thoughts on that subject before the Cabinet at your meeting on Thursday, and have just wrote to the two Secretaries of State to acquaint them you have my directions for that purpose. Indeed, my dear Lord, though the present scene is not very clear, yet with activity, decision, and zeal, things may soon wear a very different appearance.

XLIII. To John Robinson

Queen's House, 42 min. past 11 a.m., November 6, 1778.

The drafts seem highly proper, but oblige me again to repeat that the inaccuracy in stating the rations in N. America is most extraordinary, and encourages the opinion of fraud or great negligence.[1]

[1] This question of contracts was soon to become acute.

Lord North laid his plan yesterday before me, which if followed up with spirit, will I trust prove very beneficial to my service; but to deal frankly he must cast off his indecision, and bear up, or no plan can succeed. He must be more exact in answering letters or let others do it for him, and he must let measures be thoroughly canvassed before undertaken, and when adopted must not quit them.

Nothing can be more proper than the part taken by Mr. Robinson in the whole of this transaction.

Vigour before all things was needed to preserve the beauties of the Constitution; it looked as though the King himself would have to provide it. He provided, at least, a remarkable political testament.

XLIV. TO LORD NORTH

Kew, [1] min. past [1] p.m., November 14, 1778.

It has been a certain position with me that firmness is the characteristic of an Englishman, that consequently when a Minister will show a resolution boldly to advance that he will meet with support; consequently Lord North's report that the gentlemen who attended the meeting in Downing Street last night will cordially support during the next session is what I expected; and if on the opening of the session the speech from the Throne is penned with firmness, and shows no other end is sought but benevolence to all the branches, provided the empire is kept entire, and invite all who will cordially unite in that point and in a resolution to withstand the natural enemies of the country, and the Ministers in their speeches show that they will never consent to the independence of America, and that the assistance of every man will be accepted on that ground, I am certain the cry will be strong in their favour.

I should have concluded here had not the letter contained the following expression, that Lord North is *conscious and certain that he neither has the authority nor abilities requisite for the conduct of affairs at this time*; the word *authority* puzzles me, for from the hour of Lord North's so handsomely devoting himself on the retreat of the D. of Grafton, I have never had a political thought which I have not communicated unto him, have accepted of persons highly disagreeable to me, because he thought they would be of advantage to his conducting public affairs, and have yielded to measures my own opinion did not quite approve; therefore I must desire to have an explanation in writing on what is meant to be conveyed by that word; as also that *a change might be made to the benefit of my service without having recourse to the Opposition.* This is quite a new thought, and till Lord North explains what that means, the idea is quite incomprehensible to me.

If Lord North can see with the same degree of enthusiasm I do the beauty, excellence, and perfection of the British constitution as by law established, and consider that if any one branch of the empire is allowed to cast off its dependency, that the others will infallibly follow the example, that consequently, though an arduous struggle, that is worth going through any difficulty to preserve to latest posterity what the wisdom of our ancestors have carefully transmitted to us, he will not allow despondency to find a place in his breast, but resolve, not merely out of duty, to fill his post, but will resolve with vigour to meet every obstacle that may arise, he shall meet with most cordial support from me; but the times require vigour, or the state will be ruined.

Apart from an assassination plot, which the King met with his usual coolness in the face of physical danger, the only points of interest at this period are the replacement of Barrington by Charles Jenkinson at the War Office, and the quarrel between the admirals. Keppel had not done well, Palliser was little better; at all events the King thought it provided an opportunity to replace Sandwich by Lord Howe at the Admiralty, a change which was not achieved. North's attempt to form a coalition with the Chatham party met with no success.

XLV. To Lord North

Queen's House, 37 min. past 6 p.m., January 29, 1779.

. . . By Mr. Eden's note I perceive Opposition, as I expected, when they talk of coalition, mean to dictate. I thank God I am not made of materials, whatever difficulties may ever surround me, to stoop to that. . . .

Yet there is no wonder that North was depressed. There were riots over the naval affair, in which his house had been attacked: he was defeated in the House over a Bill to prevent members of the House being contractors of any kind, a defeat which he took as ' a personal affront ', and was still not happy when on a further reading the government won. ' I cannot conceive what had depressed Lord North yesterday,' the King confided to Robinson. Everything upset North unduly—the Universities losing the monopoly of almanacs, or the inquiry on Sir William Howe's action. The King wrote to the man he used as a spur to goad North on.

XLVI. To John Robinson

Queen's House, 30 min. past 7 a.m., May 11, 1779.

. . . A letter came from Lord North full of apprehensions last night after having lost the revenue of the Universities from the sale of almanacs, which ended with saying the inquiry on Sir W. Howe takes a very unpleasant turn for administration, and that if the General's conduct should be approved it must probably be attended with a change of administration; This language is not encouraging, but as I have no object but to do my duty, nothing shall abate my zeal for my country and resolution to keep out those who have from private views shown themselves enemies to it. Mr. Robinson must to-day attempt his irksome part of rousing Lord North to act as he ought.

The whole business of state, it began to appear to the King, was to keep North in office, and all the while North was trying to slip the bit. Much of the next two years was therefore occupied with changing the ministry so that North might stay in—for if he went, all was lost, the excellence and the beauty of the constitution destroyed for ever. One of the main troubles was with Wedderburn, who, restive at seeing Thurlow Lord Chancellor, aspired after a peerage. The King made North consult Thurlow, which he was not anxious to do: he was jealous of him, the King hinted to Robinson, or perhaps his ' love of indecision ' made him fear downright advice. The King was always for grasping nettles firmly and at once.

XLVII. To John Robinson

Kew, 46 min. past 9 a.m., June 6, 1779.

Mr. Robinson's account of the conduct again held by the Attorney General is by no means wonderful to me; for any one that has carefully attended to the whole of that gentleman's political walk must see that he is not guided by principle, that self-conceit and what he thinks his momentary interest alone sways him; I should think if Lord North were rid of him it would be advantageous; intrigues should never approach a man of Lord North's cast, who with many good qualities too much tends to the difficulty of the moment and procrastination, and Lord North from wanting to get out of the evil of the day but too often falls into what may prove ruin in futurity. I own my mind always inclines to meet difficulties as they arise, and I would much rather have them soon fall on my head if not to be avoided than to know that in future they must inevitably happen. Public men ought always to act on system not from the occasion of the minute; 'tis that alone has given the advantage to Franklin, 'tis by uniformly attending to that, that we may yet retrieve our affairs.

Thus when Sir William Meredith tabled a motion for peace with America, the King had once more to supply North with 'vigour'.

XLVIII. To Lord North

Kew, 25 min. past 10 a.m., June 11, 1779.

. . . The object of Sir W. Meredith pretends to be the desire of peace with America, that of Mr. Eden to be employed as a private negotiator with Franklin to effect peace with America;[1] it is therefore easy to blend my thoughts on both ideas; indeed I rather wish to convey my sentiments to Lord North on a very serious subject on paper, as it will enable him at any time to recur to this when he wants to know my ideas on the subject.

[1] To Robinson two days later: ' Mr. Robinson probably knows that Eden, unsatiated with intrigues in this country, is wanting to go to Bruges to treat with Franklin; I have given the deaf ear to it.' (Add. MSS. 37834, f. 96.)

I should think it the greatest instance among the many I have met with of ingratitude and injustice, if it could be supposed that any man in my dominions more ardently desired the restoration of peace and solid happiness in every part of the empire than I do; there is no personal sacrifice I could not readily yield for so desirable an object; but at the same time no inclination to get out of the present difficulties, which certainly keep my mind from a state of ease, can incline me to enter into what I look upon as the destruction of the empire. I have heard Lord North frequently drop that the advantages to be gained by this contest could never repay the expense; I own that, let any war be ever so successful, if persons will sit down and weigh the expenses, they will find, as in the last, that it has impoverished the state, enriched individuals, and perhaps raised the name only of the conquerors;[1] but this is only weighing such events in the scale of a tradesman behind his counter; it is necessary for those in the station it has pleased Divine Providence to place me, to weigh whether expenses, though very great, are not sometimes necessary to prevent what might be more ruinous to a country than the loss of money. The present contest with America I cannot help seeing as the most serious in which any country was ever engaged : it contains such a train of consequences that they must be examined to feel its real weight. Whether the laying a tax was deserving all the evils that have arisen from it I should suppose no man could allege that without being thought more fit for Bedlam than a seat in the Senate; but step by step the demands of America have risen : independence is their object; that certainly is one which every man not willing to sacrifice every object to a *momentary* and inglorious peace must concur with me in thinking that this country can never submit to : should America succeed in that, the West Indies must follow them, not independence, but must for its own interest be dependent on North America. Ireland would soon follow the same plan and be a separate state; then this island would be reduced to itself, and soon would be a poor island indeed, for, reduced in her trade, merchants would retire with their wealth to climates more to their advantage, and shoals of manufacturers would leave this

---

[1] A remark which seems to be some 150 years ahead of its time.

country for the new empire. These self-evident consequences are not worse than what can arise should the Almighty permit every event to turn to our disadvantage; consequently this country has but one sensible, one great line to follow, the being ever ready to make peace when to be obtained without submitting to terms that in their consequence must annihilate this empire, and with firmness to make every effort to deserve success.

Every effort indeed was necessary, for in June Spain declared war. The event stimulated the King; it ' might have been long expected; my conduct has not hurried it on; it is therefore our duty with firmness to meet it, an higher Power must decide with what effect '. And if North once more tried to escape, well, more spirit must be infused.

XLIX. To Lord North

Queen's House, 13 min. p.m., June 16, 1779.

Lord North's application to resign within two days of the prorogation of Parliament I can see in no other light than his showing his continuation in a desire of retiring whenever my affairs will permit it; for I can never suppose that he, who so very handsomely stepped forth on the desertion of the Duke of Grafton, would lose all merit by following so undignified an example. The times are certainly hazardous, but that ought to rouse the spirit of every Englishman to support me, who have no wish but for the prosperity of my people, and no view but to do my duty and to show by firmness in difficulties that I am not unworthy of the station into which it has pleased Providence to place me.

' No man has a right to talk of leaving me at this hour,' he wrote to Robinson a little later. Indeed affairs did not shape well: there was an invasion scare that summer, the militia were called out, an Impressment Bill was passed. Yet nothing much happened in America, still less at sea; and though there was trouble in Ireland, the French began to angle for peace. In the autumn there were several changes in the ministry: Gower and Weymouth resigned, Hillsborough and Stormont taking their places. The King did his best to prevent the resignations.

L. To Lord Weymouth

Kew, 50 min. past 6 p.m., November 5, 1779.

I owe it to my own feelings as well as to the public, to try
to persuade Lord Weymouth not to fly from the public business
at an hour of difficulty, and at a time when the most desperate
opposition that ever stood forth is using every means to force itself
into power, and is willing to betray every national object. . . .

*But it was no good: and still North persisted in his appeals
for release, which the King always met with pretended astonishment. ' I do not yet think he means to retire,' the King wrote
to Robinson, ' and am resolved the retreat shall be his not my
deciding.' North, one would think, had already made that plain
enough.*

*Matters, however, grew increasingly difficult. Friends of the
government grew slack in their attendance at the House: ' It is
impossible to keep one's temper on the conduct of gentlemen who
calls [sic] themselves zealous for government,' the King complained bitterly to Robinson. Furious attacks on North were
the common fare of every debate: huge meetings of protest were
organized in Yorkshire. The Prime Minister insisted upon trying to form a coalition, Thurlow negotiating. The King hated
the idea.*

LI. To Charles Jenkinson

Queen's House, 7 min. past 8 a.m., December 11, 1779.

Mr. Jenkinson will receive the first rough draft of a letter to
the Chancellor, the subject of which is so very revolting to my
mind, and from which I expect no favourable issue, that I have
found the greatest difficulty to put anything on paper; it is
greatly too long and requires much pruning. . . .

LII. To Lord Chancellor Thurlow

Queen's House, December 18, 1779.

. . . From the cold disdain with which I am thus treated
[the offers had been rejected], it is evident to me what treatment
I am to expect from Opposition, if I was to call them now to my
service. Nothing less will satisfy them than a total change of

measures and men : to obtain their support I must deliver up my person, my principles, and my dominions into their hands : I must also abandon every old meritorious and faithful servant I have, to be treated as their resentment or their mercy may incline them. These would be hard times indeed to be a sovereign in any situation. I trust to God that mine is not yet so bad as this. I will never make my inclinations alone, nor even my own opinions, the sole rule of my conduct in public measures; my first object shall be the good of my people. I will at all times consult my Ministers, and place in them as entire a confidence as the nature of this government can be supposed to require of me. You, my Lord, and all who have ever served me, can do me the justice to testify that I have not been deficient in this respect. But none of my ministers can after this trial advise me to change my government totally, and to admit Opposition without any terms. My Parliament have already shown, since their meeting, that they are in opinion against such a desperate measure; and I am confident, from all I can learn, that it is not the wish of my people at large. They wish that I would strengthen my government by bringing into it all that is eminent and respectable; but they do not wish that I should turn out one set of men merely for the purpose of bringing in another.

Nothing therefore remains for me to do but to exert myself and to call upon all those who serve me to exert themselves in support of my legal authority, and to resist this formidable and desperate Opposition; and I shall do it with more confidence and spirit from a consciousness that I have done all which it becomes a sovereign to do to reclaim the factious, to form a coalition of the great and virtuous, and to unite all my subjects. . . .

Early spring, however, brought petitions from the north, and constant attacks in the House, from Burke and others, on the questions of economy and pensions, and particularly secret service money, culminating in April with Dunning's famous motion on April 7th, that ' the influence of the Crown has increased, is increasing, and ought to be diminished'. The government was badly defeated, though it lost by only two votes a further motion Dunning introduced on the 10th, which practically amounted to a demand for publication of all secret service accounts. All these events centre round the constitutional struggle as to whether the King should be allowed to choose his own ministers, and use public money as party funds. He himself had no doubts on the point.

LIII. To LORD NORTH

Queen's House, 15 min. past 8 a.m., April 11, 1780.

It is clear that had the five members arrived in time last night, the strange resolution of the committee would have been rejected; consequently Lord North must see things begin to wear a better aspect. A little time will I am certain open the eyes of several who have been led on farther than they intended, and numbers will return, for it cannot be the wish of the majority to overturn the Constitution. Factious leaders and ruined men wish it; but the bulk of the nation cannot see it in that light. I therefore shall undoubtedly be assisted in preserving this excellent Constitution by a temperate, but at the same time firm conduct. It is attachment to my country that alone actuates my purposes, and Lord North shall see that at least there is one person willing to preserve unspoiled the most beautiful combination that ever was framed.

The King was right: on further readings the opposition were outvoted: nevertheless it would be wise to let the general election come at its appointed time: ' it would be madness,' the King wrote to Robinson, ' not to call a new Parliament as soon as we have hobbled through the next session '. With a new Parliament, surely, all would be well: North might still make wriggling efforts to get away, the King would restrain him with a firm hand.

LIV. To LORD NORTH

Queen's House, 15 min. past 8 a.m., May 19, 1780.

Lord North cannot doubt that I received with pleasure his account of Mr. Burke's Bill having been defeated in the several clauses that were before the Committee yesterday.[1]

---

[1] On economic reforms, in the earlier stages of which the government had been defeated.

But he cannot be surprised at the real sorrow occasioned by seeing he persists in the idea that his health will not long permit him to remain in his present situation. If I had the powers of oratory of Demosthenes, or the pen of an Addison, I could not say more on the subject than what I can convey in the few following lines: that I am conscious, if Lord North will resolve with spirit to continue in his present employment, that with the assistance of a new Parliament I shall be able to keep the present constitution of this country in its pristine lustre; that there is no means of letting Lord North retire from taking the lead in the House of Commons that will not probably end in evil; therefore till I see things change to a more favourable appearance, I shall not think myself at liberty to consent to Lord North's request. He must be the judge whether he can therefore honourably desert me, when infallible mischief must ensue.

In face of such an appeal, Lord North could do no less than wait to see what the general election would bring forth.

In the interim, in July, an approach was made to the Rockingham group, and North induced the King to write a declaration.

LV

His Majesty, ever desirous of promoting the welfare and happiness of his dominions, thinks it behoves every one actuated by any attachment to his country to cast aside all private pique and animosity, and cordially unite in the service of the State.

He therefore is willing to blot from his remembrance any events that may have displeased him, and to admit into his confidence and service any men of public spirit or talents who will join with part of his present ministry in forming one on a more enlarged plan, provided it is understood that every means are to [be] employed to keep the empire entire, to prosecute the present just and unprovoked war in all its branches with the utmost vigour, and that His Majesty's past measures be treated with proper respect.

But Rockingham proved 'evasive' on the point of American independence: the King would accept none of the Bills suggested, and did not find that his old ones would be treated with the respect he thought they deserved: the negotiations therefore fell through.

There is little more in the correspondence that refers to America. or the war: Rodney had some early successes, but the East and West India fleets were lost. The Armed Neutrality was formed against England, but there were the successes of Charleston and Camden in America. In the autumn there were overtures from the French which inspired hope in the King's breast, but they came to nothing. In December and January there was a broil with the Dutch, who declared war. The French landed in Jersey, but were repulsed. Gibraltar was relieved, but the French and Spaniards landed in Minorca. In 1781 matters seemed then to be marking time, except that the war seemed to be shaping well in America, till suddenly, it seemed, in the autumn there came the news of the disaster at Yorktown, where Cornwallis surrendered. The King refused to be despondent, and was encouraged by the votes on the Address, and the report on the Address.

LVI. To Lord North

Queen's House, 8 min. past 8 p.m., November 28, 1781.

I cannot say I expected the day [debate?] of to-day would have been so short, considering the great love modern orators have of hearing themselves speak; the division was certainly a very good one, and I have no doubt, when men are a little recovered of the shock felt by the bad news, and feel that if we recede no one can tell to what a degree the consequence of this country will be diminished, that they will then find the necessity of carrying on the war, though the mode of it may require alterations.

North, however, was clearer-headed. 'O God! it is all over, it is all over!' he exclaimed when he got the news. It also—though this he did not mind—sealed the end of his own administration.

*　　*　　*　　*　　*　　*

The licentiousness of the press somewhat occupied the King's mind at this time. In 1774, Horne Tooke had published an

*article against the Speaker: both he and the printer were
proceeded against.*

LVII. TO LORD NORTH[1]

Queen's House, February 13, 1774.

LORD NORTH,

I am glad the printer is committed to the custody of the
Serjeant-at-Arms, and that he has confessed Mr. Horne to be the
person that delivered the paper to him, who, in consequence, is
ordered to attend the House of Commons on Wednesday. Now
that this affair has come forward, the House must with spirit
proceed. The half-measures taken on the former occasion have
certainly taken off the dread that used very necessarily to be had
of offending that House, and therefore makes a due degree of
severity absolutely incumbent on the House to inflict on author
and also on printer.

*The House, however, was unable to inflict any punishment:
yet the King did not lose hope.*

LVIII. TO LORD NORTH

Kew, July 19, 1774.

LORD NORTH,

Having heard yesterday of a most scandalous paragraph that
appeared in the *Whitehall Evening Post* in the course of last week
laying a matter to the charge of Lord Lewisham which though
without the least shadow of truth I have reason to know has
caused much uneasiness to his worthy parents, I cannot help
mentioning it to you as his relation, and should imagine that
Lord Dartmouth is called upon to defend the amiable young man
whose exemplary conduct at Oxford so fully does credit to the
principles instilled in him; besides the prosecution of a printer
by so worthy a man as Lord Dartmouth must be attended with
success, and would greatly tend to check that licentiousness which
disgraces the freedom of the press.

*There was another form of licentiousness which perturbed
him, or something perilously near licentiousness.*

[1] See also letter VI of this chapter.

LIX. TO THE ARCHBISHOP OF CANTERBURY[1]

n.d.

MY GOOD LORD PRELATE,

I could not delay giving you the notification of the grief and concern with which my breast was affected at receiving·authentic information that *routs* have made their way into your Palace. At the same time I must signify to you my sentiments on this subject, which holds those levities and vain dissipations as utterly inexpedient, if not unlawful, to pass in a residence for many centuries devoted to divine studies, religious retirement, and the extensive exercise of charity and benevolence. I add, in a place where so many of your predecessors have led their lives in such sanctity as has thrown lustre on the pure religion they professed and adorned.

From the dissatisfaction with which you must perceive I behold these improprieties—not to speak in harsher terms—and on still more pious principles, I trust you will suppress them immediately, so that I may not have occasion to show any further marks of my displeasure, or to interpose in a different manner.

May God take your Grace into his Almighty protection,

I remain, my Lord Primate,

Your gracious friend, G.R.

An admirable letter, and no less admirable was his attitude of tolerance towards a man whose religious opinions, always changing, though he was a Nonconformist minister, and always unorthodox, was yet a distinguished man of science.

LX. TO LORD NORTH

Queen's House, 33 min. past 5 p.m., February 22, 1779.

. . . If Dr. Priestley[2] applies to my librarian, he will have permission to see the library as other men of science have had : but I cannot think the Doctor's character as a politician or divine deserves my appearing at all in it : instruments I have none in London. I am sorry Mr. Eden has any intimacy with that

[1] The Hon. Frederick Cornwallis, uncle of Lord Cornwallis.
[2] He was the discoverer of oxygen.

Doctor, as I am not over-fond of those that frequent any disciples or companions of the Jesuit in Berkeley Square.

The Jesuit of Berkeley Square was Shelburne, whose librarian Priestley was at that time: Jesuit because of the nickname 'Malagrida'.
Licentiousness of a graver sort had to be guarded against in his children, now growing into the age of temptation.

LXI. To Lord Dartmouth

Windsor, December 23, 1780.

Lord Dartmouth will easily conceive that the hour when I take my eldest son out of the hands of his governor must be an arduous one to me; I see the various rocks that surround every young man in this thoughtless and dissolute century. I therefore have had no views in forming his family but to collect men of good private characters, and have not permitted politics or arrangements to come across me; I have as much as possible found men not in the height of youth; one young man would be an exception to my rule, but that I could only make for the son of the excellent man to whom I am writing. I am certain his sons must have been bred up in the school of virtue and decorum, as such I venture to think of your second son, Mr. Legge, for one of his Grooms of the Bedchamber, that will be an office of trust and some attendance; but I think I shall not be disappointed in my choice.

But even the presence of young Legge did not prevent the Prince from being dazzled by the charms of Mrs. Robinson, Sir Joshua Reynold's famous Perdita, *writing to whom the young man would sign himself Florizel.*

LXII. To Lord North

Windsor, 40 min. past 9 a.m., August 28, 1781.

I am sorry to be obliged to open a subject to Lord North that has long given me much pain, but I can rather do it on paper than in conversation; it is a subject of which I know he is not ignorant. My eldest son got last year into a very improper

connection with an actress and woman of indifferent character
through the *friendly* assistance of Lord Malden; a multitude of
letters passed which she has threatened to publish unless he, in
short, bought them of her.   He had made her very foolish
promises, which undoubtedly, by her conduct to him, she entirely
cancelled.   I have thought it right to authorize the getting them
from her, and have employed Lieut. Col. Hotham, on whose
discretion I could depend, to manage this business.   He has now
brought it to a conclusion, and has her consent to get these letters
on her receiving £5,000, undoubtedly an enormous sum; but I
wish to get my son out of his shameful scrape.   I desire you will
therefore see Lieut. Col. Hotham and settle this with him.   I am
happy at being able to say that I never was personally engaged in
such a transaction, which perhaps makes me feel this the stronger.

The last sentence would seem unnecessary.

*During this period Ireland was giving the usual trouble,
under the leadership of Grattan: it was, in fact, almost as disaffected as America.   The King's letters, however, do not reveal
his feeling of intolerance towards his Irish subjects, whom he
understood as little as he did the Americans.   They are more
explicit on the subject of India, of which two among many are
given as examples.   The occasion of the first was no doubt the
disaster and convention of Wargaum; of which Francis, the
inveterate enemy of Hastings lately appointed for his second term
as Governor-General, had no doubt been eager to send the news.
It was not long, however, before Hastings retrieved the situation.*

LXIII. To LORD NORTH

Queen's House, 15 min. past 7 a.m., May 11, 1779.

LORD NORTH,

I have very carefully perused the two letters you have received
from Mr. Francis; the Company is ruined, and Parliament turned
into ridicule, unless Mr. Hastings be instantly removed from his
situation.   I hope, therefore, you will direct Mr. Robinson without the loss of a minute to see the Chairman and Deputy-Chair-
man, and have the legal steps taken for removing Hastings and

Barwell,[1] and that two men of integrity and firmness must be sent to fill up the commission. Harley[2] once wished that employment : I do not mention this from any other view but that a man of his spirit is best calculated for that scene; it will not be a quiet one. If Coote is not gone,[3] would it not be proper to have his opinion concerning those joined to him on this occasion? Do not let these two seats be filled by men who it may suit, but find men that suit the situation.

An earlier letter is probably of less general interest, as not involving such famous names. In 1776, there had been internal dissensions in the Council of Madras, and some of the councillors, among them Stratton, had seized and imprisoned the Governor, Lord Pigot.

LXIV. To JOHN ROBINSON

Kew, [1] *min. past* 9 *a.m., March* 29, 1777.

Mr. Robinson has judged perfectly right in supposing I should be curious to see the different accounts of the present state of the affairs at Madras. The letter from Mr. Stratton is wrote with great address, and certainly puts the conduct of the majority of the Council in as favourable a light as so irregular a transaction can be stated. I have not the smallest doubt but both parties have been stimulated by motives alone of private interest, and every fresh intelligence I have received from you confirm me in the opinion that the recalling all the parties would have been the only prudent path. I have not been void of apprehensions since your account of the turn of the General Court in favour of Lord Pigot, that his violence (which confinement will have even increased) might when reinstated in the Presidency drive him to acts of cruelty; but Mr. Stratton's letter shows that the self-created President and Council of Madras will certainly send Lord Pigot home; for if they consult the Governor and Council General at Bengal, there cannot be the smallest doubt but as matters stand

[1] Richard Barwell, of the Bengal Civil Service, was one of the Council of Five, which governed the Company under North's Regulating Act of 1773.

[2] Harley, a younger son of the 3rd Earl of Oxford, was a rich merchant, who had shown himself contemptuous of the mob during the Wilkes riots.

[3] This is curious, as Sir Eyre Coote had arrived at Calcutta in March.

this measure will be adopted as subject to the least evil in the present unhinged state of the settlement at Madras; I should hope therefore that Mr. Rumbold will still be sent to be next at the Board to Lord Pigot, consequently to be President if he is either dead or has quitted India.

Pigot died before being released, and was succeeded by Sir Thomas Rumbold, who was dismissed for malpractices after three years.

One more subject demands attention—the Gordon, or 'No Popery', Riots of 1780. For some days the mob had terrorized London, attacking coaches, burning the prisons and private houses, and getting drunk by thousands. The soldiers would take no action without an order from a magistrate, the magistrates were afraid to give orders, and Parliament did nothing.

lxv. To Lord North

Queen's House, 25 min. past 9 p.m., June 6, 1780.

Lord North cannot be much surprised at my not thinking the House of Commons have this day advanced so far in the present business as the exigency of the times requires; the allowing Lord Geo. Gordon, the avowed head of the tumult, to be at large certainly encourages the continuation of it; to which is to be added the great supineness of civil magistrates; and I fear without more vigour that this will not subside; indeed unless exemplary punishment is procured, it will remain a lasting disgrace, and will be a precedent for future commotions.

That night was the worst of all; the sky was red with the conflagrations, and it was entirely on the King's initiative that the soldiers were given the requisite power to shoot if they should see a felony being committed. He called a council on the 7th, and insisted this should be done, saying, 'There will be at all events one magistrate in the kingdom who will do his duty.' He was later attacked in the House of Lords for taking so illegal a step, but was ably defended by Lord Mansfield. He was ready not only to preach 'firmness' and 'vigour' to his ministers, but to display them when occasion arose. There is no doubt that it was to him that London owed its immediate safety; he had, most effectively, and most beneficently, been King.

CHAPTER V
THE GREAT CRISIS
1782-1783

In these years King George III reveals himself as playing the role for which he thought himself destined, the Saviour of the Constitution. What he thought the constitution was comes out clearly in several of his letters. The period was, for him, a dramatic one. There was a time of struggle, then a crushing and humiliating defeat, followed afterwards by a complete victory. Looking back on it, we, of course, can see that it was not really a victory at all, for one man could not stop the growth of a system of politics implicit in the Revolution; but circumstances, namely the ill-fame of the coalition, the greatness of Pitt, and popular feeling, made it look like a triumph. With the reign of Pitt, the stage was set for the growth of party government, the idea of which as one of the essentials of the constitution had up to this time been only embryonic. Anne had fought strenuously against party, as George II had fought against his ministers being forced upon him. By 1784 George III seemed to have scotched both ideas: in reality they were both crystallizing out, to come into operation silently during his own reign, and to make themselves manifest when in 1834 William IV tried to do exactly what George III did in 1783, and failed.

North's administration did not collapse immediately on the receipt of the news of Yorktown. Parliament was to meet two days later, on the 27th November, 1781, and it was decided that the war in America should cease to be ' continental ', but become a matter of clinging on to what was still in English possession. On this ground the administration met the opposition, successfully survived adverse motions on the Address in both Houses, and passed the Army estimates with a large majority.

1. To Lord North

Windsor, December 15, 1781.

The account of the very great majority on the first motion on the Army estimates last night gives me much satisfaction, and shows the country gentlemen begin to see that though internal continental operations in North America are not advisable, the prosecution of the war can alone preserve us from a most ignominious peace, which when once concluded would certainly occasion much greater internal uneasiness than any difficulties at present to be contended with. I have wrote to Lord G. Germain whom I did not see yesterday, on the subject of Sir Guy Carleton.

Germain was the first difficulty to be disposed of: he hated Carleton, who was to replace Clinton in America, and wished to continue the continental war: he was removed to the Upper House as Lord Sackville, to the disgust of his fellow peers, and Welbore Ellis, ' the mannikin,' took his place as Secretary of State. This showed administrative weakness, as did the fact that North retained Dundas as Lord Advocate, although he spoke against the government in the House.

It was not until after the recess that the government began to totter. There had been meetings to protest against the war, Kempenfeldt had failed at sea, most of the West Indies were lost, there had been a disappointment at the Cape, and finally, in January, the English forces at Minorca were forced to surrender. The King still remained obdurate as regards America, in which he agreed with Germain: indeed he went so far as to hint that if the war concluded badly, he would rather not remain king.

11. To Lord North

Queen's House, 10 min. past 10 a.m., January 21, 1782.

. . . I shall only add that on one material point, I shall ever coincide with Lord G. Germain, this is against a separation from America, and that I shall never lose an opportunity of declaring that no consideration shall ever make me in the smallest degree an instrument in a measure that I am confident would annihilate the rank in which the British Empire stands among European states, and would render my situation in this country below continuing an object to me. . . .

But Parliament soon showed that the administration could no longer hold together: the country gentlemen changed their minds and began to ' rat '. When in February Fox attacked its naval administration, the government majority was only 22; a fortnight later, on the same question, it dwindled to 19. When on the 22nd, Conway brought in a motion ' that the war on the Continent of North America might no longer be pursued for the

*impracticable purpose of reducing the inhabitants of that country
to obedience', the government majority fell to 1. There was,
however, a short respite, and North succeeded in carrying his
motion for a loan. It gave the King heart.*

III. TO LORD NORTH

Windsor, 30 min. past 8 a.m., February 26, 1782.

I am glad to find the House of Commons voted yesterday in
the Committee of Ways and Means the Loan, which bargain has
certainly been made on terms that do great credit to Lord North;
I have not the smallest doubt that he will use every exertion to
obtain a good attendance to-morrow, and indeed I equally believe
he did so on Friday last; undoubtedly the House of Commons
seem to be so wild at present, and to be running on to ruin that
no man can answer for the event of any question. I certainly
till drove to the wall [will] do what I can to save the Empire,
and if I do not succeed I will at least have the self-approbation of
having done my duty and not letting myself be a tool in the
destruction of the honour of the country.

*On the 27th, however, Conway moved a resolution against
any further prosecution of the war in America: the government
did not directly oppose, but on the Attorney-General moving to
adjourn the debate, North was defeated by 19 votes. He at once
wrote to the King that 'some other system' must be found:
it might be feasible to split the opposition, and take in only a
part of it, but some change must be made. In the morning of
the 28th, the King wrote,*

' I am mortified Lord North thinks he cannot now remain
in office; I hope I shall see him after the Drawing Room that I
may explain my mind to him.'

Later in the day he wrote him another letter.

IV. TO LORD NORTH

February 28, 1782.

The very extraordinary resolution carried by the opposition
last night having obliged Lord North to notify me that he thinks

it impossible he can be any longer of utility to me and the nation in his present situation, I think it proper to authorize the Lord Chancellor to sound Lord Gower and Lord Weymouth whether in conjunction with him they cannot form an administration with such others of any party they may think right to recommend; the basis of public measures being founded on keeping what is in our present possession in North America, and attempting by a negotiation with any separate provinces or even districts to detach them from France, even upon any plan of their own, provided they remain separate states.

Shelburne also was consulted. But there was one point of difference between North and the King, the former wanted to resign altogether, the latter wished him to form a new administration. It was clear that North wanted ' rousing ' again.

v. To Charles Jenkinson

Queen's House, 55 min. past 7 a.m., March 7, 1782.

Mr. Jenkinson's account of the humour in which he found Lord North last night is much what I expected. I shall certainly rather take the strong than soothing language as most likely to rouse him. . . .

But time was pressing, something must be done soon, and the negotiations did not mature. On March 8th the administration only survived a string of adverse resolutions by 10 votes. North became more emphatic.

vi. To Lord North

Queen's House, 50 min. past 6 a.m., March 9, 1782.

Lord North may easily conceive that I am much hurt at the appearance of yesterday in the House of Commons, and at his opinion that it is totally impossible for the present ministry to continue to conduct public business any longer : this leads so much, after the trials I have made of late, to my taking so decisive a step, that I certainly must maturely deliberate before I can return any answer.

Negotiations then began with Rockingham, while the administration staggered on with bare majorities: ' the rats were very bad,' as Robinson wrote to Jenkinson. By the 18th March matters grew desperate: what amounted to a vote of no-confidence was to be moved on the 20th. North wrote to the King pointing out that other kings had yielded to the House without loss of dignity, and advised him to deal with Rockingham and Shelburne. The King was more hurt than ever.

VII. TO LORD NORTH

Windsor, 21 min. past 11 p.m., March 19, 1782.

LORD NORTH,

After having yesterday in the most solemn manner assured you that my sentiments of honour will not permit me to send for any of the leaders of Opposition and personally treat with them, I could not but be hurt at your letter of last night. Every man must be the sole judge of his feelings, therefore whatever you or any man can say on that subject has no avail with me.

Till I have heard what the Chancellor has done from his own mouth, I shall not take any step, and if you resign before I have decided what I will do, you will certainly for ever forfeit my regard.

North replied that as they would certainly be beaten on the next day, he would beg to be allowed to resign rather than suffer the stigma of being removed. Permission was given, and North forestalled the vote of no-confidence by going to the House and announcing his resignation. Much against the grain, then, the King was forced to treat with Shelburne, representing the Chathamites, and Rockingham, as heading the ' old Whigs '; but they were inclined to quarrel on the question of patronage. The King did not dislike Shelburne, but he would have nothing to do with Rockingham.

VIII. TO CHARLES JENKINSON

[March 24, 1782.]

MR. JENKINSON,

I have seen Lord Shelburne; his language is fair : he dreads the R[ockingham] party, and will I believe offer to take a secondary part if he can gain them. He knows I will not treat *personally* with Lord R., and that he is therefore employed to see what arrangement on a broad basis can be formed. . . .

IX. To Lord Shelburne

Queen's House, 30 min. past 8 a.m., March 26, 1782.

Lord Shelburne's note I look upon as an instance of *personal* attention, and I feel it as such; I trust from it he has stood firm, and will have remembered that the powers entrusted to him in the ministerial line, according to his own sentiments, gives him strength with more vigour to resist all others. I shall be glad to see Lord Shelburne at seven this evening if that hour is perfectly convenient to him.

Although the King had found, as he told Thurlow, that things were going 'extremely slow', it was not long before matters were arranged. Rockingham was to have the Treasury, dividing the patronage with Shelburne, who was to be Secretary of State for home affairs, while Fox was to have the seals for foreign affairs, this natural division being at last arrived at. Lord John Cavendish was Chancellor of the Exchequer, Camden Lord President, Conway Secretary at War, while Grafton took the Privy Seal. The Cabinet consisted of five Rockinghams and five Shelburnes, while Thurlow, the only one of the North administration who remained, held the balance as Chancellor. Burke became Paymaster, but Pitt, recently come to Parliament, where he had already made his mark, refused all tempting offers of lower places: he would serve in a Cabinet, he had declared, but never in any smaller position. The King was heartbroken at the clean sweep that had been made of his old administration. On March 27th he wrote many letters of farewell, all of them expressive of deep grief.

X. To Lord North

Queen's House, March 27, 1782.

Lord North,

At last the fatal day is come which the misfortunes of the times and the sudden change of sentiments of the House of Commons have drove me to, of changing the Ministry, and a more general removal of other persons than, I believe, ever was known before: I have to the last fought for individuals, but the number I have saved except my bedchamber is incredibly few. You would hardly believe that even the Duke of Montagu was strongly run at, but I declared I would sooner let confusion follow than part with the late governor of my sons, and so unexceptionable a man; at last I have succeeded, so that he and Lord Ashburnham[1] remain. The effusion of my sorrows has made me say more than I intended, but I ever did and ever shall look upon you as a friend as well as faithful servant. Pray acquaint the Cabinet that they must this day attend at St. James's to resign; I shall hope to be there if possible by one, and will receive them before the Levee, as I think it would be awkward to have the new people presented at the Levee prior to the resignations.

XI. To the Duke of Montagu

Duke of Montagu,

Your heart which is ever affectionate must I am certain feel for my situation at an hour when not only all my ministers except the Chancellor, and most of my Court except yourself, Lord Ashburnham and my bedchamber in its different branches are also swepped; the agitation of my mind you may discover by the badness of my writing. . . . You know how I love Lord Aylesbury; I trust he will feel that this[2] goes to my soul : I have wrote him my distress, but I trust it will not make him quit the Queen's family, as he must see how I am used. Do not let him add to my distress. . . .

XII. To Lord Dartmouth

March 27, 1782.

Lord Dartmouth,

Though I have directed Lord North this morning to acquaint all the Cabinet that they must come to resign their respective offices before the Levee this day, as I think it would make an odd medley to see some there kissing hands whilst others are to resign, therefore that I shall if possible be at St. James's before one for that melancholy purpose, I own I could not let Lord Dart-

---

[1] Lord of the Bedchamber and Groom of the Stole.
[2] His dismissal from the Lord Lieutenancy of Wiltshire. He was a Lord of the Bedchamber.

mouth hear this without writing him a few lines to avow how very near he will always be to my heart, and that I have ever esteemed him in another light than any of his companions in Ministry.

What days it has pleased the Almighty to place me in when Lord Dartmouth can be a man to be removed but at his own request, but I cannot complain, I adore the will of Providence, and will ever resign obediently to His Will. My heart is too full to add more.

And when, immediately after the levee, Dartmouth wrote soliciting a Garter, the King was forced to confess he had not the power to give him one: ' A politician,' he added bitterly, ' would have been less explicit, but as I pretend to nothing but honesty, I thought it best to express what I know I cannot do.' The King was so depressed by this collapse, that he had serious thoughts of abdicating; according to Horace Walpole, the royal yacht was prepared against the event.

XIII. Draft Message

[*March*, 1782.]

His Majesty during the twenty-one years he has sat on the Throne of Great Britain, has had no object so much at heart as the maintenance of the British Constitution, of which the difficulties he has at times met with from his scrupulous attachment to the rights of Parliament are sufficient proofs.

His Majesty is convinced that the sudden change of sentiments of one branch of the Legislature has totally incapacitated him from either conducting the war with effect, or from obtaining any peace but on conditions which would prove destructive to the commerce as well as the essential rights of the British nation.

His Majesty therefore with much sorrow finds he can be of no further utility to his native country which drives him to the painful step of quitting it for ever.

In consequence of which intention His Majesty resigns the Crown of Great Britain and the Dominions appertaining thereto to his dearly beloved son and lawful successor, George Prince of

Wales, whose endeavours for the prosperity of the British
Empire he hopes may prove more successful.

The message never went further than a draft.

*The King's situation was not made any easier by the fact
that no sooner had the Shelburne-Rockingham administration
been formed than the leaders began to squabble about patronage.
It had been decided they were to share it, but Rockingham was
greedy, and eager to reserve the best posts for birth rather than
for merit. The King saw Shelburne, wrote to Thurlow to try
and arrange matters, and finally indited the following message:*

xiv. To Lords Rockingham and Shelburne

Queen's House, April 7, 1782.

That no mistake may arise in the conducting of business, and
to make things as much as is in my power both agreeable to the
Marquis of Rockingham and the Earl of Shelburne, I have drawn
up the enclosed paper, of which I send at the same time a copy
to each, and trust when they have conversed together, it cannot
fail to meet with their hearty concurrence.

Enclosure

When the King found himself necessitated to form a new
administration, he resolved to place it on a broad basis, as most
conducible to heal the divisions that distract the kingdom, as
well as most creditable to himself: this was the plan which the
Earl of Shelburne was expected to set forward; but to cement the
administration more, the King forbore to make the bottom
wider. It is for that purpose he is earnest to assure the Marquis
of Rockingham and the Earl of Shelburne that he will receive
the advice of both separately with great attention, but certainly
with the more if it meets with the concurrence of the other, and
he flatters himself persons like the above noblemen who have
accepted offices only from a view of being serviceable to their
country at a perilous time, can have no other wish than to
recommend the best and ablest men on all occasions, and consequently must rejoice at being obliged to consult together, as
the means most conducible of having such vacancies filled up to
the advantage of the state.

Not that the King really held such exalted views as to the noble characters of his servants: to Thurlow he had declared that he feared patronage to be ' the real object of an English modern minister '.   Nor was ambition confined to the ministers, for Lord Ashburnham resigned from the Bedchamber when the King told him he was unable to bestow a Garter upon him.   The harried monarch's state of mind may be judged from the words he wrote when he had had to deal somewhat sharply with North over the old accounts.

xv. To Lord North

April 21, 1782.

Lord North cannot be surprised that a mind truly tore to pieces should make me less attentive to my expressions.   I certainly did and still think the accounts ought to have been regularly given in; but I did not mean by that to express any intention of withdrawing my good opinion of him.   He must recollect I foretold the consequences if a total change was made, and every hour only convinces me more and more of the truth of my assertions.

Among the consequences that the King foresaw was an attempt to bring about an ' innovation ' (and as such dangerous) in the already. perfect constitution.   In his view apparently, legislation, even though it might not issue from the royal mind, must seem to do so.   Writing to Shelburne on a point that need not concern us here, he declared (April 29th):

Certainly it is quite new for business to be laid before the Cabinet and consequently advice offered by the Ministers to the Crown unasked; the Minister of the Department used always to ask the permission of the King to lay such a point before the Cabinet, as he couldn't choose to venture to take the direction of [the] Crown upon [it] without such sanction; then the advice came with propriety.

Yet his own views do not seem to have been quite clear, for

*on June 15th we find him writing to Fox as follows on a point
which had arisen with respect to the Armed Neutrality:*

XVI. To C. J. Fox

Windsor, 55 min. past 7 a.m., June 15, 1782.

There is no doubt but the Empress of Russia seems to continue in better humour, but there are points in the communication of so serious a nature, and that must affect so much in
futurity, that I am certain Mr. Fox must see the propriety of
laying the dispatch of Sir James Harris[1] before the Cabinet
before he offers me any opinion on the subject, and consequently
takes any steps on it. . . .

*The new ministry, however, never rode easily in the saddle,
apart from quarrels over patronage. Burke brought in his
Economy Bills, but they were much curtailed by Rockingham's
own action: Thurlow, still Chancellor, continually spoke against
government measures: the one thing the Cabinet seemed agreed
on was the recall of Rodney from the West Indies ('I hope Lord
Keppel has a proper Admiral in his eye to succeed him,' the King
wrote caustically to Shelburne), but luckily before the order to
return reached him, Rodney won the great Battle of the Saints,
capturing De Grasse and his famous flagship. Peace negotiations were, of course, put in train: both Secretaries of State had
an emissary in Paris, Shelburne as including America within his
sphere of 'home' action, and Fox naturally sending his as
foreign minister. Fox, eager to make peace with France, surrendered America too easily for Shelburne's taste. Pitt's motion
for Parliamentary reform, though supported by Sheridan and
Fox, was allowed to sink out of view by the other Rockinghams.
One sore place in the Empire was, however, temporarily healed
by, on May 17th, giving Ireland almost complete autonomy, and
'Grattan's Parliament' continued to sit until the Union. The
King appears to have thought this somewhat weak, writing to
Shelburne on the 13th:*

The sooner some arrangement with Ireland can be formed the
better, but if the same spirit which seems to direct the foreign

---

[1] The Mr. Harris whom we saw at Madrid, now Ambassador at St.
Petersburg, afterwards Lord Malmesbury.

negotiations is adopted in that business, this poor island will be no great gainer.

At the end of June, the peace negotiations had gone some way, the King agreeing with Shelburne and most of the Cabinet as against Fox that peace was to be the price of American independence: Fox wished to put it to the test. But at that time Rockingham became dangerously ill, a fact his friends tried to hide. The King at once saw that if Rockingham died, it would be difficult for Shelburne to continue with Fox, so critical was the divergence over America and peace.

XVII. To Lord Shelburne

Windsor, 21 min. past 7 a.m., July 1, 1782.

Lord Shelburne must see I am certain with resentment the total ignorance that those who have governed Lord Rockingham cautiously try to keep both me and him as to the desperate state of that Lord, which certainly is with a view to some arrangement of their own.

I am apprised Lord Shelburne, though he has gone great lengths at the expense of his opinion in giving way as to American independence, if it can effect peace, would think he received advice in which his character was not attended to, if it tended to give up that without the price set on it, which alone could make this kingdom consent to it. Besides, he must see that the success of Lord Rodney's engagement has again so far roused the nation, that the peace which would have been acquiesced in three months ago would now be matter of complaint.

From the language of Mr. Fitzpatrick[1] it should seem that Lord Shelburne has no chance of being able to coalesce with Mr. Fox; it may not be necessary to remove him at once, but if Lord Shelburne accept the head of the Treasury, and is succeeded by Mr. Pitt as Secretary for the Home Department and British Settlements, that it will be seen how far he will submit to it; the quarrelling with the rest of the party as a party would not be wise; if they can be got to remain it would be advisable, but it would

---

[1] Lieutenant-Colonel: Chief Secretary for Ireland.

not be right if only to be obtained by Lord Shelburne's being placed in the shoes of Lord Rockingham, that is, the head of a party when in reality he would be the slave of it. He must be the minister placed on a broad bottom.

When on the same day Rockingham died, the King offered the premiership to Shelburne, and told him to make arrangements according to the above letter and his conversations. A number of the Rockinghams, however, put forward the Duke of Portland, at this time Lord Lieutenant of Ireland, as successor: they were 'the violent party', headed by Fox. Their object not being attained, Fox resigned, to be followed by Portland and Cavendish, and, among the lesser officials, Burke and Sheridan. Some, however, remained, angered at Fox's apparent adherence to the oligarchic principle, the 'old Whigs' exhibiting what we should now call extreme reactionary Toryism. Pitt, at the age of twenty-three, now took office as Chancellor of the Exchequer, his cousin, the second Earl Temple, took Ireland, Lord Grantham, an ex-ambassador, became Secretary for Foreign Affairs, and Thomas Townshend, Pitt's friend, accepted the Home Department.

The policy, of course, was to be Shelburne's: the King was glad to find that Fox was going to test the feeling of the House and country on a motion of unconditional surrender: he felt sure his views would prevail. Sir George Savile, who had split from Fox on the resignations, and remained an adherent of Shelburne, seems to have thought differently.

XVIII. TO LORD SHELBURNE

Kew, 16 min. past 7 a.m., July 11, 1782.

. . . The enclosed papers Lord Shelburne left yesterday in my hands, the one from Sir George Savile may be fine metaphysical reasoning, I am the avowed enemy of that ingenious nonsense, therefore no judge of its supposed merit; but common sense tells me that if unconditional independence is granted, we cannot ever expect any understanding with America, for then we have given up the whole and have nothing to give for what we want from thence. Independence is certainly an unpleasant gift at best, but then it must be for such conditions of peace as may justify it. Lord Camden yesterday said to me that under the present Act he thought any minister would risk his head that advised granting independence but as the boon for peace. . . .

It was on this day that Parliament was prorogued, Fox making the most violent onslaughts which brought forth a protestation of loyalty from Jenkinson: the King in thanking him wrote: ' The mask is certainly cast off; it is no less than a struggle whether I am to be dictated to by Mr. Fox.' It seemed to him a personal battle.

This feeling persisted. Since a ' broad bottom' had to be found for Shelburne (Camden only promised temporary adherence; Conway and Grafton were uneasy), it was necessary to apply to some other group. The King and Shelburne decided to sound North, in spite of Pitt saying that he could not serve with him. But the alternative was Fox, and this the King would not hear of.

XIX. To Lord North

Windsor, August 7, 1782.

Lord North has so often whilst in office assured me that whenever I would consent to his retiring he would give the most cordial support to such an administration as I might approve of, that I should not think I either acted properly to my own affairs or placed that confidence in his declarations if I did not express my strongest wishes that he will give the most active support the next session of Parliament to the administration formed with my thorough approbation on the death of Lord Rockingham, and that during the recess he will call upon the country gentlemen who certainly have great attention for him to come early and show their countenance by which I may be enabled to keep the Constitution from being entirely annihilated, which must be the case if Mr. Fox and his associates are not withstood. Many strange scenes have occurred in this country, but none more so than the present contest; it is no less than whether the sole direction of my kingdoms shall be trusted in the hands of Mr. Fox; Lord North has long known my opinion of that gentleman, which has been if possible more riveted by three months' experience of him in office, which has finally determined me never to

employ him again : consequently the contest is become personal
and he indeed sees it also in that point of view.   Lord Shelburne
is acquainted with my intention of writing to Lord North, and
will I am confident be desirous of showing every mark of attention for the assistance my administration may desire in consequence of this letter.

*This was not yet an invitation, and meanwhile during the
summer the peace negotiations went on.   The King, with
Shelburne, and many other statesmen of that century, would
have been glad to barter Gibraltar for some more valuable
possession, thinking that ' the brightest jewel in the Crown', as
Keppel regarded it, was more likely to be a cause of future
contention than a useful ornament.   The whole peace question
agitated the King profoundly.*

xx. To Lord Shelburne

Windsor, 2 min. past 10 a.m., September 16, 1782.
 . . . The holding Gibraltar very high is quite judicious and
if not taken I should hope Porto Rico may be got for it. . . .

I am glad Lord Shelburne is coming to Town more fully to
investigate the bounds of Newfoundland and the East India
points, that the interest of this country may not wantonly be
sacrificed.

As to the general question on Peace, I am too much agitated
with the fear of sacrificing the interests of my country by hurry-
ing it on too fast, which indeed has been uppermost in my
thoughts since the beginning of the war, that I am unable to add
anything on that subject but the most fervent prayers to Heaven
to guide me so to act that posterity may not lay the downfall of
this once respectable Empire at my door; and that if ruin should
attend the measures that may be adopted, I may not long survive.

*The sole responsibility was not, however, the King's: negotia-
tions went forward, though the Bourbons were in no hurry until
it was clear that they would not recapture Gibraltar.   By November the preliminaries were ready.*

M

XXI. To Thomas Townshend

Windsor, 23 min. past 10 p.m., November 19, 1782.

Mr. Townshend may send the messenger to Paris with the draft of the preliminary articles and the dispatches as soon as they are ready, without waiting for my seeing the latter. He cannot be surprised at my not being over anxious for the perusal of them, as Parliament having to my astonishment come into the ideas of granting a separation to North America has disabled me from longer defending the rights of this kingdom. But I certainly disclaim thinking myself answerable for any evils that may arise from the adoption of this measure, as necessity not conviction has made me subscribe to it.

Parliament was postponed from 26 November to 5 December so that the proposed treaty might be laid before it. It was not really a bad peace, in the circumstances, though the King was bitterly ashamed of it: yet any peace was better than no peace.

XXII. To Lord Grantham

Windsor, 25 min. past 9 a.m., December 3, 1782.

. . . I think peace so essential, and that the dreadful resolution of the 27th of February last of the House of Commons[1] has so entirely removed the real cause of the war to the utter shame of that branch of the Legislature, that it would be madness not to conclude peace on the best possible terms we can obtain.

The preliminaries were not ready by the 5th, difficulties over Gibraltar not having been settled. In his Address the King stated that he had agreed to separation, provided peace with France was attained: he went on:

XXIII. Address to Parliament

In thus admitting their separation from the Crown of these Kingdoms, I have sacrificed every consideration of my own to the wishes and opinion of my people. I make it my humble and earnest prayer to Almighty God, that Great Britain may not feel the evils which might result from so great a dismemberment of

---

[1] See letter IV of this chapter.

the Empire; and that America may be free from the calamities which have formerly proved in the mother country how essential monarchy is to the enjoyment of constitutional liberty. Religion, language, interest, affections may, and I hope will, yet prove a bond of permanent union between the two countries; to this end neither attention nor disposition on my part shall be wanting.

Fox inveighed furiously against the preliminaries: independence, he declared, should have been granted without any question of peace: but North, faithful to an assurance he had given the King that he and the country gentlemen would support the administration, led his party into the opposite lobby, and Fox was heavily defeated.

During the recess, several defections took place. Keppel resigned from the Admiralty, the Duke of Richmond and Lord Carlisle also refused further service, and the King was persuaded to allow Pitt to approach Fox, who said nothing would induce him to work with Shelburne. This ended the interview, for, as Pitt said, he had not come to betray Shelburne. The King was not displeased at the result of the interview: had he not said he would never employ Fox again?

XXIV. To Lord Shelburne

Queen's House, 20 min. past 9 a.m., February 11, 1783.

I am not in the least surprised at Mr. Pitt's interview with Mr. Fox having ended as abruptly as the hastiness and impoliteness of the latter naturally led me to expect. I·shall certainly not object to any other quarter Lord Shelburne may with the advice of Mr. Pitt choose to sound; but I must insist on Lord Shelburne's remaining in his present situation be the basis of any plan that may be prepared for my inspection; by this clear instruction Lord Shelburne must feel himself at liberty to act as he may find it necessary, and I can trust his own sentiments are too much exalted to think of supplicating any party, but that whoever he treats with must be expected to feel obliged for any offer that is made.

Then it was decided to approach North: but it was too late: he had already entered upon that astounding league with Fox, who had showered opprobrium upon him for years, that ' unnatural alliance' which shocked even some members of their own parties. In a debate on the peace in the House of Commons on the 17th of February, the government was defeated by sixteen votes: on the 21st it was defeated by one vote more. The King was almost past words.

XXV. TO THOMAS TOWNSHEND

Windsor, 47 min. past 1 p.m., February 22, 1783.

I cannot help on coming home and receiving Mr. Secretary Townshend's note with the list of the speakers and the numbers of the division this morning, just to express that I am sorry it has been my lot to reign in the most profligate age, and when the most unnatural coalition seems to have taken place, which can but add confusion and distraction among a too much divided nation.

Another administration was about to fall: ' I am again from necessity left to extricate myself; to the assistance of Providence and the rectitude of my intentions I can alone hope for succour,' the King wrote to Shelburne: but he would not throw himself into the hands of a party. He sent for Pitt, and offered the premiership to a young man of twenty-four. Pitt, however, counting up his supporters, found he could not undertake it. Negotiations dragged on for a month. On Thurlow's advice the King applied to North, who refused to join the administration on any terms: on the same advice he appealed to Gower, with the same result: he returned to North, he told him to approach Portland, who, however, would not think of forming a ministry on a ' comprehensive plan': in despair he applied once more to Pitt.

XXVI. TO LORD CHANCELLOR THURLOW

Queen's House, 10 min. past 10 p.m., March 2, 1783.

MY LORD,

I have seen Lord Guilford[1] and sent him to Lord North with the offer of placing him again in the Treasury and consulting him on the formation of a ministry on the most compre-

[1] Lord North's father.

hensive lines, that if he declines that particular employment I am willing to place him in another suitable Cabinet office to advise with him on the formation of a new administration; but then reserving to myself the appointing of a peer not connected with any of the strong parties that distract this kingdom to preside at the Treasury. . . .

XXVII. To Lord Chancellor Thurlow

Queen's House, 33 min. past 8 a.m., March 7, 1783.

My Lord,

I shall certainly with very great pleasure instantly send for Lord Gower agreeable to your advice, and refer to him the thinking of such an administration as may be sufficient to take on them the conducting of public affairs, and if he shall not be able to form such a plan, I shall certainly still attempt to find whether there is no man willing at this crisis to stand by the Crown against a desperate faction in whose hands I will never throw myself.

XXVIII. To Lord Grantham

Queen's House, 40 min. past 7 a.m., March 10, 1783.

Lord Grantham is desired to acquaint those of the expiring ministry likely to attend at St. James's this day, that I shall not appear there as usual, being fully employed in attempting to form without further delay an administration : it is to not my fault but to the knavery and indolence, perhaps I might add timidity, of the times that my incessant labours have as yet proved unsuccessful : things must speedily come to a conclusion.

XXIX. To Lord North

Queen's House, March 18, 1783.

Lord North,

I received your letter late the last evening enclosing the one you had received from the D. of Portland; the clearest manner in which I can answer yours is by recalling to you what has passed. When first I sent to you I desired to place you again at the head of the Treasury, and that you should try to form an administration on the most extensive basis, from a conviction that no party could alone conduct the public affairs, and my uniform wish from the hour I first mounted the throne, and from which I have never departed, to extinguish all odious party distinctions, and have the assistance of the best and ablest men the kingdom might produce. You declined from want of health accepting that situation; I then proposed that you should have any other cabinet office that might suit you, and that you should assist me in pointing out how an administration could be formed on such a wide basis, the treasury being based in the hands of some peer, not the head of any large party, whom when the other outlines were stated on paper to be laid before me for my consideration I should name. You soon wrote that as to the Duke of Portland and his friends, they would not make part of any such extensive plan, unless he was nominated to preside at the Treasury. After some consideration I, on Wednesday last, authorized you to continue to try to have such a plan formed for my inspection, and that if it can be effected, the D. of Portland's being at the head of the Treasury shall not be objected to by me. Your letter does not, nor does that from the D. of Portland to you, seem to recollect that I cannot enter into any detail till you have sent me such a plan on paper for my inspection; I certainly shall not bind myself by giving any separate approbation or disapprobation to any proposal till the whole is sent to me on paper, when I shall coolly judge whether such a proposal is likely to effect my only object, the removing all dissensions, and thus forming an administration that may have weight both at home and abroad.

To prevent delays and mistakes, I authorize you to communicate this wherever you may think it necessary.

But Portland steadily refused to produce a plan.

XXX. To the Duke of Portland and Lord North

Queen's House, 35 min. past 10 p.m., March 23, 1783.
The Duke of Portland having uniformly declined drawing up the plan of arrangement and continuing to do so after my

having this day at St. James's acquainted him that I would not longer delay coming to some resolution if he did not send such a plan for my consideration this evening, I therefore take this method of acquainting him that I shall not give him any further trouble.

Lord North must therefore see that all negotiation is at an end.

He had written to Pitt a couple of hours earlier telling him that the negotiations had broken down, and desired his presence at the Queen's House. Pitt had advised the above letter, and moreover the meeting was promising.

xxxi. To Lord Chancellor Thurlow

Queen's House, March 24, 1783.

My Lord,

I shall be extremely glad to see you this morning as early as it may suit you; I shall not detain you now by a long epistle. After every sort of chicanery from the Coalition, to which I have opposed the only weapon an honest man can employ, straight dealing, I have brought it to the repeated refusal of laying a plan of arrangements before me for my consideration; upon which with the consent of Mr. Pitt, I broke off all further negotiation last night. He has said everything but that he will remain at the head of the Treasury, which his delicacy made him wish to defer saying till this morning, when I am to expect him. I wish therefore your attendance here may be as early as possible.

xxxii. To William Pitt

Queen's House, 10 min. past 11 a.m., March 24, 1783.

Mr. Pitt's idea of having nothing announced till the debate of to-day meets with my thorough approbation. I have just seen the Lord Chancellor, who thinks that if Mr. Pitt should say, towards the close of the debate, that after such conduct as the coalition has held, that every man attached to this Constitution must stand forth on this occasion, and that as such he is determined to keep the situation devolved on him, that he will meet with an applause that cannot fail to give him every encouragement. . . .

*The debate, however, on a motion by Coke of Norfolk
entreating the King to appoint an administration that had the
confidence of the country, was so tepid, that, as Pitt told the
King, nothing passed ' very strongly to mark the precise sentiments of the House'. Therefore he made no move, and wrote
a temporizing letter to his anxious monarch. Was Pitt too going
to fail him? The King feared so, but tried to ignore the
possibility.*

XXXIII. To William Pitt

Windsor, 5 past 12 at night, March 24, 1783.

I am not surprised, as the debate has proved desultory, that
Mr. Pitt has not been able to write more fully on this occasion.
After the manner I have been personally treated by both the Duke
of Portland and Lord North, it is impossible I can ever admit
either of them into my service : I therefore trust that Mr. Pitt will
exert himself to-morrow to plan his mode of filling up the offices
that will be vacant, so as to be able on Wednesday morning to
accept the situation his character and talents fit him to hold, when
I shall be in town before twelve ready to receive him.

Yet he could not disguise his fears from himself.

XXXIV. To Lord Weymouth

Windsor, 15 min. past 7 a.m., March 25, 1783.

Lord Weymouth must be better apprised than I can possibly
be of the debate in the House of Commons yesterday, the short
note I wrote to him must have shown I had some suspicion of
the conduct Mr. Pitt might hold; I received the enclosed letter
from him to which I sent the following answer;[1] as I have no
copies of them I trust Lord Weymouth after showing both to the
Chancellor will return them by my servant, who has orders to
wait for your directions. I am clear Mr. Pitt means to play
false, and wants I should again negotiate with the Coalition; but
no consideration in life could bring me to that : I am decided
sooner to yield the game to them, and let my son be the puppet

[1] i.e. letter XXXIII above.

which Mr. Pitt's letter seems to indicate the House of Commons not disinclined to see their Sovereign. . . . All I shall add is that the Chancellor can tell you my plan is not unformed if I find all combine to say that nothing but the Opposition can come forward.

Pitt decided that he could not form an administration: he had determined, in the King's view, to 'play false'.

XXXV. TO WILLIAM PITT

Windsor, 35 min. past 4 p.m., March 25, 1783.

MR. PITT,

I am much hurt to find you are determined to decline at an hour when those who have any regard for the Constitution as established by law ought to stand forth against the most daring and unprincipled faction that the annals of this kingdom ever produced.

For two or three days the King cogitated his not unformed plan, but still he would make one more attempt along the normal lines.

XXXVI. TO LORD CHANCELLOR THURLOW

Queen's House, 30 min. past 7 p.m. [?a.m.], March 28, 1783.

MY LORD,

I wish to see you before you go to Lincoln's Inns this day, having Lord Weymouth's opinion that it would be right again to try Lord Gower; indeed, my Lord, I am the more pressing to attempt to catch at every thing, as I feel is some one will not assist me, I must within a couple of days take the step I have so often hinted to you.

What the mysterious step was, the not unformed plan, which seemed to involve making his son a puppet, is made clear from the following abdicating speech which he prepared.

XXXVII. THE KING TO PARLIAMENT

I cannot at the most serious, as well as most painful moment of my life, go out of this great assembly without communicating to you my intentions, not asking your advice.

The first time I appeared as your Sovereign in this place now above twenty two years, I had the pleasing hope that being born among you I might have proved the happy instrument of conciliating all parties, and thus collecting to the service of the State the most respectable and most able persons this kingdom produced. Of this object I have never lost sight, though sad experience now teaches me that selfish views are so prevalent that they have smothered the first of public virtues, attachment to the country, which ought to warm the breast of every individual who enjoys the advantage of this excellent Constitution, and the want of sentiment has prevented that unanimity which must have rendered Great Britain invulnerable, though attacked by the most powerful combinations.

My own inclination to alleviate the distresses of my people, added to the change of sentiments of one branch of the legislature, which rendered the real object of the war impracticable, made me undertake the arduous task of obtaining the blessings of peace, rendered indeed more difficult by the resolution above alluded to.[1] I cannot sufficiently acknowledge the candour with which the Courts of France and Spain have conducted themselves during the negotiation of the preliminary articles, which greatly accelerated that desirable work.

Circumstances have arisen that might make those Courts more doubtful of the stability of the councils of this country, *in forming the definitive treaties*. I have *therefore* again attempted to collect the most efficient men of all parties, who under my inspection might with dispatch and confidence proceed in forming the definitive treaties. But this patriotic attempt has proved unsuccessful by the obstinacy of a powerful party that has long publicly manifested a resolution not to aid in the service of the Empire unless the whole executive management of affairs is thrown entirely into its hands, from which it has not on this occasion departed; at the same time want of zeal prevents others from standing forth at this critical conjuncture. My obedience to the oath I took at my coronation prevents my exceeding the powers vested in me, or submitting to be a cipher in the trammels of any self-created band.

[1] Of February 27, 1782, against continuing the American war.

I must therefore end a conflict which certainly puts a stop to every wheel of government, make a final decision, and that I think myself compelled to do in this assembly of the whole legislature.

A long experience and a serious attention to the strange events that have successively arisen, has gradually prepared my mind to expect the time when I should be no longer of utility to this Empire; that hour is now come; I am therefore resolved to resign my Crown and all the dominions appertaining to it to the Prince of Wales, my eldest son and lawful successor, and to retire to the care of my Electoral dominions, the original patrimony of my ancestors. For which purpose I shall draw up and sign an instrument to which I shall affix my private seal. I trust this personal sacrifice will awaken the various parties to a sense of their duty, and that they will join in the support and assistance of the young successor.

You may depend on my arduous attention to educate my children in the paths of religion, virtue, and every other good principle that may render them if ever called in any line to the service of Great Britain, not unworthy of the kindness they may hereafter meet with from a people whom collective I shall ever love.

May that All Wise Providence who can direct the inmost thoughts as well as actions of men give my son and successor not only every assistance in guiding his conduct, but restore that sense of religious and moral duties in this kingdom to the want of which every evil that has arisen owes its source; and may I to the latest hour of my life, though now resolved for ever to quit this island, have the comfort of hearing that the endeavours of my son, though they cannot be more sincere than mine have been, for the prosperity of Great Britain, may be crowned with better success.

A moving and dignified document, but a terrible confession of failure. He had not succeeded in bringing about the reconciliation of parties, he had lost America, his dominions were to be curtailed by the peace, and virtue had made no strides. He was at the end of his tether. Better to rule in Hanover than serve under Fox in England, the dust of which he would shake off his feet.

But Thomas Pitt, William Pitt's first cousin, afterwards Lord Camelford, having been taken into the King's confidence, suggested a less hysterical course. He pointed out that if he let Portland form a ministry, virtually Fox's, in combination with North, internal disagreements would weaken it, the interested who could not be gratified with plums would become disaffected; that men of principle would disclaim them for deserting their principles, and the people would execrate them because they would impose heavy taxes and scotch any projects of reform. There was already considerable odium attaching to the monstrous coalition, and these sentiments of abhorrence would increase. His advice was to give the dogs rope to hang themselves with, and the King accepted it.

XXXVIII. MEMORANDUM

The total stagnation of public business by no administration in reality subsisting at a time when the definitive treaties ought to be prosecuted; the Navy and Army reduced to a state of peace, and taxes laid for defraying the expenses of the State and for settling the unpaid debt, obliged me no longer to defer submitting to the erection of an administration whose conduct as individuals does not promise to deserve collectively my confidence.

I therefore on Tuesday evening, April 1st, 1783, sent for Lord North and inquired if the seven persons named by the Duke of Portland and him were ready to accept the employments proposed; on his answering in the affirmative, I authorized him to acquaint them they might accept them the next day, after which the Duke of Portland and he should plan the arrangements of employments.

The seven persons were, the Duke of Portland at the Treasury, Fox and North Secretaries of State, Cavendish Chancellor of the Exchequer, Lord Carlisle Privy Seal, Lord Stormont President of the Council, and Keppel at the Admiralty. The King had to admit a heavy defeat, one indeed that looked decisive and final. The beauty of the Constitution, the perfection of which depended upon his being allowed to choose his own ministers, was seriously impaired: in short this miraculous instrument was apparently ruined: but Thomas Pitt had made him feel much more cheerful.

XXXIX. TO LORD TEMPLE

Queen's House, April 1, 1783.

MY LORD,

I had the pleasure on the 26th of last month to receive from your truly amiable and right headed brother and Secretary,[1] your very able letter of the 23rd on the state of Ireland, couched in terms that also conveyed the warmest attachment to my person and government, which makes me not deem among the least of public misfortunes that the want of resolution in some, and of public zeal in others, will oblige you to quit a station which you fill so much to the satisfaction of all honest men as well as mine.

Since the last conversation I had with Mr. William Grenville, on the 16th of last month, I have continued every possible means of forming an administration; an experience of now above twenty-two years convinces me that it is impossible to erect any stable one within the narrow bounds of any faction, for none deserve the appellation of party, and that in an age when disobedience to law and authority is as prevalent as a thirst after change in the best of all political constitutions; it requires that temper and sagacity which can alone be expected from a collection of the best and most calm heads and hearts the kingdom possesses.

Judge therefore of the uneasiness of my mind at having been thwarted in every attempt to keep the administration of public affairs out of the hands of the most unprincipled coalition the annals of this or any nation can equal; I have withstood it till not a single man is willing to come to my assistance, and till the House of Commons has taken every step but insisting on this faction by name being elected ministers. To end a conflict which stops every wheel of government, and which would affect the public credit if it continued much longer, I intend this night to acquaint that *grateful* man Lord North that the seven Cabinet councillors the coalition has named shall kiss hands to-morrow,

---

[1] William Grenville, who had gone to Ireland as Secretary to his brother Temple, afterwards Marquis of Buckingham, who was Lord Lieutenant.

and then form their arrangements, as [in] the former negotiations they did not condescend to open to me any of their intentions.

A ministry which I have avowedly attempted to avoid, by calling on every other description of men, cannot be supposed to have either my favour or confidence, and as such I shall most certainly refuse any honours that may be asked by them; I trust the eyes of the nation will soon be opened, as my sorrow may prove fatal to my health if I remain long in this thraldom: I trust you will be steady in your attachment to me, and ready to join other honest men in watching the conduct of this unnatural combination, and I hope many months will not elapse before the Grenvilles, the Pitts, and other men of abilities and character will relieve me from a situation that nothing but the supposition that no other means remained of preventing the public finances from being materially affected would have compelled me to submit to.

It shall be one of my first cares to acquaint those men that you decline remaining in Ireland.

It was one of the first resignations that had ever pleased the King: this, at least, was not a ' desertion'. But who would have thought, fifteen years earlier, that the King, fighting hard to rid himself of the dominance of ' the Family', namely the first Earl Temple, George Grenville, and the elder Pitt, would have declared that he looked forward to the day when the Grenvilles and Pitts would step forward to rescue him!

The unnatural combination might carry on, but the King would hold as aloof as possible.

XL. To C. J. Fox

Queen's House, 25 min. past 9 a.m., April 19, 1783.

The projects of the Definitive Treaties with France and Spain, and the Dispatch which is to accompany them to Mr. Fitzherbert,[1] must so fully state the reasons of the alterations from the Preliminary Articles, that I do not mean to call on Mr. Fox for further explanations on this subject: unnecessary discussions are not my taste, and the Cabinet having by a minute approved of the projects,

---

[1] Afterwards Lord St. Helen's. He had been sent as emissary to Paris.

I do not propose to give myself any additional trouble with regard to them.

He seldom missed an opportunity of gibing at the adminis-tration.

XLI. To LORD NORTH

Windsor, 8 min. past 9 p.m., July 24, 1783.

Undoubtedly there is less regularity in the modes of conduct-ing business in this kingdom than in any other European, or the mode of calling a new Parliament in Ireland ought to have been so clearly stated in the change of that Constitution that no room ought to have left for doubt as to the proper method of effecting it; but I fear folly, not reason, dictated the measure, and therefore it is not surprising every step has not been well weighed.

XLII. To C. J. Fox

Windsor, 40 min. past 7 a.m., July 19, 1783.

It is a very untoward circumstance that a Definitive Treaty cannot be concluded without leaving clear ground for fresh dis-putes . . . [for] every difficulty in concluding peace this country has alone to blame itself; after the extraordinary and never to be forgot vote of Feb. 1782, and the hurry for negotiation that ensued, it is no wonder that our enemies, seeing our spirit so fallen, have taken advantage of it.

The famous resolution of February 27th, 1782, was always a splendid whip to beat the dogs with.

XLIII. To C. J. Fox

Windsor, 48 min. past 9 a.m., August 16, 1783.

I cannot say the supposed letter of Mr. Hastings gives great lustre to his prudential as well as moral character, though it does not destroy the idea of his activity.

I cannot say I am surprised at France not putting the final stroke to the Definitive Treaty as soon as we may wish, as our having totally disarmed in addition to the extreme anxiety shown for peace during the whole conduct that has ensued [since] the end of February 1782, certainly makes her feel that she can have no reason to apprehend any evil from so shifting a proceeding.

And when the peace was made, the King was no more gracious.

XLIV. To Lord North

Windsor, 44 min. past 5 p.m., September 7, 1783.

I have signed the warrant for the attendance of the heralds for the proclamation of peace; I have no objection to that ceremony being performed on Tuesday; indeed I am glad it is on a day I am not in Town, as I think this completes the downfall of the lustre of this Empire : but when religion and public spirit are quite absorbed by vice and dissipation, what has now occurred is but the natural consequence; one comfort I have, that I have alone tried to support the dignity of my crown, and feel I am innocent of the evils that have occurred, though deeply wounded that it should have happened during my reign.

Only once did he oppose his ministers, and then scored a victory.

This was on the question of the Establishment of the Prince of Wales, who was about to come of age. The Prince, having already exhibited the natural reaction against a strict and pietistic upbringing in his liaison with Perdita Robinson, had now become an intimate of Fox, whom he used to address in his letters as 'Dear Charles'. The classic Hanoverian struggle of the heir-apparent against the monarch had already begun, and Carlton House was soon to become an opposition focus. The ministers, led by Fox, who was naturally all in favour of attaching the Prince to himself, proposed the outrageously large annual income for him of £100,000 (somewhat in contradistinction with their schemes for reducing the Civil List), and proposed to foist all his debts upon the King. The latter, by no means pleased with his son on account of his associates, not only because of their political position, but because of the 'vice and dissipation' he had referred to in his last quoted letter to North as a direct cut at Fox, was furious. Apart from other considerations, he did not see why he should subsidize the opposition. Thus when the Duke of Portland brought the scheme up to him, he blasted him in a tremendous letter.

xlv. To the Duke of Portland

Windsor, 59 min. past 10 a.m., June 16, 1783.

It is impossible for me to find words expressive enough of my utter indignation and astonishment at the letter I have just received from the Duke of Portland; these words are certainly strong, and would be inexcusable if not authorized by the following facts. When the Duke of Portland desired I would turn my thoughts to fixing a sum for the separate establishment of the Prince of Wales, when he arrives at the age of twenty-one years, I desired he would with the rest of the efficient ministers consider what proposal should be made to me on that subject; about a fortnight since he acquainted me that it was their unanimous opinion that a sum of one hundred thousand pounds, including the revenue of the Duchy of Cornwall, should be obtained from Parliament. I instantly showed my surprise at so lavish an idea, and the more so when my subjects are so much loaded with taxes, and said I thought fifty thousand pounds in addition to the revenue of Cornwall, which would nearly exceed twenty-seven thousand per annum of what the late King thought sufficient for me in a similar station, was all that could with reason be granted; and consequently desired that Duke to acquaint the ministers with my opinion, and of my wish that they should reconsider this business. On the 6th of this month the Duke of Portland told me they continued to think it right to propose that sum to Parliament, from whom they meant the whole sum should come; that the reasons of putting it so high arose from a knowledge that the Prince of Wales had debts which must be paid out of his annual income, besides the expense of fitting himself out; and that they meant to acquaint him of this, and that no addition could be made whenever he married. I did not deny that I still thought the sum too large, though I acknowledged if no increase was made whenever he married that I would make no further objection.

I was therefore surprised on the 13th to find the Duke of Portland had not the drafts of the messages, but that they would soon be sent to me, from which time I have been in expectation of them; but this suspense is now fully explained, for the whole proposition is changed : I am to be saddled with the whole odium of this measure, and the expense at the same time ultimately to fall entirely on me, who am not, from my numerous progeny, in a situation to bear it, though I had been assured no part was to be paid by me; and in addition I am pressed to take twenty-nine thousand of debts on myself which I have not incurred, that the public may blame me, and the Prince of Wales with so unreasonable an income not be subject to this sum which can alone have arisen from shameful extravagance.

I therefore must declare that unless the proposal is brought back to the mode in which the Duke of Portland first stated it to me, and that all expenses are thrown on the Prince of Wales, I cannot proceed in this business, and shall think myself obliged to let the public know the cause of the delay and my opinion of the whole transaction. I cannot conclude without saying that when the Duke of Portland came into office I had at least hoped he would have thought himself obliged to have my interest and that of the public at heart, and not have neglected both to gratify the passions of an ill advised young man.

XLVI. To Lord North

Windsor, 35 min. past 11 a.m., June 16, 1783.

Lord North,

The treatment I have received from the Duke of Portland, if the other ministers are not equally privy to the transactions concerning the establishment of the Prince of Wales is such that I have thought it necessary to send an immediate answer to the letter I have received from the Duke of Portland, of which the enclosed is a copy; I can scarcely suppose you and Lord Stormont can have known the whole and acquiesced in it; I therefore send you this for the perusal of both and that you may exculpate yourselves; though it may not be necessary to assure you of the truth of every syllable of my letter, yet as it is so strong it may not be wrong to add that I could take an oath with regard to every circumstance.

Portland wrote a very humble letter of apology, but in which there was not much retraction.

XLVII. TO THE DUKE OF PORTLAND

Windsor, 22 min. past 10 p.m., June 16, 1783.

The letter I have this instant received from the Duke of Portland does not in the least alter my opinion with regard to the one I have received this morning, and to which I wrote the feelings of my heart. If the Prince of Wales's establishment is to fall on me it is a weight I am unable to bear, if on the public I cannot in conscience give my acquiescence to what I deem a shameful squandering of public money, besides an encouragement of extravagance and likely to prevent the Prince of Wales at a proper time wishing to marry, as it would be a lessening his expenditure; to show that my ideas do not arise from any other motive than duty towards the public, I make the proposal on the adjoining sheet.

The proposal suggested fifty thousand a year besides the revenues of the Duchy of Cornwall, and further to ask Parliament to pay the debts, as well as to supply a sum for furnishing the new establishment. It was some time before the ministers—all of whom had known all about the whole matter—would withdraw from their position: it seemed that this question might be made the occasion of their dismissal. The King, however, was persuaded by Temple that the occasion was not suitable for bringing about another crisis; the Prince exonerated Fox from his promise; and the matter was brought before Parliament as the King had wished.

It was not very long before the desired opportunity arose for the King to provoke a crisis. In November Fox brought forward his East India Bill, the chief objection to which, from the King's point of view, was that it put a preponderating amount of patronage into Fox's hand, a patronage which could continue for five years even if Fox went out of office. The notion of taking the Indian question outside the realms of party politics was, of course, sound, but in the circumstances aroused not only the King's indignation, but also of those who thought the Coalition already far too venal. The Bill passed in the Commons, but the King sent Temple to 'whip' the Lords, making it known that he would consider as his enemy any peer who voted for the Bill.

The Lords threw out the Bill on the 17th. On the 18th the House of Commons, by a large majority, resolved that it was a high crime and misdemeanour to report the King's opinion on any Bill before Parliament if the object were to influence votes. This was a constitutional issue, and the moment the King heard of it he flung down the challenge.

XLVIII. To Lord North

Queen's House, 43 min. past 10 p.m., December 18, 1783.

Lord North is by this required to send me the Seals of his department, and to acquaint Mr. Fox to send those of the Foreign department. Mr. Frazer or Mr. Nepean will be the proper channel of delivering them to me this night: I choose this method as audiences on such occasions must be unpleasant.

It was a bold stroke, and it was dangerous. Could the attitude be maintained? Had he smashed the Coalition? He did indeed, on the 20th, tell Temple, whom he had sent for late at night on the 19th and at once made Secretary of State, that it was impossible for him to retract: but yet, after having sworn that it was impossible for him ever to employ North, or Fox, or Portland, he had employed them all. The excitement was terrific. No one knew what would happen, but, with an enormous majority behind them, Fox and North were convinced that in the end they would win. It did not much disturb them when on the afternoon of the 19th a writ was moved in Parliament for the borough of Appleby, ' in the room of the Right Honourable William Pitt, who since his election has accepted the office of First Lord of the Treasury and Chancellor of the Exchequer'. At the worst there would be a General Election, and they would come triumphantly back.

It was, of course, extremely doubtful if Pitt would be able to form an administration at all: the difficulties were immense, and did not at first seem to become less so, especially as Temple suddenly and inexplicably resigned.

XLIX. To William Pitt

Queen's House, 46 min. past 10 a.m., December 23, 1783.

To one on the edge of a precipice every ray of hope must be pleasing. I therefore place confidence in the Duke of Richmond,

Lord Gower, Lord Thurlow, and Mr. Pitt, bringing forward some names to fill up an arrangement; which if they cannot, they already know my determination. One will be an hour perfectly agreeable to me.

Gower, as President of the Council, was a great accession: Thurlow resumed the Seals, which had been in commission since the fall of Shelburne: Richmond took office without a seat in the Cabinet: Lord Sydney (lately Thomas Townshend) took a Secretaryship: Howe went to the Admiralty. It was an extremely weak administration.

Hardly anybody expected it to last, especially as at the very beginning Fox insisted on a short recess, and carried his point. When Parliament met on January 12th, five motions were carried against Pitt without division, and he was left in minorities of 39 and 54 when the House did divide. The King, however, was steadfast.

L. To William Pitt

Windsor, 43 min. past 10 a.m., January 13, 1784.

Mr. Pitt cannot but suppose that I received his communication of the two divisions in the long debate which ended this morning with much uneasiness, as it shows the House of Commons much more willing to enter into any intemperate resolutions of desperate men than I could have imagined. As to myself, I am perfectly composed, as I have the self-satisfaction of feeling I have done my duty.

Though I think Mr. Pitt's day will be fully taken up in considering with the other Ministers what measures are best to be proposed in the present crisis, yet that no delay may arise from my absence I will dine in Town, and consequently be ready to see him in the evening, if he shall find that will be of utility. At all events, I am ready to take any step that may be proposed to oppose this faction, and to struggle to the last period of my life; but I can never submit to throw myself into its power. If they in the end succeed, my line is a clear one, and to which I have fortitude enough to submit.

*Pitt then brought in his India Bill, and on a resolution of
going into committee, Fox again defeated the government, but
this time by only 21 votes.   On the 23rd, on the second reading
of the Bill, it was thrown out on the motion for commitment, but
by only 8 votes.   It seemed as though Pitt would after all win
through, and the King was eager for dissolution, as he had been
in December, but had been dissuaded.   Too early a dissolution
would give a handle to the Foxites, who declared that it would
be a perversion of the prerogative.*

LI. To WILLIAM PITT

17 min. past 9 a.m., January 24, 1784.

I own I cannot see any reason, if the thing is practicable, that
a dissolution should not be effected; if not, I fear the constitution
of this country cannot subsist.

*One of the members, Powys, having raised the question in
the House, the King made further efforts.*

LII. To WILLIAM PITT

25 min. past 6 p.m., January 24, 1784.

I desire Mr. Pitt will assemble the confidential ministers this
evening, that he may state what passed this day.   I should think
it cannot give any reason for preventing a dissolution on Monday;
but if it should, he must be armed with the opinion of the other
ministers.   I fear Mr. Powys's candour has drawn him into a
trap; delay must be of the worst of consequences, and the
Opposition cannot but be glad he should be the author of it. . . .

*He was in favour of cutting ' those threads that cannot be un-
ravelled.   Half measures are ever puerile, and often destructive ',
or so he informed Pitt the next day.*

*Pitt, however, felt that the moment had not yet come. Fox's
prestige was sinking, but had not yet sunk far enough.   Pitt,
therefore, held firm all along the line.   When the ' independents ',
or St. Alban's Tavern group, besought him and the Duke of
Portland to meet, he expressed willingness, but the Duke refused
unless Pitt would resign his offices.   On February 2nd, their
chairman moved that a ministry on a broader basis should be
formed: Coke moved that the continuance of the ministers in*

*office was a barrier to any other administration being formed.
Whereupon, two days later, the Lords by a large majority
declared that the House of Commons had in some of its late
resolutions infringed the spirit of the Constitution, by, in fact,
denying the King's right to choose his own ministers. In
writing about this to Pitt, the King revealed clearly what, in his
view, the Constitution was.*

LIII. To WILLIAM PITT

Queen's House, 38 min. past 7 o'clock, February 3, 1784.

. . . It will highly become the House of Lords to throw off
their lethargy, and also vote an Address that shall show they
feel that each branch of the legislature has its fixed bounds, and
that the executive power is vested in the Crown, and not to be
infringed by the Commons.

LIV. To WILLIAM PITT

8 min. past 8 o'clock, February 4, 1784.

The whole conduct of Opposition confirms the opinion I
gave very early of its dangerous intentions of going step by step
as far as the House of Commons can be led, avoiding if possible
any avowed illegality of conduct : but not looking to the spirit
either of the constitution or of justice. The directing of the
resolution of Monday to be brought to me, without having proved
any charge against Administration, or indeed pretending to any,
must make every man of reflection grieve that the House can be
carried such lengths.

I trust the House of Lords will this day feel that the hour is
come for which the wisdom of our ancestors established that
respectable corps in the State, to prevent either the Crown or the
Commons from encroaching on the rights of each other. Indeed
should not the Lords stand boldly forth, this Constitution must
soon be changed; for if the two only remaining privileges of the
Crown are infringed—that of negativing Bills which have passed
both Houses of Parliament, and that of naming the ministers to
be employed—I cannot but feel, as far as regards my person,
that I can be no longer of any utility to this country, nor can with
honour continue in this island.

The vote of the House of Lords being such as it was, and the feeling in the country being clearly in Pitt's favour, the King was, as he said, in perhaps the most singular situation that ever occurred. For once he was inclined to value popularity, for on this occasion it arose from rectitude of conduct, or so he told Pitt in a long letter of February 15th, where also he agreed that Pitt should once more approach Portland. The Duke, however, made impossible stipulations, to the King's great delight.

LV. To WILLIAM PITT

Queen's House, 40 min. past m., February 26, 1784.

I should not deal with that openness towards Mr. Pitt which his conduct deserves, if I did not state my hopes that the Duke of Portland will not come into what I may deem reasonable; a subject requiring from his Sovereign exact words agreeable to which he can alone enter into negotiation is very revolting; but as the other ministers seem to advise that this last trial should be made, I will not object to it, provided in addition to the words proposed, Mr. Powys shall explain specifically to that Duke that his being called upon is to give him no right to anything above an equal share to others in the new administration, not to be the head of it whatever employment he may hold.

Portland boggled at equality, and nothing came of the attempt.

Meanwhile Pitt was carrying on a terrific oratorical battle in the House, and the City was covering him with honours: gold boxes and addresses continually came his way. His popularity was increased by an attack made on him outside Brook's Club when he was returning from a City function. Fox's attempt to stop supplies failed: on March 8th what he called a great State Paper was passed by only one vote: he dared make no attempt the next day to oppose the Mutiny Bill. Pitt hurried through the supply stages, polished off odds and ends of legislation, and told the King he was now ready for a dissolution.

LVI. To WILLIAM PITT

Windsor, 16 min. past 9 a.m., March 9, 1784.

Mr. Pitt's letter is undoubtedly the most satisfactory I have received for many months. An avowal on the outset that the proposition held forth is not intended to go further lengths than a kind of manifesto; and then carrying it by the majority of only one, and the day concluding with an avowal that all negotiation is at an end, gives me every reason to hope that by a firm and proper conduct this faction will by degrees be deserted by many, and at length be forgot. I shall ever with pleasure consider that by the prudence as well of rectitude of one person in the House of Commons this great change has been effected, and that he will be ever able to reflect with satisfaction that in having supported me he has saved the Constitution, the most perfect of human formations.

The King was only too happy to declare a dissolution.

LVII. To William Pitt

48 min. past 8 p.m., March 23, 1784.

This instant I have received Mr. Pitt's letters, and a draft of the Speech, which entirely meets with my ideas: I therefore desire the proper copy may be prepared for to-morrow. I have, in consequence of Mr. Pitt's intimation that the Bills will be ready for my assent, sent orders for the equipages to be at St. James's to-morrow at half-past two. I desire notice may be given that I may be expected a quarter before three at Westminster, that those necessary to attend may be there.

Only one thing remained: the support of the country. A victory at the polls was essential to complete the victory on the inner political stage. It soon appeared that all would be well.

LVIII. To William Pitt

April 5, 1784.

I cannot refrain from the pleasure of expressing to Mr. Pitt how much his success at Cambridge has made me rejoice, as he is the highest on the return, and that Lord Euston[1] is his colleague. This renders his election for the University a real honour, and reconciles me to his having declined Bath.

[1] The Duke of Grafton's son.

I shall only add that as yet the returns are more favourable than the most sanguine could have expected.

In fact matters had turned out exactly as Thomas Pitt, now Lord Camelford, had predicted. When Parliament met in May, Pitt won the first motion by 149 votes, the second by 168. The victory was overwhelming.

At last, the King might think, the great object of his reign had been attained: he had saved the Constitution by making good his right to select his own ministers whatever the composition of the Commons might be. It was, of course, an illusory triumph, for it rested, not on prerogative, but on the temper of the people as a whole at that time. Twenty-two harried years had culminated in a twenty-third of the bitterest humiliation, in which he had twice almost thrown up the sponge, but the end had been a glorious reversal. Having gained his point, he seems from now on to fade curiously out of the drama: his feelings were very largely those of his people, those of his ministers. He continued to take an active interest, but as a spectator rather than as a participant. The only grand point on which his opinion was at all decisive was on that of Catholic Emancipation: and until this brought about Pitt's retirement, the history of England no longer centres about the monarch, but about the man who at the age of twenty-four had the audacity to take the helm, and hold it for twenty years.

It was during this period that George III lost two of his 'numerous progeny'. The first was Prince Alfred, who did not survive infancy. These letters are addressed to Hurd, who had been tutor to some of his children, whom he had made a bishop, and then transferred to a better see, one suitable to the admirable scholar. The King also offered Hurd the Primacy, but this was refused.

LIX. TO THE BISHOP OF WORCESTER

Windsor, August 20, 1782.

MY GOOD LORD,

There is no probability, and indeed scarce a possibility, that my youngest child can survive this day. The knowing you are acquainted with the tender feelings of the Queen's heart, convinces me you will be uneasy till apprised that she is calling the only solid assistant under affliction—religion—to her assistance.

She feels the peculiar goodness of Divine Providence in never having before put her to so severe a trial, though she has so numerous a family. I do not deny [that] I also write to you, my good Lord, as a balm to my mind. As I have not you present to converse with, I think it the most pleasing occupation by this means to convey to you, that I place my confidence that the Almighty will never fill my cup of sorrow fuller than I can bear; and when I reflect on the dear cause of our tribulation, I consider his change to be so greatly for his advantage, that I sometimes thing it unkind to wish his recovery had been effected. And when I take this event in another point of view, and reflect how much more miserable it would have been to have seen him lead a life of pain, and perhaps end thus at a more mature age, I also confess that the goodness of the Almighty appears strongly in what certainly gives me great concern, but might have been still more severe.

The next letter refers to Prince Octavius, who was born in 1779.

lx.To the Bishop of Worcester

Windsor, May 6, 1783.

My good Lord,

The humanity which is not among the least conspicuous of your excellent qualities, would, I am persuaded, make you feel for the present distress in which the Queen and I are involved, had you not the farther incitement of a sincere attachment to us both.

The little object we are deploring was known to you, and consequently his merits: therefore you will not be surprised that the blow is strong. We both call on the sole assistant to those in distress—the dictates of religion. I have proposed to the Queen, and she approves of it, that I should desire you to come on Saturday, and bring Mr. Fisher with you, that on Sunday, in my chapel in the Castle, we may have the comfort of hearing you preach, and receiving from your hands the Holy Communion. I think this is a very proper time for renewing the baptismal vow; and though greatly grieved, I feel a true submission to the decrees of Providence, and great thankfulness for having enjoyed for four years that dear infant.

It was to Hurd too, as Clerk of the Closet, and as a man for whom he had great affection, that he confided his feelings about Hanover, which at this stage, with abdication in his mind, was no longer so wretched a country. There is a certain bitterness in the phrase, ' where my opinion must be of weight'.

LXI. To the Bishop of Worcester

Windsor, July 23, 1782.

My good Lord,

It is with infinite satisfaction I received on Sunday your letter, by which I find that at last the German books, wrote in Latin and collected by Professor Heyne by my directions for you, have arrived at Hartlebury. I own the reputation of the University of Göttingen I have much at heart, from an idea that if ever mankind reflect, they must allow that those who encourage religion, virtue, and literature, deserve as much solid praise as those who disturb the world, and commit all the horrors of war, to gain the reputation of being heroes.

Indeed, my good Lord, we live in unprincipled days; and no change can be expected but by an early attention to the education of the rising generation. Where my opinions must be of weight—I mean in my Electoral dominions—it shall be the chief object of my care; and should it be crowned with success, it may incline others to follow the example. . . .

Your very affectionate friend,

George R.

CHAPTER VI

CALMER YEARS

1784-1790

For the rest of his reign, except on one or two occasions, and of course in family matters, King George III, as already suggested, appears to have been chiefly a spectator, doing what was required of him as head of the State, but no more. He gave his opinions, but hardly expected them to be acted upon: it was as though his great struggle against the Coalition had exhausted him. He was ready, it seems, to acquiesce in all that Pitt did, even though he did not approve of it. He was naturally pleased with Pitt's first successes, especially in ordering the finances of the country: he was aware, however, that Parliament, besides, no doubt, being the guardian of the people's liberties, sometimes came in useful for furthering vested interests.

1. TO WILLIAM PITT

Kew, 1 min. past 9 a.m., July 1, 1784.

It is with infinite satisfaction that I learn from Mr. Pitt's letter that the various Resolutions proposed yesterday to the House of Commons on the subjects of the loan, the subscription for the unfunded debt,[1] and the taxes, were unanimously agreed to. Nothing is more natural than that, such heavy charges requiring many new taxes, those particularly affected by some will from that selfish motive, though conscious of the necessity of new burdens, attempt to place them on others rather than on themselves. Mr. Fox's moderation and candour will cease if any strong opposition to particular taxes should arise; but I trust Mr. Pitt will be able to carry all of them. It seemed to be an opinion yesterday that the brick tax was the one most likely to be opposed, but Mr. Pitt not having mentioned it, I suppose that branch of trade has not so many friends in the House as the coal pits which are the property of more considerable persons, and therefore more clamorous, though not less able to support a new charge on their profits.

[1] The Sinking Fund, now first introduced.

The brick tax passed, though not without considerable opposition; the coal tax had to be abandoned.

As soon as he could, Pitt introduced his India Bill, which replaced Fox's, and continued in operation, with a few modifications, until 1858. The King was too wise to consider it final.

II. To William Pitt

Windsor, 20 min. past 9 a.m., July 17, 1784.

It is with infinite pleasure I have received Mr. Pitt's note containing the agreeable account of the Committee on the East India Bill having been opened by the decision of so very decided a majority. I trust this will prevent much trouble being given in its farther progress, and that this measure may lay a foundation for, by degrees, correcting those shocking enormities in India that disgrace human nature, and if not put a stop to, threaten the expulsion of the Company out of that wealthy region. I have the more confidence of success from knowing Mr. Pitt's good sense, which will make him not expect that the present experiment shall at once prove perfect; but that by an attentive eye, and an inclination to do only what is right, he will, as occasions arise, be willing to make such improvements as may by degrees bring this arduous work into some degree of perfection.

The King's pliancy in Pitt's hands is shown by his attitude towards his Prime Minister's Parliamentary Reform Bill, for he hated the idea of Parliamentary reform, here siding with the opposition, especially Burke. But everything might be allowed to Pitt.

III. To William Pitt

54 min. past 8 a.m., March 20, 1785.

I have received Mr. Pitt's paper containing the heads of his plan for a Parliamentary Reform, which I look on as a mark of attention. I should have delayed acknowledging the receipt of it till I saw him on Monday, had not his letter expressed that there is but one issue of the business he could look upon as fatal, that is, the possibility of the measure being rejected by the weight of those who are supposed to be connected with government.

Mr. Pitt must recollect that though I have thought it unfortunate that he had early engaged himself in this measure, yet that I have ever said that as he was clear of the propriety of the measure, he ought to lay his thoughts before the House; that out of personal regard to him I should avoid giving any opinion to any one on the opening of the door to Parliamentary Reform except to him; therefore I am certain Mr. Pitt cannot suspect my having influenced any one on the occasion. If others choose for base ends to impute such a conduct to me, I must bear it as former false suggestions. Indeed on a question of such magnitude I should think very ill of any man who took a part on either side without the maturest consideration, and who would suffer his civility to any one to make him vote contrary to his own opinion. . . .

Even when the opposition attacked Hastings—which would be enough to make the King want to protect Hastings—he could not find it in him to blame Pitt for siding with the opposition on the second charge, that of unjust action towards Cheyte Singh, Rajah of Benares.

iv. To William Pitt

30 min. past 9 a.m., June 14, 1786.

Mr. Pitt would have conducted himself yesterday very unlike what my mind ever expects of him, if, as he thinks Mr. Hasting's conduct towards the Rajah was too severe, he had not taken the part he did, though it made him coincide with [the] adverse party. As to myself, I own I do not think it possible in that country to carry on business with the same moderation that is suitable to an European civilized nation.

How far Pitt always had his sympathy is amusingly shown by animadversions on Burke, at the period when Pitt was suffering reverses on the Irish trade question, and that of the fortifications of Portsmouth.

v. To William Pitt

February 18, 1786.

It is very unpleasant to me to observe by Mr. Pitt's note that he has been detained at the House of Commons by the fertile

o

imagination of Mr. Burke . . . a good division after a pretty general call for the question is the only means of counteracting those who only stir up debate for the purpose of delay.

The King, in short, trusted everything to Pitt, even withdrawing himself from notice wherever possible, as in the vexed question of the commercial treaties with Ireland. Where family matters were concerned, however, he could not keep aloof.

The trouble was once more the Prince of Wales, again in debt, and spending large sums on Mrs. Fitzherbert, whom he wished to follow abroad, and whom he was soon to marry: but even here the King was prepared to let others do the business.

VI. To WILLIAM PITT

St. James's, 20 min. past 1 p.m., September 10, 1784.

. . . On Monday I received through the hands of Lord Southampton[1] the enclosed letter from the Prince of Wales; the copy of my letter to the Lord Chancellor will explain what was intimated on delivering it; I also send the Lord Chancellor's answer : unless I hear something more, I do not see I am required to take any steps. I trust Mr. Pitt when I see him on Wednesday will return these papers, which I cannot want before. Whether the Prince of Wales will apply on the subject of his debts I have no guess : Lord Southampton thinks he cannot avoid it : he dropped that they are supposed to amount to £100,000, which in one year and without gaming seems hardly credible. I shall certainly give no answer should such an application be made that can engage me to anything : I must see the whole before I can guess whether anything can be done, and then not without the fullest communication with Mr. Pitt.

VII. To WILLIAM PITT

42 min. past 7 p.m., March 24, 1785.

This morning I received the enclosed from Lord Southampton, on which I appointed him to be at St. James's when I returned from the House of Peers. He there delivered to me the letter from the Prince of Wales. All that I could collect

---

[1] The Prince's Groom of the Stole.

further from him was that the idea is that I call for explanations and retrenchments as a mode of declining engaging to pay the debts; that there are many sums it cannot be honourable to explain; that Lord Southampton has reason to believe they have not been incurred for political purposes; that he thinks the going abroad is now finally resolved on; that perhaps the champion of the Opposition has been consulted on the letter now sent. I therefore once more send all that has passed to Mr. Pitt, and hope to have in the course of to-morrow from him what answer ought to be sent to this extraordinary epistle, which though respectful in terms, is in direct defiance of my whole correspondence. I suppose Mr. Pitt will choose to consult the Chancellor.

The King had rarely consulted any one on Hanoverian matters, but now he turned to Pitt. The situation was complicated. Frederick the Great was forming his alliance of German Princes, the Fürstenbund, *a counterstroke to Joseph II to exchange the Netherlands for Bavaria, in which the Emperor was supported by Catherine of Russia. In 1784 England had been negotiating for a treaty with Russia, but when in 1785 Hanover joined Frederick's league, the Russian ambassador, Woronzow, delivered a sharp note to both Secretaries of State, threatening that unless the Electorate seceded, Russia would form combinations unpleasing to England. The matter was all the more difficult in that Frederick would have nothing to do with England.*

VIII. To WILLIAM PITT

Windsor, 42 min. past 1 p.m., August 7, 1785.

I have this instant received Mr. Pitt's letter enclosing the one brought him by Count Woronzow's secretary and the paper that accompanied it, which is a copy of the one given on Friday to Lord Carmarthen. Count Woronzow also visited Lord Sydney and insisted a Council was to be held the next day to give him an answer whether I should break the treaty I have in my Electoral capacity finally concluded with the King of Prussia and the Elector of Saxony to prevent all measures contrary to the Germanic Constitution. If no one has such dangerous views, this association cannot give umbrage; but the time certainly required this precaution. My only difficulty in giving any answer to the Empress of Russia is that her declaration bears so strongly the shape of a command, that it requires a strong one.

Pitt, and the Cabinet in general, were chary of Prussian engagements, and hankered after an understanding with Russia; but the events of 1787 forced their hands in the other direction. These had to do with the affairs of Holland. For generations the English had supported the Orange party while France had helped the Republicans, who, encouraged by their country having lately fought against England, and by its recent treaty with France, decided in 1786 to abolish the hereditary stadtholdership. France, under Vergennes's direction, would tolerate no interference by other powers in Holland: Frederick the Great would offer no help to the Orange party. Frederick, however, died in 1786, and Vergennes in 1787, and the Princess of Orange made a bold bid for her husband's reinstatement: she was insulted, and appealed to the new King of Prussia, who was her brother. This gave Sir James Harris, now Ambassador at the Hague, a brilliant chance, which he took, and a crisis was precipitated which led to a re-grouping of Europe, the immediate issue for the moment being whether England or France should dominate the United Provinces. It was here that Pitt scored his first great international victory, and the occasion marks the re-entry of England on the stage of European politics, from which she had been virtually absent since the accession of George III: thus in a sense it also marks the end of the King's determining influence in foreign affairs. In Holland itself, so far were the 'patriots' from representing the mass of opinion, that the Prussian invasion was more like the triumphal entry of an army of liberation.

IX. To William Pitt

Windsor, 30 min. past 8 a.m., September 16, 1787.

On returning to the Secretary of State's office the dispatch from Mr. Eden[1] of the 13th, I cannot help accompanying it with a few lines to Mr. Pitt; though the language of M. de Montmorin[2] is so very *offensive* that I can scarcely mention it with *temper*. I disapprove of it, and consequently cannot recommend its being

---

[1] William Eden had been sent as a special commissioner to Paris to negotiate the Treaty of Commerce.

[2] Who had succeeded Vergennes.

retorted. We have held a fair conduct during the whole business, and France has been double to the greatest excess. I think they feel they cannot do much, and therefore from spleen indulge themselves in this unjustifiable language, which anyone but Mr. Eden would have declined hearing and still more reporting. I trust temper may still bring things into the line of negotiation; and while we are desirous of that, France should with politeness be told that we must stand by the United States [*sic*] against the faction in the Province of Holland if France persists in the idea now communicated of supporting it with arms.

I suppose our ships, if M. de Barthélemy's language shows France means to act without hearing farther from us, ought to appear off the Dutch coast for a few days which might decide measures previous to the arrival of any material force from France.

Ought not some one instantly to go to France who may know better how to talk with M. de Montmorin than Mr. Eden?

x. To WILLIAM PITT

Windsor, 44 min. past 8 p.m., September 16, 1787.

The drafts of dispatches to Sir James Harris, Sir William Faucitt,[1] and Mr. Ewart[2] are very proper, and the delaying answering Mr. Eden for a couple of days is natural, that it may be done with a thorough consideration. I have sent provisional orders for a state of what force can in a short space of time be collected; till this arrives I cannot take any farther step, and then I must know that England means to take them into pay, and must also enable me to put the rest of my forces in a state of defence, for I cannot leave Germany unprotected for a Dutch quarrel. The King of Prussia has really a military government, and consequently more ready for immediate action than other powers, yet his collecting 30,000 men has taken above two months: I cannot pretend to move with greater velocity.

---

[1] See note to letter XXII, chapter IV. He had been sent to negotiate the hire of Hessians.

[2] Secretary, and the next year Ambassador, at Berlin. He was at this time only twenty-eight years old. His death in 1792 put an end to the promise of a brilliant career.

The news of the reception of the Prussians made it seem that Pitt's warlike preparations might be discontinued.

XI. TO WILLIAM PITT

Windsor, 17 min. past 11 p.m., September 21, 1787.

It is impossible that any political event can give me more satisfaction than the account just received from the agent at Helvetsluys, as I think it gives a fair prospect of this country escaping a war, and at the same time shows France that though England has no grasping ideas, that yet she is not of a temper tamely to let her rival succeed in her ambitious projects. I think Mr. Grenville's good judgement will make the negotiations prosper, which will add to his own character as well as to that of his relation.[1]

Grenville did negotiate well, or the French, in their pre-Revolution confusion, negotiated badly: there was no war, but the result was the Triple Alliance between England, Holland, and Prussia, which thus opposed themselves to the Russo-Austrian Alliance. France could have been the determining factor, had her internal situation admitted.

A new threat of war, however, appeared the next year: the campaign of Russia and Austria against the Turks induced Gustavus of Sweden to attack Russia. The Triple Alliance by no means approved of Gustavus's action, but when the dismemberment of Sweden was threatened by the intervention of Denmark, it looked as though steps would have to be taken. It seems to have been the fear of war, coupled with the disgraceful behaviour of his two eldest sons, that brought about the King's first attack of definite insanity.

XII. TO WILLIAM PITT

Kew, 6 o'clock p.m., October 20, 1788.

I have not been able to answer Mr. Pitt's letter sooner this day, having had a very indifferent night; the medicine which Sir George Baker found necessary to be taken to remove the

---

[1] William Wyndham Grenville, afterwards Lord Grenville, Pitt's cousin, had been sent to replace Eden: Pitt had previously sent him to Holland, and his dispatches from there had much pleased the King. See also note to letter XXXIX, chapter v.

spasm has now greatly relieved me. Indeed I think myself nearer getting rid of my complaint than since the attack.[1] If I should have a good night, I will write and desire Mr. Pitt to come here previous to the meeting of the Cabinet.

We happily got through the business last year, but then our enemy was weak indeed, and the Prussian arms succeeded beyond expectation. In the present scene it is the contrary. The King of Sweden seems to have what often go together—great want of courage and as little good faith. The sentiments of his subjects are not known here, for Mr. Elliot's[2] dispatches are yet to be composed, and the Danish troops have advanced much farther than any one supposed; even Bensdorf[3] owns it in a letter I believe drawn up for our inspection. All I mean by this is, that we must try to save Sweden from becoming a province of Russia; but I do not think this object can only be obtained by a general war, to run the risk of ruining the finances of this country, which, if our pride will allow us to be quiet for a few years, will be in a situation to hold a language which does not become the having been driven out of America.

To speak openly, it is not the being considerably weakened by illness, but the feelings that never have day or night been at ease since this country took that disgraceful step, that has made me wish what years I have still to reign not to be drawn into a war. I am now within a few days of twenty-eight years having been not on a bed of roses. I began with a successful war; the people grew tired of that, and called out for peace. Since that the most justifiable war any country ever waged—there in few campaigns, from being popular again peace was called for. After such woeful examples, I must be a second Don Quixote if I did not wish, if possible, [to avoid] falling again into the same situation. The ardour of youth may not admire my calmness, but I think it fairer to speak out thus early than by silence be supposed to have changed my opinion if things should bear a more warlike appearance than I now expect, and if I should then object to a general war.

[1] Diagnosed as a bilious attack.
[2] Hugh Elliot, Envoy at Copenhagen, a diplomat of great brilliance, but who took too much upon himself. He was a friend of Mirabeau.
[3] Count Bernstorff, all-powerful minister in Denmark.

I am afraid Mr. Pitt will perceive I am not quite in a situation to write at present, but I thought it better even to write as loosely as I have here than to let the box return without an answer to his letter.

Rumours of the real nature of the King's illness soon got about—his feverishness, his volubility, his stiffness—and caused much alarm in the City. On the 25th he wrote to Pitt:

Mr. Pitt seemed really distressed at seeing my bodily stiffness yesterday, which I alone exhibited to stop further lies and any fall of the Stocks. . . . I am certainly weak and stiff, but no wonder,

and added that he could never think that whether Sweden was to be governed by a corrupt King or a corrupt Senate was worth going to war about. On November 3rd he wrote to say that he could sign warrants without inconvenience. His next letter was not written until February 23rd, 1789.

With the Regency difficulties, the jubilation of the opposition, the tergiversations of Thurlow, and the abominable behaviour of the King's two eldest sons during his lunacy, we have nothing to do. The King was not unaware of the latter, as we see from the first note he wrote to Pitt on his recovery, in which he virtually says he must withdraw from active participation in politics.

XIII. To William Pitt

Kew, February 23, 1789.

It is with infinite satisfaction I renew my correspondence with Mr. Pitt by acquainting him of my having seen the Prince of Wales and my second son. Care was taken that the conversation should be general and cordial : they seemed perfectly satisfied. I chose the meeting should be in the Queen's apartment, that all parties might have that caution which at the present hour could but be judicious.

I desire Mr. Pitt will confer with the Lord Chancellor that any steps which may be necessary for raising the annual supplies, or any measure that the interests of the nation may require, should not be unnecessarily delayed; for I feel the warmest gratitude for the support and anxiety shown by the nation at large during my tedious illness, which I should ill requite if I did not wish to prevent any further delay in those public measures which it may be necessary to bring forward this year, though I must decline entering into a pressure of business, and indeed for the rest of my life shall expect others to fulfil the duties of their employments, and only keep that superintending eye which can be effected without labour or fatigue. . . .

Yet by April he was in a stout enough frame of mind to tell Pitt that he was ' thoroughly determined not to yield to my deputy in Ireland', Lord Buckingham (lately Temple), over the matter of a small appointment, though four days later he wrote, ' my mind is not strong enough as yet to stand little ruffles, and still more so when they relate to Lord Buckingham, who does not stand well in my mind'. Again, a few days later, he referred to ' a certain lassitude and want of energy both of mind and body'.

In May, however, he was called upon to stand a larger ruffle, due to the behaviour of his third son, whom he had placed in the Navy. The letters connected with it are self-explanatory.

xiv. To William Pitt

Windsor, 48 min. past 9 a.m., May 1, 1789.

Mr. Pitt cannot be surprised at my being unpleasantly affected by the information of the arrival of my third son from his station in the West Indies at Portsmouth; at the same time it is impossible to have had it communicated with more delicacy than was used by Lord Chatham;[1] I am not surprised as every one knew the step of sending him leave to return must be disagreeable to me for a variety of reasons that no one chose ever to hint to me, consequently I had not the smallest suspicion that any one had proposed this measure. I certainly think Lord Chatham could not in my then unfortunate illness take it upon him to refuse the leave; but the quarter from whence the application came has certainly by this given me a proof how little any wish of mine will ever be attended to. It will be now absolutely necessary to give him the same allowance that his brother the

[1] First Lord of the Admiralty since Howe's retirement in 1788.

Duke of York has, and had my illness not put a stop to my private business, Colonel Hotham could have laid before Mr. Pitt the exceeding he has made on his sea allowance. He must also now have his seat in the House of Lords.[1] In truth I have but too much reason to expect no great comfort by an additional member of the opposite faction in my own family. It would be highly unjust in me not to add that I have every reason to be thankful to Divine Providence for the affectionate conduct of the Queen and of all my daughters, and certainly after having had so strong a warning of their having nearly lost the only protector they can look up to, I must be desirous of having them secured, whenever it shall please the Almighty to end my days, from a total dependence on a successor who does certainly show that their loss would be irreparable; their situation and the want of a provision that the executive government may go on unmolested should not I entirely recover the vigour of mind and the inclination of taking the same active part I have done for above twenty-eight years, are points that hang heavily on my mind : were they arranged by the help of a total change of scene and thorough relaxation I should hope by degrees to recover the great shock that so severe an illness has certainly given to my whole nervous system.

xv. To William Pitt

Kew, May 29, 1789.

I choose to communicate the enclosed letters from my second and third sons, and the answer I wrote to the latter, as it is to a degree a political letter as well as perfectly affectionate. Mr. Pitt may be surprised to see them all in another hand, but I own I am not as yet able to copy my own papers : time, air, and sea bathing will I trust restore that tone to my constitution which I am taught to believe I am too unreasonable in having expected would have been effected before this time. I mean these copies for Mr. Pitt, therefore they need not be returned, and I am confident it was necessary to deal openly though temperately with my sons, that they might not plead ignorance of my sentiments.

[1] He became Duke of Clarence that year—and joined the opposition.

XVI.TO PRINCE WILLIAM

Windsor, May 25, 1789.

DEAR WILLIAM,

On Saturday evening the letter you had left here for me was delivered : it contained your application for an increased allowance, and a list of those you wish to take into your family. I should neither act the part of a parent nor of a friend if I did not fairly state to you how little either met with my approbation, or passed by how little your conduct since your return from sea corresponds with the language you held to me on that occasion. Instead of feeling that fourteen thousand pounds per annum for each of my younger sons must be a considerable diminution of my income, and that therefore no more can be expected from that source, which indeed is the exact sum the late King settled on his only younger son, you are laying in a plea for an application to Parliament for an immediate addition to this sum. I cannot suppose this arises from yourself, but is the suggestion of others, for the hour of receiving a favour is not the natural one of applying for another. Should Parliament at a further period be inclined to settle any additional sum on my younger sons, it certainly can only be obtained by their having lived with real economy on the sum allotted, and Parliament thinking an addition would enable them to live with a splendour more suitable to their rank; but whilst the dignity of the character is forgot, and only dissipation and extravagance is pursued, the assistance of Parliament can neither with decency be applied for, nor any willing success be obtained. Though I choose to cast a veil over the unkindness I met with during my illness from the ill advised conduct of my sons, yet I cannot but feel it, and as well as the Parliament, and indeed the whole nation, [be] sure this is not the moment that I can be supposed to encourage such an application. You have an easy method of diminishing your expenses, and that by the laudable plea of forwarding your nautical knowledge by applying for foreign service. As to the names you have submitted, I suppose for my opinion, I cannot but repeat what I told you at our first interview, that Captain Elphinstone is in open and direct opposition to every measure of government, and you having one of that description at the head of your family would bear an aspect to the public of you being at least very inattentive to the inclinations of your father; Captains Pole and Christian are deserving sea officers; as to the other gentlemen I am silent on their characters as not sufficiently acquainted with them, though I rather doubt most of them are of sentiments that would encourage opinions being formed of your not looking alone to your profession and to the welfare of your family. As to your personal conduct towards me since your return, though I certainly neither wish nor expect you should live entirely with me, yet your having entirely estranged yourself from your parents can not but be unpleasant to them, and the being entirely a follower of those who are certainly not attentive to me, can not but incline me to think your assurances on the day you have arrived have soon been obliterated.

xvii. To William Pitt

Kew, June 9, 1789.

The enclosed is the copy of the answer I have written to the letter I on Friday showed Mr. Pitt which I had received from my third son. I think I have not [now?] closed the correspondence in the fairest manner, and considering the inclination of some desperate persons to increase the venom which has been but too effectually conveyed, the less room is given for altercation at present, the more chance there is that young minds may cool, and come to a temper that cannot but be more to their credit as well as to the satisfaction of more rational minds.

xviii. To Prince William

Kew, June 9, 1789.

Dear William,

When I wrote to you I did not intend getting into an unpleasant correspondence, but that you should have my sentiments on paper rather than a conversation, which like most others might have not afterwards been rightly understood; I should therefore not have answered your letter of the 1st of this month had I not on farther inquiry found I had mistaken the allowance I give to Frederick;[1] my orders were that you should have the

---

[1] Duke of York.

same, which proves to be twelve thousand pounds a year. In some degree to remove any disappointment this may occasion, I have authorized Mr. Pitt to lay before me any reasonable application you may make for your first expenses. I cannot omit mentioning that I think you will repent the not returning to sea, which would have kept you out of many inconveniences, as well as increased your nautical knowledge.

Prince William led the gay life of the Fox circle, and entered into a liaison with Mrs. Jordan, the actress: this was no doubt very grievous to the King: but the Duke of Clarence might have asked how it was, that if his father was so eager for him to go to sea, raising him to the rank of Admiral of the Red, he was never given a command?

In 1790 the King-Elector once more had his mind turned towards foreign affairs. The Continental situation had been considerably eased by the death of Joseph II, but a dispute with Spain had arisen over trading rights in Nootka Sound, which at one time seemed to be leading direct to war; thanks to Pitt's negotiations, however, it was made plain to the Spanish Court that France would not uphold the Family Compact.

xix. To W. W. Grenville[1]

Queen's House, May 26, 1790.

On coming to town I have found Mr. Grenville's note conveying a wish that I would furnish a body of Hanoverians to augment the garrison of Gibraltar; the idea is new to me, I therefore can only express at present an inclination to furnish them for that service; but as it requires some arrangement, I will try to-morrow evening to write more fully on the subject; it is impossible I can collect them under six weeks, so that there is no immediate hurry for ordering the transports.

xx. To William Pitt

Windsor, October 26, 1790.

From a thorough conviction how essential peace is to the prosperity of this country, it is impossible to me to object to any means that may have a chance of affecting it; though not sanguine

---

[1] Now Secretary of State for the Home Department.

that Mr. H. Elliot and his French friend are likely to succeed where caution and much delicacy are necessary. While our ambassador and official correspondence are kept clear of this business it will certainly be wise to keep up the proposed communication for the sole purpose of restoring peace, but no encouragement must be given to forwarding the internal views of the democratic party. We have honourably not meddled with the internal dissensions of France, and no object ought to drive us from that honourable ground.

The means were certainly mysterious, for Elliot's French friend was Mirabeau, whom he had known from youth: the King also was justified in questioning Elliot's discretion, for though his action at Copenhagen (see letter XII) had been effective, it had been rash to the point of romanticism. However, this negotiation, and another of the same kind, both screened from the British ambassador in Paris, was successful in averting war.

As to war, however, honourable restraint from meddling, and the democratical party, these were matters which were soon to occupy the royal mind to a far larger degree, as the next chapter will show. So far, however, the French Revolution had not assumed those terrifying proportions which were soon to shock, not only the King, but some of his fiercest opponents.

Other letters of this period reflect the King's more private tastes.

XXI. TO LORD CARMARTHEN

St. James's, 46 min. past 1 p.m., March 23, 1786.

Lord Carmarthen's list of music for next Wednesday is very excellent, and meets with the approbation of those whose opinion on the subject he wished to know; his introducing Mrs. Billington if he can get her to sing pathetic songs and not to over *grace* them will be doing an essential service to the concert.

XXII. TO WILLIAM PITT

Cheltenham, 1 min. past 7 p.m., August 14, 1788.

I am this instant returned from seeing the most beautiful sight I ever beheld, namely the colliery country near Stroud: above forty thousand people were assembled, and they all confess the trade is now brisker than the oldest person ever remembers. . . .

This, while showing his appreciation of music, allowed him to be a trifle satirical of the protracted trial of Hastings.

XXIII.TO THE DUKE OF LEEDS

Queen's House, February 27, 1790.

I have just received the Duke of Leeds's note enclosing the letter addressed to him by his brother directors of the Ancient Concert on the subject of resuming the Festival at Westminster Abbey; its having subsided for the last two years was not of my instigation but from the trial of Mr. Hastings in Westminster Hall. If the Duke of Leeds can find means of securing certain days for the musical performances in Westminster Abbey I shall most willingly attend them, and considering how thoroughly the public as well as the House of Peers seem tired of the attendances in Westminster Hall, I should not think this difficult to be effected.

No portrait of the King would be complete without a glimpse of him as Farmer George.

XXIV.TO ARTHUR YOUNG

January 1, 1787.

. . . Without farther preface, I shall mention that the dispute which has lately arisen on the subject of summer-fallows had made me secretly wish that Mr. Ducket, the able cultivator of Petersham, would have communicated his thoughts, not only on that subject, but would have benefited the public by a full explanation of that course of husbandry which has rendered his farm at Petersham, which has now been above nineteen years in his hands, so flourishing, though his three predecessors had failed on it.

When he first entered on it, all the land, except the meadows, appeared to be hungry sand, and several acres were covered with gorse and brambles, which now produce excellent crops of corn. . . .

Mr. Ducket's system of agriculture is a medium between the old and the drill husbandry. He adapted his present mode of culture six years before he came to Petersham, on a small farm at Esher, as also at the Duke of Newcastle's villa of Claremount, where he used his three ploughs, but at that time hand-hoed all his corn.

His course of husbandry seems to be the employment of clover, turnips, and rye, as fallow-crops, and as intermediate ones between wheat, barley, oats, and rye, changing these occasionally according to the nature and state of the land. Of these intermediate crops, those which serve only to fill up the winter-interval are of the greatest use for winter and spring food, and what these take from the ground is amply re-supplied by the dung and treading of the cattle which feed on them; thus his ground, although never dormant, is continually replenished by a variety of manure, and thus unites the system of continued pasture with cultivation. . . .

He drills for all the crops, but sows the seeds broad-cast (turnips excepted), as the seeds fall naturally into the drills, or what escape the hoe eradicates; turnips when eaten by the fly are well renewed by drilling; he has had good crops after the first sowings have been destroyed by the fly. Clover drilled among the corn he finds very advantageous, much seed being saved, and the crop better secured from the fly, which feed on this plant as well as turnips. If his clover fails, he sows bents broad-cast when the corn is near in the ear, which, from the ground being loosened by the preceding drillings, are by the first rain washed into the earth, and ensure him a crop of grass; but he prefers a crop of clover alone, being the better preparation for wheat. . . .

Mr. Ducket has lately adopted two new implements; the one for sowing is a frame on which are fixed five tin boxes, each holding about one pound of seed, which drops through the bottom of them into the drills. It is carried in a man's hand, and, being continually shook, the seed is prevented from clogging the holes in the bottom of the boxes by a wire playing across them, and is thus dribbled regularly into the drills. . . .

I shall not take up more of your time than to assure you that I am,

Sir, your most humble servant,
RALPH ROBINSON.

CHAPTER VII

THE FRENCH REVOLUTION

1791-1801

The year 1789, which to us looking back was so pregnant with great events, did not seem so important to Englishmen living in that age. The French were indeed in a troubled state, but that was due to bad finance and bad harvests: the 'Eastern question', the machinations of the Emperor and of the Tsarina, the Swedish affair, the ambitions of Prussia, the attitude of Spain, all, or indeed any of these, seemed far more important than the events occurring in France. Thus the last hardly receive mention in the King's correspondence. But once the movements there were seen to be clearly anti-monarchical, the King's attention was aroused; for him the wars which followed were always Royalist wars; everything must be done to crush those scoundrels who dared assail the quasi-divinity of kingship. Seemingly indifferent to the Revolution till 1791, the attempted flight of Louis XVI awakened him with a start.

I. To Lord Grenville

Windsor, June 25, 1791.

Lord Grenville has judged very properly in immediately transmitting the account of the King and Queen having left Paris; I feel thoroughly interested in whatever regards them, and, as such, fearful lest the messenger's intelligence of the supposed interruption to their escape at Quinault. Should they providentially get out of France, it will bring to the test whether the nobility, clergy, and law will join the regal cause.

II. To Lord Grenville

Windsor, June 27, 1791.

I am much pleased at Lord Grenville's attention in sending me the intelligence he has received from Sir Robert Woodford of the King of France being stopped by a *maître des postes* at St. Menehout. I own I am much affected by this step, as I fear he will again fall into the hands from which he has escaped; I desire Lord Grenville will continue to send me every information

211

he may receive till the King shall either be released by those who may effect that step, or that he be reconducted to Paris.

III. To Lord Grenville

Windsor, June 27, 1791.

It is with infinite concern that I find by the letter of Lord Gower[1] that the French King is not only in the hands of his enemies but on the road for Paris; it is but the common fate of all attempts to be blamed if not crowned with success. The situation at Paris was so horrid that no one can justly be surprised any attempt was made to get out of it.

I trust I shall receive any further accounts that may arrive, for this business will occasion many strong measures and further restraints.

The affairs in France had, contrary to Pitt's expectation, roused radical feeling in England, the reformist movement gaining strength from the rejection of Fox's Bill for the relief of dissenters, a rejection highly agreeable to the King. The Jacobin element, however, called forth a loyalist party, who at Birmingham wrecked not only Priestley's chapel, but also his private house and scientific instruments. These two letters show not only the King's reaction to this, but also his extreme interest in the details of military administration.

IV. To Henry Dundas[2]

Windsor, 28 min. past 4 p.m., July 16, 1791.

The order for three troops of the 15th Regiment of Dragoons to march towards Birmingham to restore order if the civil magistrates have not been able is incumbent on government; though I cannot but feel better pleased that Priestley is the sufferer for the doctrines he and his party have instilled, and that the people see them in their true light; yet cannot approve of their having employed such atrocious means of showing their discontent.

[1] Ambassador at Paris.
[2] Now Home Secretary.

v. To Henry Dundas

Kew, 2 min. past 9 p.m., July 20, 1791.

The accounts seem to be so confident that the riot at Birmingham has subsided, that I trust the mischief in the neighbouring places will also cease. This is sufficient reason to prevent the taking up the horses of the cavalry except of the Royal Regiment of Horse Guards, which should yet continue to go to Coventry to relieve the three troops of the 15th, which ought to return to Nottingham, and another troop of the Blues may be sent from Coventry to Wolverhampton. Those regiments that have taken up their horses should not turn them again to grass, as the expense of grass money will not be equal to the loss that will attend turning out the horses again, particularly if they have begun their march.

Foreign policy at this juncture was strong for a strict neutrality as regards the affairs of France: at the same time, the King did not attempt to disguise his hostility towards, and his contempt for, the French emissaries. This was to some extent shared by Pitt and Grenville, who would not officially recognize the ci-devant Marquis de Chauvelin as ambassador.

vi. To the King of France

St. James's, August 13, 1791.

Monsieur mon Frère et Cousin,

In consequence of the friendly letter I have just received from your Majesty, I seize the opportunity to say how much I esteem your assurances of regard and personal friendship. It will always be a real pleasure to me to cultivate those sentiments, as well as to preserve and strengthen the good understanding which has so long and so happily subsisted between our countries.

My conduct in respect of the troubles which have so greatly disturbed the Kingdom of France has been directed by principles of an exact and perfect neutrality; and I have never, on any occasion that has arisen, departed from this system. I am very far from wishing to meddle with the internal affairs of that Kingdom, so as to profit from a moment of crisis, or to snatch advantages which circumstances might offer me. As a result of these principles I intend to take no part whatever in the measures which the other powers of Europe may adopt in this matter, either in supporting them or in opposing them. My hopes in this respect are all for the happiness of their Most Christian Majesties and their subjects, and the establishment and tranquillity and public order in a Kingdom so near my own, and with which my subjects have relations both friendly and commercial. . . .

VII. TO LORD GRENVILLE

Windsor, April 28, 1792.

. . . I authorize [Lord Grenville] to appoint M. de Chauvelin to deliver his letters on Wednesday. I am very happy, however, M. de Talleyrand and du Roveray may be directed by the French Secretary of State to Lord Grenville, that they have no credence to me, and therefore may receive the contempt their characters entitle them to. I know I need not recommend the greatest caution to Lord Grenville in conversing with persons much fitter to be employed with the new club in St. James's Street[1] than with any servants of the Crown.

Curious negotiations, however, went on with France, for Pitt was anxious not to lose the fruits of an entente *he had worked to procure: but the King was from the first against them, and occasional acid comments enliven his correspondence with his Foreign Secretary.*

VIII. TO LORD GRENVILLE

Windsor, May 14, 1792.

The brutality and cowardice that has attended the outset of the French hostilities does not augur either a successful or honourable issue of their warlike furor, but indeed from the commencement of the Revolution, more acts of barbarity have been committed than by the most savage people.

[1] ' The Friends of the People ', including Sheridan, Whitbread, and other prominent members of the opposition; but not Fox.

IX. TO LORD GRENVILLE

Kew, June 20, 1792.

. . . I cannot help expressing . . . my surprise at the fresh memorial from the French Court; it seems calculated for no one good purpose but to keep up a constant intercourse of papers which cannot effect any good, and may prove inconvenient. The more coldly and shortly it is answered the better to prevent a continuance of it.

The September massacres, however, began to bring about a different state of mind towards intervention.

X. TO LORD GRENVILLE

Weymouth, September 3, 1792.

. . . The idea of trying the French Queen and adding her death to their many other crimes is most shocking, and must alienate the minds of all who have the least sentiments of humanity and does not add much lustre to their having decreed the rights of a French citizen to Mr. Wilberforce.

XI. TO LORD GRENVILLE

Weymouth, September 4, 1792.

Lord Grenville may be desirous of knowing that Lord Gower arrived here about eight this morning.[1] His language conveys nothing different from what the various former accounts have contained; that the desire of destroying all religion, law, and subordination seem to be the only prevailing idea, without the smallest inclination after this destruction to build up anything. . . .

The execution of Louis XVI stirred him still further: the order to Chauvelin to leave, however, only precipitated the ambassador's departure by a few days.

XII. TO LORD GRENVILLE

Queen's House, January 24, 1793.

I have received Lord Grenville's note enclosing that from the post-office at Dover confirming the shocking account but too

[1] It was considered too dangerous for a noble to stay in Paris.

certain from the news arrived yesterday. I trust the Privy
Council will be ready immediately after the Drawing Room this
day for giving the necessary order that Monsieur Chauvelin may
instantly leave the kingdom.

*Thus it was with no restraining thought that the monarch
so ardent for peace, who on appointing Grenville Foreign
Secretary had told him he had chosen him on account of his
peaceful proclivities, welcomed a declaration of war. The immediate subject of dispute, as it was to be again in 1803 and
1914, was the occupation of Belgium by a power dangerous to
England.*

XIII. To Lord Grenville

Windsor, February 9, 1793.

The confirmation of the step taken by the faction that governs
in France of jointly declaring war against this kingdom and the
Dutch Republic is highly agreeable to me, as the mode adopted
seems well calculated to rouse such a spirit in this country that
I trust will curb the insolence of those despots, and be a means
of restoring some degree of order to that unprincipled country,
whose aim at present is to destroy the foundations of every
civilized state.

*The campaign in Flanders, with his favourite son, the Duke
of York, in command of the British contingent, was closely
followed by the King. Indeed, seeing that his three most
important advisers knew nothing of military matters, it is
supposed that it was he who laid down the lines on which the
operations of 1793 were conducted, namely an attack on
Valenciennes and Dunkirk. His scheme was marred by a
frittering away of troops in scattered attacks on the French coast.*

XIV. To William Pitt

Queen's House, March 29, 1793.

I return to Mr. Pitt the packet he received yesterday from
the Duke of York, whose conduct since called forth into his
present arduous situation has completely answered my most
sanguine expectation, and I am most happy at perceiving his

judgement and prudence are as conspicuous as his activity and intrepidity; these are not the sentiments alone of an affectionate father, but grounded on the basis of the propriety of his conduct.

It is easy to see that the Prince of Coburg,[1] though deserving every commendation for the ability and activity of his military conduct, is not void of negotiating qualities, and that though it is impossible he should not be apprised that no concert as yet exists between this country and the two great German Courts on the best mode of repelling the French, yet he keeps calling both on the Duke of York and the Dutch as if he was empowered to call for unlimited assistance, and also states his own situation as much more perilous than the real fact.

I think so far we may with safety concur as to authorize the moving of the English forces and the Hanoverians to Bergen op Zoom, and by that movement making a demonstration on the right of the Austrians, from whence they may advance to Antwerp; but if it can be effected the most advantageous step that can be taken, and most conducive to shorten both the sea and land operations of France, would be the English and combined forces, with some addition from the Dutch, getting possession of Dunkirk, as this would enable battering trains of artillery to be embarked in Holland and landed in the most advantageous situation for the Austrians to carry on regular sieges; this seems to me the real assistance that this country and Holland can give to the two German powers, and to which extent I am ready to concur, but not to giving them the command of the combined army to be employed agreeably to their own plans or views.

His pleasure in the campaign was largely the result of family pride.

xv.To Henry Dundas

Kew, 46 min. past 8 p.m., August 13, 1793.

The dispatches Mr. Secretary Dundas has transmitted from Sir James Murray give me infinite satisfaction which has been greatly increased by the letters I have received from my son the Duke of York.   He mentions in that of the 6th the very gallant

[1] Coburg commanded the Austrian contingent.

behaviour of my fifth son, and also commends him for the coolness as well as spirit he showed; he saved his life by killing a French chasseur, and fairly cutting his way through the enemy.

He saw that the failure of the Dunkirk expedition was due to a splitting up of forces.

XVI. To WILLIAM PITT

Windsor, 30 min. past 10 p.m., September 14, 1793.

The misfortune of our situation is that we have too many objects to attend to, and our force consequently must be too small at each place, yet it seems to me that the Hessian infantry are the only corps we can soon get at to send to Toulon. . . .

XVII. To WILLIAM PITT

Queen's House, 46 min. past 1 p.m., December 5, 1793.

Mr. Pitt's note is just arrived. I am sorry there is any idea of still farther lessening the force on the side of Flanders; if it must be done I agree to its being of British troops, but can by no means consent that any of my Hanoverians shall be employed but in Flanders. I send this directly that any arrangement may be effected without expecting from me what I on many accounts will never consent to.

At the end of that year Pitt tried to remove the Duke of York, and substitute Cornwallis, a move which the King skilfully parried by making difficulties over precedence. As regards other theatres he seemed acquiescent enough: he never had a very high opinion, however, of the emigrés, *whom he supported grudgingly, guessing that they would quarrel among themselves, and feeling that they should not take refuge in England.*

XVIII. To LORD GRENVILLE

Windsor, August 2, 1794.

I cannot have a doubt in the present state of the war, of the propriety of Lord Grenville's and Mr. Pitt's opinions that the Count d'Artois,[1] accompanied by Maréchal de Castries, should

---

[1] Afterwards Charles X.

come over to settle the mode of collecting to one point such force of different descriptions of emigrant Frenchmen as can be brought to act for the restoration of monarchy in France; indeed my own inclination would tend to oblige every one of that perfidious nation here, either to go on that service, or, by the Alien Act, be removed from this country.

I trust the Count d'Artois will appear entirely incognito, and, when the business is concluded, not think of prolonging his stay.

At the end of 1794 Pitt did succeed in removing the Duke of York, whom he made Commander-in-Chief at home—an excellent appointment. The King was deeply wounded, did not hesitate to show his displeasure with Pitt, and eventually refused to discuss the matter with him.

XIX. TO WILLIAM PITT

Windsor, 25 min. past 9 a.m., November 24, 1794.

Mr. Pitt cannot be surprised at my being very much hurt at the contents of his letter. Indeed he seems to expect it, but I am certain that nothing but the thinking it his duty could have instigated him to give me so severe a blow. I am neither in a situation of mind nor from inclination inclined to enter more minutely into every part of his letter; but I am fully ready to answer the material part, namely, that though loving very much my son, and not forgetting how he saved the Republic of Holland in 1793,[1] and that his endeavours to be of service have never abated, and that to the conduct of Austria, the faithlessness of Prussia, and the cowardice of the Dutch, every failure is easily to be accounted for without laying blame on him who deserved a better fate, I shall certainly now not think it safe for him to continue in his command on the Continent, when every one seems to render his situation hazardous by either propagating unfounded complaints against him or giving credit to them.

No one will believe that I take this step but reluctantly, and the more so since no successor of note is proposed to take the command. Truly I do not see where any one is to be found that can deserve that name now the Duke of Brunswick has declined;

[1] A pardonable exaggeration.

and I am certain he will fully feel the propriety of the resolution he has taken when he finds that even a son of mine cannot withstand the torrent of abuse.

xx. To William Pitt

Queen's House, 40 min. past 8 a.m., November 27, 1794.

There could have been no advantage in discussing with Mr. Pitt yesterday the subject of his letter, as I had though reluctantly consented to his proposal. I have written to my son simply that the present complication of affairs required his presence here, but thought it more advisable not to enter any farther as to the end this business may take.

The King's influence in military affairs still continued, however, to be effective—unfortunately, since his ideas now were not so good. One would have thought that seeing what was ' the conduct of Austria, the faithlessness of Prussia, and the cowardice of the Dutch ', he would not have insisted upon retaining troops in Flanders, to the detriment of the expeditions to Quiberon Bay, and in closer support of the Vendéens. No doubt he was actuated by a desire to protect Hanover.

xxi. To Henry Dundas

Windsor, 46 min. past 8 a.m., January 14, 1795.

Mr. Secretary Dundas's letter forwarding the heads of the intended minute of Cabinet naturally inclines me to write a few lines to him. The question for consideration is one of the most weighty that can be at any time discussed. The fate of the little remains of the Dutch Republic may depend on it, as on the other side the total annihilation of the troops to be moved to the right; I undoubtedly should wish more time to deliberate previous to my giving any opinion were I not convinced that should the Dutch accept of the proposal it must in the end be of no avail, and the troops employed inevitably sacrificed. I think the only step to be taken is to permit the whole remains of the army to move to the left and retire to Germany, from whence they can return to Holland if with Austria a sufficient army can be formed to drive the French in the Spring from thence; if not, they, the British troops, may at that season by Emden if the King of Prussia shows acquiescence, or by the Weser in all cases embark for Britain. There is nothing I dread more than the Dutch from cowardice entrapping us again to defend the right, which must end in losing the British and Hessian troops employed in that service. . . .

XXII. To Henry Dundas

Weymouth, September 9, 1795.

Mr. Secretary Dundas cannot be surprised at my having read the minute of the Cabinet of the 7th this morning with some degree of pain; the proposition of withdrawing the British cavalry from Germany plainly shows that this kingdom no farther concerns itself in the fate of the Empire, which I must suppose will naturally drive the Emperor into such measures as may end the contest there with France. It certainly puts my Electoral Dominions into a most perilous situation, and must of necessity make me in my Electoral capacity submit to Prussian neutrality, and then I cannot with safety to the original possessions of my forefathers consent to leave any of my Hanoverian infantry in British pay, as the object is to employ them out of Germany, where it will be my duty to keep as many national troops as I can, to withstand as long as possible the evils that must attend the present unhappy proposition.

The King's views on naval strategy were as firm as upon other points, and many of them were quite sound.

XXIII. To Lord Spencer[1]

Queen's House, 15 min. past 11 p.m., April 17, 1795.

I am much pleased at the agreeable information received from Earl Spencer of the captures of the *Promptitude* and *Gloire* frigates by the squadron under the command of Rear-Admiral Colpoys, which event is proof of the necessity of keeping constantly detached squadrons to keep the Channel, the Bay, and North Sea clear of the enemy's ships. Had that measure been

---

[1] Who had succeeded Chatham as First Lord of the Admiralty.

uniformly adopted by the Admiralty, I am certain that by this time the trade of France would have been annihilated.

The peace negotiations of 1796 filled him with horror.

XXIV. To HENRY DUNDAS

Windsor, 30 min. past 8 a.m., February 6, 1796.

It is impossible I can think any time thrown away that is engaged in reading any pamphlet on the prospect of peace that is recommended by Mr. Secretary Dundas, whose sentiments as to the impropriety of treating at the present hour are as steady as mine. I think the language of those who were most eager for it in the Cabinet now they see the open language of the Court of Vienna must be at least staggered, but I should hope if not *cursed with mulish obstinacy,* resolved to give up the former timid opinion. You may easily believe this remark does not extend to Mr. Pitt, who may have been too much affected by the jaundiced opinion of others, but who I am certain has all along at bottom sided with us in opinion, for his arguments have not been of his own sterling growth, but as on the slave trade a display of those hatched by others.

The letter is a curious example of the ability to attribute to others the opinions we would wish them to have. Pitt was, of course, extremely eager for peace; as a good Chancellor of the Exchequer, he hated the expense of war. But however adverse the King might be to peace, he would not interfere with his ministers: yet he would not disguise his feelings.

XXV. To LORD GRENVILLE

Queen's House, February 9, 1796.

I certainly have not expressed myself clearly if what I wrote to Lord Grenville carries an idea of postponing the dispatching the messenger with the instructions that have been drawn up with the concurrence of the Cabinet; I therefore consent to his proceeding according to their advice; but I should not have acted either openly or honestly had I not expressed my own sentiments on the subject, and no reasoning of Lord Grenville on this subject could move me from what I think the line of morality, though perhaps not of politics; Italian politics are too complicated paths for my understanding.

The complications of foreign politics had never interested him much, and it seemed to him that dispatches were becoming intolerably prolix; he indicated to his Foreign Secretary that their style was susceptible of improvement.

XXVI. To Lord Grenville

Windsor, April 5, 1796.

I am much pleased at Lord Grenville's having selected part only of the papers arrived yesterday for my perusal this day, and keeping back the rest till to-morrow. I confess when the load is too great I find that I cannot retain in my mind any part of the contents, and therefore am always better pleased when the contents are not so voluminous; indeed the whole mode of carrying on public correspondence is so much more diffuse and indigested than thirty years ago, that I do not think it has made public subjects of discussion so clear as when foreign ministers thought the matter of their dispatches and not the length of them their true merit.

He was getting tired, but he was delighted when a graceless answer from France provoked a sharper tone from his own ministers on the 10th: he had expected no other style from the French, but, he added, ' I should have hoped the courage of this nation had not been so sluggish as to require this insolence to bring it to its proper tone.' Well, the ministers might do as they pleased; only when there was a threat to the status of Hanover, owing to the cupidity of Vienna and Berlin, did he burst out into a long and detailed tirade to Grenville, in which the political ideas are not altogether un-' Italian '.

XXVII. To Lord Grenville

Windsor, July 30, 1796.

. . . I am certain no one of my ministers can be surprised that I feel great repugnance at the idea of giving up any conquests made by this country, and still more when it is so vaguely stated

that the King of Prussia may suppose this goes to any extent to
obtain the object of an immediate peace; but unpleasant as that
may be, that is a point that is for the consideration of this country,
and necessity may oblige one to submit; but what right England
has to give away the rights and interests of other Princes, who
have either by England or Austria been brought forward into a
business their own inclinations did not covet, I cannot either see
a shadow of justice or the pretence of interference; and whether
the violence of France or the encouragement of Britain effect this,
I must look on it as equally hard on the individual, and subversive
of every idea that ought to actuate the stronger to support not
oppress the weaker. . . .

He was infuriated by the rebuffs met with from France.

XXVIII. TO LORD GRENVILLE

Windsor, September 23, 1796.

After the highly insolent answer to the Danish *Chargé
d'Affaires* on a demand for a passport that a person may be sent
to treat at Paris, I cannot suppose any one can be so lost to the
sentiments of self-respectability to think any other measure necessary than the letting Parliament know the offensive turn given
to what *some* might think an humiliating step taken by this
country; if such a communication will not rouse the British lion,
he must have lost his wonted energy.

XXIX. TO LORD GRENVILLE

Windsor, September 24, 1796.

As Lord Grenville and Mr. Pitt think a further step of
humiliation necessary to call forth that spirit which used to be
characteristic of this island, I will not object to the proposed
declaration being sent by a flag of truce.

*He was of the opinion that no man of note should be sent
to France, and believed that Malmesbury would think the mission
beneath him: Malmesbury, however, went; but since the French
would only make peace on the basis of their retaining all con-*

*quests, and England giving up all hers, the negotiations fell
through. The King was delighted.*

xxx. To Lord Grenville

Windsor, October 31, 1796.

I have perused the dispatches received this morning from
Lord Malmesbury which Lord Grenville had forwarded to me.
I perfectly concur in the opinion that there is not the smallest
appearance of the negotiation advancing, which, as I never
thought the present an advantageous moment for concluding
peace, cannot but give me pleasure.

*He had written to Pitt eighteen months earlier of peace with
France, that ' till the bad principles propagated by that unfortunate nation are given up, it cannot be safe for any civilized part
of the globe to treat or trust that people'.*

*But if the behaviour of his ministers was not quite what he
could wish as regards foreign affairs, at home, with the exception
of the Irish question, to which we shall return, he was more
than satisfied. It is true that he resisted, on personal grounds,
Pitt's dismissal of Thurlow from the Woolsack and his substitu-
tion of Loughborough (once Wedderburn) whom he hated, but
he does not seem to have noticed the significance of this. For
this action of Pitt's in insisting that a minister with whom he
could not get on must go, implied the principle that the Prime
Minister, and not the King, chose the Cabinet: in fact in 1792
the King let slip out of his hands the principle he had so valiantly
fought for. But he does not seem to have struggled against the
inclusion of some of the ' old Whigs' such as Portland in the
Ministry in 1794. He forgave even Burke, and willingly granted
him a pension.*

xxxi. To William Pitt

Weymouth, 4 p.m., September 5, 1794.

I have received Mr. Pitt's note enclosing the letter he has
received from Mr. Burke; misfortunes are the great softeners of
the human mind, and has in the instance of this distressed man
made him own what his warmth of temper would not have
allowed in other circumstances, viz. that he may have erred;

225

R

one quality I take him to be very susceptible of, that is gratitude, which I think covers many failings, and makes me therefore happy at being able to relieve him; his choosing the pension to be settled on his wife I thoroughly approve of, and it will with the better grace enable the other pension to be settled on him.

But then something very curious and interesting had happened: the old Whig and Tory divisions had evaporated in confusion, and the Conservative and Liberal parties had been born. It is possible to date the birth to a day, May 6th, 1690, when Fox and Burke parted company, not without tears publicly shed. For the future there was to be the party of conservation, and that of change or progress; for the first few years it is possible to call the former the party of reaction, the latter that of revolution. Pitt deserted his liberal principles and became repressive in the extreme, and Burke helped him by spreading the terror. Act after Act was passed, on treasonable correspondence, on seditious meetings, and, during the naval mutinies of '97, an Incitement to Sedition Bill was rushed through, which successive legislators thought stringent enough until the wisdom of the National Government saw fit to render it still more extreme in the year of peace and recovery, 1934. The King approved all these measures, as he did the rejection of any measure of Parliamentary reform—now judged 'inopportune' by Pitt, who also half-heartedly shelved the measures for the abolition of the slave trade so strenuously advocated by his friend Wilberforce. There was not really much fear of Jacobinism, but Burke's terror had certainly spread to the King, whose reaction it is easier to understand.

XXXII. To William Pitt

Queen's House, 53 min. past 7 a.m., May 8, 1793.

It is with infinite satisfaction I have received Mr. Pitt's note communicating the sense of the House of Commons on the renewed debate on the motion of Mr. Grey,[1] which was so clearly shown by the division of 282 against 41; and I most devoutly pray to Heaven that this Constitution may remain unimpaired to the latest posterity, as a proof of the wisdom of the nation, and its knowledge of the superior blessings it enjoys.

[1] On Parliamentary reform. Grey was afterwards the famous Earl Grey of the successful Reform Bill.

XXXIII. To William Pitt

Queen's House, 40 min. past 9 p.m., January 24, 1795.

Though I am always sorry for the unprofitable time spent in the debates of Parliament, yet at the present moment it is material that the Opposition should be entirely unmasked, and the opposing of so necessary a measure as the continuation of the partial suspension of the Habeas Corpus must in the opinion of all friends of civil order clearly show that confusion is no bar to their ambitions.[1]

XXXIV. To William Pitt

Windsor, 35 min. past 7 a.m., November 11, 1795.

The House of Commons having by so handsome a majority approved of bringing in a Bill for more effectually preventing seditious meetings and assemblies cannot but give me the greatest pleasure, as the most convincing proof of attachment to our happy Constitution and resolution to continue that blessing to future generations, which cannot be ensured if a stop is not made to the seditious meetings. I have equal satisfaction in finding by Mr. Pitt's note that the small minority was imprudent enough to express violence on this occasion, as it must still more open the eyes of well intentioned persons as to the designs of those champions.

The year 1797 brought two events of first-class importance, the suspension of cash payments by the Bank, and the naval mutinies.

It is perhaps only recently that the importance of the first event has been recognized, though the extremely interesting debates which followed upon Pitt's action in giving the Bank the nation's credit as backing for bank credit show that some members of Parliament realized that this might be to make government subservient to finance: what appeared more important to the King was that the action was taken, not by Parliament, but by an Order in Council. The panic run on the Bank made immediate action imperative.

---

[1] Confusion was no bar to the King's expressing his feelings, but a moment's thought will show what he meant.

xxxv. To William Pitt

Windsor, 10 min. past 8 a.m., February 26, 1797.

I have received Mr. Pitt's note by which I find that timidity, which I have ever thought but too probable to arise in this country, has already got to an extent that is truly unreasonable, but that calls the more for the exertions of those who look with a more judicious eye to lose no time in taking measures to prevent that alarm from being fatal to public credit. I believe the idea of restraining the Bank from paying cash till men's minds are more calm is the only solid plan that can be adopted.[1] . . . I suppose the predatory attack and landing in Pembrokeshire[2] will rather add to the dismay of the timid; but I trust that cool firmness which used to be the national attendant of Englishmen will again appear.

xxxvi. To William Pitt

Queen's House, 20 min. past 10 p.m., February 26, 1797.

The messages of the two Houses of Parliament which having signed I return to Mr. Pitt, so fully make me a party with the Privy Councillors who have signed the Order to the Bank to discontinue issuing cash till the sense of Parliament had been taken, that I do not in the least object to that method having been preferred to an order in my name countersigned by them. I cannot conclude without again expressing that the times require that no measure which may appear on consideration necessary must be deferred for want of the sanction of law; the safety of the country is the supreme law, and must at all hazards be effected, and when no stretch of authority is made but where that is the object, I trust the candour of Parliament will ever approve the motive of the exertion.

The candour of Parliament, however, might have its disadvantages, as the King saw when he wrote the following letter,

[1] It was originally intended to suspend cash payments for a month only: it was some twenty years before the country returned to gold.

[2] A tiny force, consisting mainly of banditti, had raided Ilfracombe, then gone across to Fishguard, where they were captured by the local militia—*not* by a body of Welsh women dressed in red cloaks, as the legend has it.

*in which is to be seen running fully that curious braggart vein
which crept increasingly into his correspondence: he was once
more becoming over-excited, as a looseness of grammar, unusual
even for him, tends to show.*

XXXVII. TO WILLIAM PITT

Queen's House, March 2, 1797.

Mr. Pitt knows I did not like the having given a little way
towards the motion brought forward yesterday by what was
thought prudent on Tuesday,[1] and to that alone do I attribute
the majority being less this morning than might have been wished
on so material a subject as what regards public credit.   It is unpleasant to touch upon errors, but how are we to act right but
by avoiding former ones?   I think Parliament generally enters
warmly into all measures brought forward, but of late years
unfortunately the subsequent steps got a languor that often shows
a want of energy, which I fear often arises from too much
candour, and that those who are disinclined to any exertion somehow or other are too much attended to and consequently that
whilst the object is getting through its various stages it is totally
different to the original proposition.   My nature is quite different; I never assent till I am convinced what is proposed is right,
and then I keep them—I never allow that to be destroyed by after
thoughts which on all subjects tend to weaken never to strengthen
the original proposal.

*The gravity of the naval mutiny, which broke out at Spithead
on April 16th, was at once apparent to everyone.   It was not
so much a mutiny as a strike for better pay and improved
conditions.   Spencer led an Admiralty Board to Portsmouth to
investigate.*

XXXVIII. TO HENRY DUNDAS

Windsor, 26 min. past 8 p.m., April 21, 1797.

I received last night Mr. Secretary Dundas's note accompanied
with copies of the two letters he had received from Lord Spencer

---

[1] On Tuesday Pitt had proposed a secret committee to inquire into the
affairs of the Bank; the next day Fox moved that the cause of the crisis
might be inquired into.

at Portsmouth, with copies of the papers that had been drawn up by the Board of Admiralty there, as means of restoring tranquillity in the Line of Battle ships riding in the road of Spithead. The spirit seems to be of a most dangerous kind, as at the same time that the mutiny is conducted with a degree of coolness it is not void of method; how this could break out at once without any suspicion before arising seems unaccountable; I hope by the few words stated by the tellograph that the men will return to some obedience, but it must require a cruise and much time before any reliance can be placed on a restoration of discipline.

Though the Board conceded most of the men's demands, there was such delay in passing the necessary Bill through Parliament that the mutiny broke out afresh.

XXXIX. To Lord Spencer

Queen's House, 50 min. past 7 o'clock, May 9, 1797.

I cannot sufficiently express my concern at the account received last evening from Earl Spencer of the fresh mutiny in the Channel Fleet, which is accompanied by more serious outrages than the first. It would be idle to lament that the measures for increasing their pay have been delayed for two weeks coming forward in Parliament, or that the wind has not proved easterly which would have carried them out to sea. It is very difficult to decide what can with any degree of propriety be now proposed. . . . If I could fix on any idea that seemed proper I should not have failed to have communicated it to Earl Spencer.

The measure proposed, perhaps by the King, was that Howe should be sent down to talk to the seamen, which he did to their satisfaction. But before this mutiny was composed, another had broken out at the Nore. A Board went down there, determined, with the King's hearty backing, to make no concessions whatever. This being the case, the King's pardon proved ineffectual, and it was determined to starve the sailors out.

XL. To Lord Spencer

Queen's House, 18 min. past 8 p.m., May 30, 1797.

I am sorry to find the humiliating step of a Board of Admiralty being themselves the bearers of the pardon I had prepared has not had its due effect; but I highly approve that no concessions have been made to the mutinous ships; I trust all must now see that vigour with temper can alone restore discipline in the fleet, and the steps now taken will I trust in a little time bring the men to a sense of their duty, and that the preventing their getting fresh water will soon oblige them to submit.

The King was, naturally, gratified at the collapse of the mutiny.

XLI. TO LORD SPENCER

Queen's House, 55 min. past 6 p.m., June 14, 1797.

The account I have received from Earl Spencer of the arrival of the *Sandwich* and *Monmouth* in the harbour of Sheerness, and that troops have been placed in each of them, and Richard Parker and several others carefully lodged in different places of confinement, gives me great satisfaction. I trust no means will be omitted of getting, if possible, at the instigators on shore of this outrageous mutiny. . . .

Richard Parker, the leader, but not the instigator, of the mutiny was hanged, with twenty-eight others; the instigators on shore, among whom the more excitable included Fox and Whitbread, were never found, for the simple reason that they did not exist. The mutinies were a spontaneous protest against loathsome conditions.

For the rest the war dragged on, the King being enthusiastic enough about successes, hating, but acquiescing in any overtures for peace, while at home he continued to be jubilant over checks to all attempts to ease repressive measures, or to introduce any measure of Parliamentary reform.

XLII. TO WILLIAM PITT

Queen's House, 50 min. past 7 a.m., May 27, 1797.

After what had been reported for some days, I had supposed that the division against Mr. Fox's motion for a reform of Parliament would have been as large as stated but the minority less; but his art has succeeded in keeping his party together, and of course some speculative men as on former occasions have joined him in this vote: many of whom probably were solely biased from desire of a little apparent consequence; but I am certain every freeholder in the kingdom as well as the inhabitants of boroughs must feel their consequence hurt by the proposal.

XLIII. To Lord Grenville

Queen's House, June 1, 1797.

I shall not do justice to my feelings if I did not in confidence state to Lord Grenville that the many humiliating steps I have been advised to take in the last nine months have taken so deep an impression on my mind that I undoubtedly feel this kingdom lowered in its proper estimation much below what I should have flattered myself could have been the case during the latter part of my reign; that I certainly look on the additional measure now proposed as a confirmation of that opinion; at the same time that Lord Grenville has certainly worded it as little exceptionally as its nature would permit. I cannot add more on this occasion but that if both Houses of Parliament are in as tame a state of mind as it is pretended, I do not see the hopes that either war can be continued with effect or peace obtained but of the most disgraceful and unsolid tenure.

XLIV. To Henry Dundas

Weymouth, October 9, 1799.

My mind is greatly relieved by the receipt the last evening of Mr. Secretary Dundas's letter accompanied by the public letter he has received from the Duke of York; after this glorious success we must wait till we hear from him, for I look upon it that from home the duty is to consider how far the proposals from the army can be fulfilled, not to plan the measures the general is to adopt; which is the fatal line of the Court of Vienna which has been the true cause of the Austrian army's ill success after having by the gallantry of the generals and troops given reason to form the most promising hopes of success which the directions from Court have ever thwarted; indeed it is impossible without being on the spot and seeing the face of the country that any well grounded directions can be given, further than pointing out what is the general object wished, but how to be effected or when must be left to those who are on the spot.

It cannot be said that the success in Holland had been very brilliant, especially as it was immediately succeeded by a retirement; but the Duke of York had been in command, and the scheme had been Dundas's, so such a letter is not surprising. The remainder of the letter is a commonplace seldom acted on in actual practice. A rather earlier letter to Spencer was a better justified piece of congratulation, and expresses very clearly the King's idea of what the war was really about. The cynical may find it naïve, but on the surface there was a good deal to be said for the attitude.

XLV. To Lord Spencer

Weymouth, September 4, 1799.

I cannot return the Admiralty box to Lord Spencer without expressing the joy I feel at the surrender of the Dutch fleet. We having taken their ships by force of arms[1] might have been more brilliant, but not so agreeable to the upright conduct followed alone by this nation; the restoring the established governments of Europe, not a thirst for conquest or plunder.

The King's opinions, however, had little if any effect on the war measures: he would write to Dundas criticizing the frequency of orders and counter-orders: he was anxious that the troops destined for Ferrol should be brought home to be refitted, a piece of advice that was ignored. Where, however, his opinions did have an effect, perhaps disastrous, was on the question of Ireland, which at this time came to a head.

The idea of a union had long been in the King's mind, as has been seen, but in his view it was in no way associated with Catholic emancipation. In the minds of his ministers the two had been closely connected, and not only Pitt, but the members of the ' old Whig' faction whom he had brought in to strengthen his government, favoured emancipation to the length of allowing Roman Catholics to sit in the Union Parliament. They were aware, however, that the matter would have to be approached

[1] They had capitulated, being bottled up in the Texel by the British fleet, and cut off from land supplies by the Duke of York's force.

carefully in Ireland, where the Castle group would be opposed to it, and with infinite discretion where the King was concerned. Unfortunately, when Lord Fitzwilliam, Portland's nominee, was appointed Viceroy in 1794, he at once made advances to the Romanists; and when he landed in 1795, promptly dismissed the more stubborn Protestants in the Irish government. The King was immediately up in arms at what he called ' the strange conduct of Earl Fitzwilliam '. He poured out his sentiments to his Prime Minister.

XLVI. To WILLIAM PITT

Queen's House, February 6, 1795.

Having yesterday, after the Drawing Room, seen the Duke of Portland, who mentioned the receipt of letters from the Lord Lieutenant of Ireland, which to my greatest astonishment propose the total change of the principles of government which have been followed by every administration in that kingdom since the abdication of King James the Second, and consequently overturning the fabric that the wisdom of our forefathers esteemed necessary, and which the laws of this country have directed; and thus after no longer stay than three weeks in Ireland venturing to condemn the labours of ages, and wanting an immediate adoption of ideas which every man of property in Ireland and every friend to the Protestant religion must feel diametrically contrary to those he has imbibed from his earliest youth.

Undoubtedly the Duke of Portland made this communication to sound my sentiments previous to the Cabinet meeting to be held to-morrow on this weighty subject. I expressed my surprise at the idea of admitting Roman Catholics to vote in Parliament, but chose to avoid entering further into the subject, and only heard the substance of the propositions without giving my sentiments. But the more I reflect on the subject, the more I feel the danger of the proposal, and therefore should not think myself free from blame if I did not put my thoughts on paper even in the present coarse shape, the moment being so pressing, and not sufficient time to arrange them in a more digested shape previous to the Duke of Portland's laying the subject before the Cabinet.

The above proposal is contrary to the conduct of every

European government, and I believe to that of every State on the globe. In the States of Germany, the Lutheran, Calvinist, and Roman Catholic religions are universally permitted, yet each respective State has but one Church establishment, to which the States of the country and those holding any civil employment must be conformists; Court offices and military commissions may be held also by persons of either of the other persuasions, but the number of such is very small. The Dutch provinces admit Lutherans and Roman Catholics in some subsidized regiments, but in civil employments the Calvinists are alone capable of holding them.

Ireland varies from most other countries by property residing almost entirely in the hands of the Protestants, whilst the lower classes of the people are chiefly Roman Catholics. The change proposed, therefore, must disoblige the greater number to benefit a few, the inferior orders not being of rank to gain favourably by the change. That they may also be gainers, it is proposed that an army be kept constantly in Ireland, and a kind of yeomanry, which in reality would be Roman Catholic police corps, established, which would keep the Protestant interest under awe.

It is but fair to confess that the whole of this plan is the strongest justification of the old servants of the Crown in Ireland, for having objected to the former indulgences that have been granted, as it is now pretended these have availed nothing, unless this total change of political principle be admitted.

English government ought well to consider before it gives any encouragement to a proposition which cannot fail sooner or later to separate the two kingdoms, or by way of establishing a similar line of conduct in this kingdom adopt measures to prevent which my family was invited to mount the throne of this kingdom in preference to the House of Savoy.

One might suppose the authors of this scheme had not viewed the tendency or extent of the question, but were actuated alone by the peevish inclination of humiliating the old friends of English government in Ireland, or from the desire of paying implicit obedience to the heated imagination of Mr. Burke.

Besides the discontent and changes which must be occasioned by the dereliction of all the principles that have been held as wise by our ancestors, it is impossible to foresee how far it may alienate the minds of this kingdom; for though I fear religion is but little attended to by persons of rank, and that the word *toleration*, or rather *indifference* to that sacred subject, has been too much admitted by them, yet the bulk of the nation has not been spoiled by foreign travels and manners, and still feels the blessing of having a fixed principle from whence the source of every tie to society and government must trace its origin.

I cannot conclude without expressing that the subject is beyond the decision of any Cabinet of ministers—that, could they form an opinion in favour of such a measure, it would be highly dangerous, without previous concert with the leading men of every order in the State, to send any encouragement to the Lord Lieutenant on this subject; and if received with the same suspicion I do, I am certain it would be safer even to change the new administration in Ireland, if its continuance depends on the success of this proposal, than to prolong its existence on grounds that must sooner or later ruin one if not both kingdoms.

Fitzwilliam in fact was recalled, and the King insisted that all whom he had dismissed should be restored to their posts under his successor, the second Earl Camden. In the meantime the King sought to strengthen his position by taking legal opinion, and addressed himself to the Lord Chief Justice, Lord Kenyon.

XLVII. TO LORD KENYON

Queen's House, March 7, 1795.

The question that has been so improperly patronized by the Lord Lieutenant of Ireland in favour of the Papists, though certainly very properly silenced here, yet seems not to have been viewed in what seems to me the strongest point of view—its militating against the Coronation oath and many existing statutes. I have, therefore, stated the accompanying queries on paper, to which I desire the Lord Kenyon will, after due consideration, state his opinion in the same manner, and should be glad if he would also acquire the sentiments of the Attorney-General[1] on this most serious subject.

[1] Sir John Scott, afterwards Lord Chancellor and Earl of Eldon. George III had from the first had a very high opinion of him.

Enclosure. The following queries on the present attempt to abolish all distinctions in religion in Ireland, with the intention of favouring the Roman Catholics in that kingdom, are stated from the desire of learning whether this can be done without affecting the constitution of this country; if not, there is no occasion to view whether this measure, in itself, be not highly improper.

The only laws which now affect the Papists in Ireland are the Acts of Supremacy and Uniformity, the Test Act, and the Bill of Rights. It seems to require very serious investigation how far the King can give his assent to a repeal of any one of these acts, without a breach of his Coronation oath, and of the Articles of Union with Scotland.

The construction put on the Coronation oath by the Parliament at the Revolution seems strongly marked in the Journals of the House of Commons, where the clause was proposed by way of rider to the Bill for establishing the Coronation oath, declaring that nothing contained in it should be construed to bind down the King and Queen, their heirs and successors, not to give the royal assent to any Bill for qualifying the Act of Uniformity, so far as to render it palatable to Protestant dissenters, and the clause was negatived upon a division. This leads to the implication that the Coronation oath was understood, at the Revolution, to bind the Crown not to assent to any repeal of any of the existing laws at the Revolution, or which were then enacted for the maintenance and defence of the Protestant religion, as by law established.

If the oath was understood to bind the Crown not to assent to the repeal of the Act of Uniformity in favour of Protestant dissenters, it would seem to bind the Crown full as strongly not to assent to the repeal of the Act of Supremacy, as the Test Act, in favour of Roman Catholics.

Another question arises from the provisions of the Act limiting the succession to the Crown, by which a forfeiture of the Crown is expressly enacted if the King should hold communication, or be reconciled to, the Church of Rome. May not the repeal of the Act of Supremacy, and the establishing of the Popish religion in any of the hereditary dominions, be construed as amounting to a reconciliation with the Church of Rome?

Would not the Chancellor of England incur some risk in affixing the Great Seal to a Bill for giving the Pope a concurrent ecclesiastical jurisdiction with the King?

By the Articles of Union with Scotland, it is declared to be an essential and fundamental article that the King of Great Britain shall maintain the Church of England as by law established in England, Ireland, and Berwick-upon-Tweed.

The bargain made by England in 1782, by Yelverton's Act,[1] gives rise to the question whether the repeal of any of the English statutes adopted by that Act would not be a direct violation of the compact made by the Parliament in Ireland with Great Britain.

The law was thus invoked to buttress up the King's ineradicable prejudice.

Fitzwilliam's gesture, his recall, the repressive policy of Camden, all served to fan a growing flame, which threatening enough in 1797 through the agitation of the United Irishmen, burst out in the rebellion of 1798.

XLVIII. TO WILLIAM PITT

Windsor, 43 min. past 7 a.m., June 10, 1798.

. . . This country remains in a very naked state by the large detachment sent to Ireland, which nothing but the greatest necessity can justify; but I cannot think any forces sent there can be of real avail unless a military Lord Lieutenant, and that the Marquis of Cornwallis, with Mr. Pelham as his secretary, be instantly sent there. The present Lord Lieutenant is too much agitated at the present hour, and totally under the control of the Irish Privy Councillors, whose hurry has been the real cause of the two failures,[2] which, if repeated, will by degrees teach the Irish rebels to fight.

Cornwallis was perhaps not quite the man the King had hoped for, since he proved almost as liberal as Sir Ralph Aber-

[1] Barry Yelverton, at that time Irish Attorney-General, now Baron Avonmore in the Irish peerage, later in the English, as a reward for his services in furthering the union. His Act relieved the Catholics from some of the restraints placed on their education and the exercise of their religion.

[2] Presumably the early rebel successes near Wexford.

cromby had done the year before, who had been recalled because he would not permit unbridled licence among his soldiers. By the time Cornwallis arrived the rebellion was nearly crushed, and he proved a conciliatory Viceroy. The utility of the rebellion to the idea of union did not escape the King.

XLIX. To WILLIAM PITT

Windsor, 36 min. past 7 a.m., June 13, 1798.

Mr. Pitt has in my opinion saved Ireland by engaging Mr. Pelham in the present state of that kingdom to return there as soon as his health will permit, which should be known there at least when the Marquis Cornwallis arrives. That gentleman's knowledge of the country must be of great utility to the new Lord Lieutenant, who must not lose the present moment of terror for frightening the supporters of the Castle into an union with this country, and no farther indulgences must be granted to the Roman Catholics, as no country can be governed where there is more than one established religion; the others may be tolerated, but that cannot extend farther than leave to perform their religious duties according to the tenets of their Church, for which indulgence they cannot have any share in the government of the State.

The question of the union, then, began to be openly discussed, but all the while the King kept a wary eye open for any step which might lead, however little, in the direction of the horrid monster Emancipation.

L. To WILLIAM PITT

Queen's House, 56 min. past 8 a.m., January 24, 1799.

. . . I cannot help . . . expressing to Mr. Pitt some surprise at having seen in a letter from Lord Castlereagh to the Duke of Portland on Monday an idea of an established stipend by the authority of government for the Catholic clergy of Ireland. I am certain any encouragement to such an idea must give real offence to the Established Church in Ireland, as well as to the true friends of our constitution; for it is certainly creating a second Church establishment which could not but be highly injurious. The tolerating Dissenters is fair; but the trying to perpetuate a separation in religious opinions by providing for the support of their clergy as an establishment is certainly going far beyond the bounds of justice or policy.

Since nothing whatever was said about the Catholics as the measures for the union proceeded, the King was highly pleased at their progress.

LI. TO WILLIAM PITT

Queen's House, 7 a.m., May 6, 1800.

The information of the last night from Mr. Pitt that all the resolutions on the Articles of Union with Ireland had been agreed to by the House of Commons, and ordered to be communicated to the House of Lords with an Address, laying them before me, gives me sincere satisfaction: I therefore trust there can now be no doubt that either on Thursday, or at latest on Friday, I shall receive the joint Address of the two Houses, which will, I trust, effect one of the most useful measures that has been effected during my reign, one that will give stability to the whole empire, and from the want of industry and capital in Ireland be but little felt by this country as diminishing its trade and manufactures. For the advantages to Ireland can only arise by slow degrees, and the wealth of Great Britain will undoubtedly, by furnishing the rest of the globe with its articles of commerce, not feel any material disadvantage in that particular from the future prosperity of Ireland.

It is not a particularly generous view of the Irish situation, nevertheless here was a perpetual *trouble apparently removed, and the King might well congratulate himself. But there was a bombshell in store for him. For though nothing about emancipation had appeared in the Articles of Union, there was an implicit understanding between the Cabinet and the Irish that emancipation would be granted almost at once, and that Roman Catholics would be allowed to occupy seats at Westminster. This, however, had been carefully kept from the King. In August, Castlereagh, who since 1798 had been Irish Secretary in succession to Pelham, and had materially helped the union by promising emancipation, came over to England to urge Pitt to proceed with the measure. The Cabinet then asked Lough-borough to go to Weymouth to talk the King over, but, appar-ently, Loughborough as usual played double: he seems to have advised the King that to grant Catholic emancipation would be contrary to the coronation oath. The Cabinet, however, con-tinued to lay its plans, and the King's speech designed for the opening of the first Imperial Parliament contained a guarded reference to future benefits to be conferred on the Irish, a refer-ence which the King unsuspiciously agreed to on January 23rd, 1801. But on the 27th or 28th some whisper reached him: at all events on the latter day there was a curious outburst at a levée to Windham and Dundas. What was this the young Lord had brought from Ireland and that they were going to throw at his head? The most Jacobinical thing he had ever heard! He would regard any one who agreed to it as his personal enemy. He does indeed seem to have been taken by surprise, for some ten days later he wrote to Dundas.*

LII. To Henry Dundas

Windsor, February 7, 1801.

I cannot but regret that on the late unhappy occasion I had not been treated with more confidence, previous to forming an opinion which to my greatest surprise I learnt on Thursday from Earl Spencer has been in agitation even since Lord Castlereagh came over in August, yet of which I never had the smallest sus-picion till within very few weeks; but so desirous was I to avoid the present conclusion that except what passed with Earl Spencer and Lord Grenville about three weeks past and an hint I gave to Mr. Secretary Dundas on Wednesday sevennight, I have been silent on the subject, and indeed hoping that Mr. Pitt had not pledged himself on what I cannot with my sentiments of religious and political duty think myself at liberty to concur. Mr. Secretary Dundas has known my opinions when he corresponded with the Earl of Westmoreland the Lord Lieutenant of Ireland,[1] and at least will do me the justice to allow that both then, and when afterwards brought forward by the Earl Fitzwilliam, my language perfectly coincided with my present conduct.

[1] Who had been displaced to make room for Fitzwilliam.

241

In the meantime matters had come to a head. On January 31st Pitt wrote the King his famous letter putting forward the case for Catholic emancipation, saying that his view was unalterably fixed, and that though he promised not to agitate the matter for the moment, he felt that if the King would not allow a measure to be brought forward at some time with the full weight of the government behind it, he must resign.

LIII. TO WILLIAM PITT

Queen's House, February 1, 1801.

I should not do justice to the warm impulse of my heart if I entered on the subject most unpleasant to my mind without first expressing that the cordial affection I have for Mr. Pitt, as well as high opinion of his talents and integrity, greatly add to my uneasiness on this occasion; but a sense of religious as well as political duty has made me, from the moment I mounted the throne, consider the Oath that the wisdom of our forefathers has enjoined the Kings of this realm to take at their Coronation, and enforced by the obligation of instantly following it in the course of the ceremony with taking the Sacrament, as so binding a religious obligation on me to maintain the fundamental maxims on which our Constitution is placed, namely the Church of England being the established one, and that those who hold employments in the State must be members of it, and consequently obliged not only to take oaths against Popery, but to receive the Holy Communion agreeably to the rites of the Church of England.

This principle of duty must therefore prevent me from discussing any proposition tending to destroy this groundwork of our happy Constitution, and much more so that now mentioned by Mr. Pitt, which is no less than the complete overthrow of the whole fabric.

When the Irish propositions were transmitted to me by a joint message from both Houses of the British Parliament, I told the Lords and Gentlemen sent on that occasion that I would with pleasure and without delay forward them to Ireland; but that, as individuals, I could not help acquainting them that my inclination to an Union with Ireland was principally founded on a trust that the uniting the Established Churches of the two kingdoms would for ever shut the door to any further measures with respect to the Roman Catholics.

These two instances must show Mr. Pitt that my opinions are not those formed on the moment, but such as I have imbibed for forty years, and from which I never can depart; but, Mr. Pitt, once acquainted with my sentiments, his assuring me that he will stave off the only question whereon I fear from his letter we can never agree—for the advantage and comfort of continuing to have his advice and exertions in public affairs I will certainly abstain from talking on this subject, which is the one nearest my heart. I cannot help if others pretend to guess at my opinions, which I have never disguised : but if those who unfortunately differ with me will keep this subject at rest, I will on my part, most correctly on my part, be silent also; but this restraint I shall put on myself from affection for Mr. Pitt, but further I cannot go, for I cannot sacrifice my duty to any consideration.

[*The full flavour of that paragraph can only be appreciated by realizing that this was an answer, too naïve by half to be quite straightforward, to the last paragraph of Pitt's letter, where the Prime Minister had very tactfully, but very firmly, told his sovereign that such outbursts as he had been guilty of to Dundas and Windham at the* levée *must really not be repeated. The King seemed to think—and he repeated the idea in a later letter —that if he kept mum about Catholic emancipation, Pitt would only be playing the game if he refrained from bringing it forward. It was really quite childish; but the King was approaching one of his periods of lunacy.*]

Though I do not pretend to have the power of changing Mr. Pitt's opinion when thus unfortunately fixed, yet I shall hope his sense of duty will prevent his retiring from his present situation to the end of my life; for I can with great truth assert that I shall, from public and private considerations, feel great regret if I shall ever find myself obliged at any time, from a sense of religious and political duty, to yield to his entreaties of retiring from his seat at the Board of Treasury.

Nevertheless he at once began to try to form another govern-
ment, with Addington at its head. Indeed in three days Pitt,
followed by most of the important ministers—Grenville, Spencer,
Dundas, Windham—resigned. The new ministry, however,
was not immediately ready to take over, thus the farewell was
delayed.

LIV. To William Pitt

Queen's House, 8 p.m., February 18, 1801.

My dear Pitt,

As you are closing much to my sorrow your political career,
I cannot help expressing the joy I feel that the Ways and Means
for the present year have been this day agreed to in the Committee
without any debate and apparently to the satisfaction of the
House.

George R.

It seems a curious note to write to a man who has served you
faithfully for nearly twenty years: but there is ' My dear Pitt '.
Pitt thanked him, and on the 20th received another note:

. . . His Majesty cannot help expressing infinite satisfaction
at Mr. Pitt's feeling the expressions of the note the King wrote
him on Wednesday evening : they were only the effusions of the
real affection His Majesty will ever have for Mr. Pitt.

One may wonder what the ' effusions ' were to which the
King so complacently referred; but then, he was already ill. The
excitement had been too much for him: already on the 16th the
usual feverish symptoms had appeared; on the 22nd his condition
became alarming, on the 23rd he was definitely ill. But the
attack was very short, and on March 9th he was to all intents and
purposes well again: but it was not until March 14th that Pitt
was able to hand his place over to Addington.

It seems that, to assist the King's recovery, Pitt had given him
some sort of pledge that he would never again bring forward this
vexed question of emancipation. And for the rest of his reign,
while he did reign, any suggestion of bringing the matter up
again elicited from him a threat that he would once more go mad.

LV. TO LORD SPENCER[1]

Windsor Castle, February 10, 1807.

The King had received Earl Spencer's letter transmitting a minute of the Cabinet with the dispatch from the Lord Lieutenant of Ireland, and the draft of the proposed answer to which it refers. Whilst His Majesty approves of that part of the answer which instructs the Lord Lieutenant to keep back any petition from the Roman Catholics of Ireland, and to prevent the renewal of a question upon which His Majesty's sentiments and the general sense of the country have already been so clearly pronounced, the King cannot but express the most serious concern that any proposal should have been made to him for the introduction of a clause in the Mutiny Bill which would remove a restriction upon the Roman Catholics, forming in his opinion a most essential feature of the question, and so strongly connected with the whole that the King trusts his Parliament never would under any circumstances agree to it. His Majesty's objections to this proposal do not result from any slight motives. They have never varied, for they arise from the principles by which he has been guided through life, and to which he is determined to adhere. On this question a line has been drawn from which he cannot depart; nor can Earl Spencer be surprised that such should be His Majesty's feelings upon this occasion, as he cannot have forgotten what occurred when the subject was brought forward seven years ago, and he had hoped in consequence that it would never again have been agitated.

The proposal was mild enough; it was only to allow Roman Catholics to rise to the rank of Colonel, not only in Ireland, as they had been enabled to do since 1793, but also in England and Scotland. Writing two days later to his Prime Minister, Grenville, he signified his painful assent to the change; yet it was, he felt, the thin end of the wedge. The letter concluded with the King's hope ' that this proof of his forbearance will secure him from being at a future period distressed by any further proposal connected with this question'. On this assurance not being given Parliament was dissolved, and the King, being once

---

[1] Then Secretary of State for the Home Department.

more united in feeling with most of his subjects—at least the voting portion of them—again experienced a triumph not unlike the one brought him by the elections of 1784.

Even though in the latter years of his reign the King could wield little influence in the political field, on this question, which had become an idée fixe with him, his view was still of paramount importance. It was this which prevented Pitt, when he came back to power in 1804, from including in his ministry not only Fox, but many of his old ministers: when Pitt died in 1806, and the Ministry of All the Talents was formed, Fox promised to leave the Test Act immaculate. The royal influence here was disastrous enough, but for the rest the King had little say in affairs. If he had been a spectator during Pitt's long ministry, it was because he approved of what Pitt did; if he was only a spectator from now until his final illness, it was because he could be nothing else.

*　　　*　　　*　　　*　　　*　　　*

The two following letters exhibit the King in his more personal relations. The first was written on the occasion of the death of Lady Mary Howe, only a few months after the death of her father, Admiral Earl Howe.

LVI. TO THE HON. MRS. HOWE

Queen's House, April 9, 1800.

The King would not for one moment have diverted Mrs. Howe from her heroic efforts to support Countess Howe on the fresh severe affliction she has met with, but from the strong desire he has that, on the first proper occasion, she will express in his name to the Countess how sincerely he participates in her grief. It is impossible to have known the truly angelic mind now departed, and be insensible to the feelings of the excellent mother.

The King trusts that the true confidence the Countess has always placed in Divine Providence will be her true stay on this most trying occasion, and that both she and the Baroness Howe will not too strongly struggle against the real feelings of nature. Tears are the necessary indulgence on such an occasion; and Divine Providence certainly cannot blame humanity for giving way to what alone in the first moments can give ease. The mind must have attained some calm before the only true assistant, religion, can give its real aid. My mind is so full I could add much more, but stop on reflecting that I am detaining Mrs. Howe, whose good sense and singular resolution are necessarily employed in supporting the mother and daughter.

LVII. TO THE BISHOP OF ST. DAVID'S[1]

Windsor, December 29, 1799.

MY LORD,

The cordial satisfaction I have derived from hearing the five sermons you have preached during your residence, and that most excellent one at my chapel on Christmas Day, obliges me to thank you on paper, and to assure you that I shall feel most happy when I shall judge it the proper opportunity to advance you to a more lucrative Bishopric. Your talents and exemplary conduct would alone stimulate me, had I not the additional motive of your being a son of the truest and best friend I ever had, and out of regard to his memory I truly rejoice that he has in the Church and Army[2] two sons who will ever reflect credit on the name of Stuart.

I cannot conclude without expressing my warmest hopes that you will publish some treatise in defence of the Christian Religion.

It was with great satisfaction, therefore, that in about six months' time, the King was able to advance to the Primacy of Ireland the son of his old mentor. It is a pity that the King did not mention whether or not the notion of more lucrative Bishoprics should enter into the defence of the Christian religion.

---

[1] William Stuart, fifth son of the Earl of Bute.
[2] Lieutenant-General the Hon. Sir Charles Stuart, K.B.

CHAPTER VIII

LAST YEARS

The King's virtual retirement is not surprising, for the strain of forty years of being a hard-working party manager, in some respects his own Prime Minister, would have told on minds more stable than his; only on points which excited him could he be roused to his old furious energy, and this was not good for him. He had another attack of his illness in the summer of 1801, and again in 1804, and he was always haunted by the terror of a Regency, with his abhorred son misruling the country, whilst Fox, like the envenomed toad, sat at his ear. Moreover in 1805 he began to lose his sight, and had at long last to employ a secretary. The ordinary routine work of constitutional monarchy, addresses to Parliament, reviewing his troops, the petty business of signing papers, was enough to occupy his working energies.

Besides this, there were the family squabbles, intrigues, and misdemeanours, which increased at this period. We get a glimpse of acute household tension in the postscript to a note he wrote to Lord Hawkesbury from Kew as early as April 24th, 1800.

Lord Hawkesbury is desired to send the enclosed to my son Prince Adolphus at Kew by a messenger, as difficulties are made of letting me send it to him though but two rooms off.[1]

Most of his seven sons gave him trouble; during the last few years of his sane life the Queen refused to be left alone with him, and his only solace was in his daughters.

It had seemed a few years before that family matters might clear up, especially as regards the tenderest point, the Prince of Wales, who in 1794, though he had only a little earlier stated his determination never to marry (within the bounds of the Royal Marriage Act), declared his willingness to marry his cousin.

1. To William Pitt

Weymouth, August 24, 1794.

Agreeable to what I mentioned to Mr. Pitt before I came here, I have this morning seen the Prince of Wales, who has acquainted me with his having broken off all connection with Mrs. Fitz-

---

[1] Holograph. Add. MSS. 38190, f. 1.

herbert, and his desire of entering into a more creditable line of life by marrying; expressing at the same time that his wish is that my niece, the Princess of Brunswick, may be the person. Undoubtedly she is the person who naturally must be most agreeable to me. I expressed my approbation of the idea, provided his plan was to lead a life that would make him appear respectable, and consequently render the Princess happy. He assured me that he perfectly coincided with me in opinion. I then said that till Parliament assembled no arrangement could be taken except my sounding my sister, that no idea of any other marriage may be encouraged.

The Prince, as we know, did not suddenly adopt a more respectable way of life: he did not permanently give up Mrs. Fitzherbert, he constantly accumulated further debts, and he made his wife miserable.

A legal marriage was all the more gratifying, since the year before, Prince Augustus had morganatically married Lady Augusta Murray. He lived abroad, but in 1800 much perturbed the King by suddenly returning, an occasion which gave the Prince of Wales an opportunity of acting with exemplary correctitude.

11. To William Pitt

Queen's House, May 13, 1800.

I am desirous of acquainting Mr. Pitt that to my great surprise, on Tuesday, May 6th, I received a packet from the Prince of Wales containing a note from Lady Augusta Murray to the Earl of Moira desiring him to come to her, and a letter from him to the Prince of Wales stating that though not acquainted with the lady he had gone to her, and to his utmost astonishment found Augustus there, who desired him to acquaint the Prince of Wales with his arrival. I instantly sent back the papers and desired that the Lord Chancellor might be acquainted with the event. On returning from Kew, the Prince of Wales came and stated that it was by the Chancellor's advice he had forwarded the papers to me, that he thought it highly improper Augustus should remain in the house with Lady Augusta, and that he (the Prince of Wales) would persuade him to remove to

Carlton House if it met with my approbation. I encouraged this as I thought it highly indecent that in addition to the great impropriety of coming over in stealth, it should bear the additional appearance of being in defiance of me by the quarters he had taken. When I saw the Chancellor I mentioned what has past; that he had my leave to visit Augustus when at Carlton House if it was desired; but that I could as yet have no directions to communicate; that I saw no objection to Augustus's seeing Lord Thurlow and Mr. Erskine[1] as they could not but convince him of the nullity of his marriage. He has seen them both, and they have in the most decided manner held the language he [I?] expected. On Friday the Prince of Wales wrote me the enclosed letter accompanied by one from Augustus; I forwarded them to the Chancellor with my opinion that Augustus's letter not stating his relinquishing the idea of his marriage and no proper excuse for his sudden arrival, I did not think without farther explanation that I would receive him. Instead of giving any opinion the Chancellor wrote the enclosed letter. . . . On coming to Town I found the Prince of Wales, whom I informed that I was not satisfied with Augustus's letter, that what he now said and the Chancellor's letter made me hope he saw the nullity of his marriage, but I was not personally informed of it, that I did not require a letter to that effect as it would oblige me to write an answer; but that if Augustus would write to that effect to the Prince of Wales and he send it to me for my information, I would certainly return it to him. I[n] the course of the evening I got such a letter, but to clear up all further doubts I wrote to the Prince of Wales. . . . I have just seen Augustus, and on that unpleasant business touched no farther than that understanding that a cloud was to be drawn over all passed unpleasant subjects. I should only look forward.

The Prince, we gather, sighed as a lover and obeyed as a son, and was the next year rewarded by being created Duke of Sussex.
It was, however, the Prince of Wales who gave the most trouble. When war with France once more broke out in 1803, he did just as his father had done almost half a century before, and George III behaved just as George II had done.

[1] Thomas Erskine, first Baron. He became Lord Chancellor in 1806.

III. TO THE PRINCE OF WALES

Windsor, August 7, 1803.

MY DEAR SON,

Though I applaud your zeal and your spirit, of which, I trust, no one can suppose any of my family wanting; yet considering the repeated declarations I have made of my determination on your former applications to the same purpose, I had flattered myself to have heard no farther on the subject. Should the implacable enemy so far succeed as to land, you will have an opportunity of showing your zeal at the head of your regiment. It will be the duty of every man to stand forward on such an occasion; and I shall certainly think it mine to set an example in defence of every thing that is dear to me and to my people.

I ever remain, my dear son,

Your affectionate father,

G.R.

This was part of a correspondence in which the Duke of York and Addington were also involved. What most aroused the King's ire in the matter was the fact that the Prince saw fit to have the correspondence published in the Morning Chronicle, *an action which his father never forgave.*

Thus when the next controversy arose, the King refused to write direct to his son, and risk further publication: he carried on the correspondence through the Chancellor, Lord Eldon, who was to write to the Prince in the King's name. The occasion was the disposal of the Princess Charlotte, for whom some arrangement had to be made, since the Prince of Wales had separated from Princess Caroline and returned to Mrs. Fitzherbert. The King interested himself keenly in the future of the child who seemed likely to succeed to the throne.

IV. TO LORD HAWKESBURY[1]

Windsor Castle, December 30, 1804.

The King has received Lord Hawkesbury's note this morning; he thought it so material to acquaint the Princess of Wales of a glimmering hope (for in truth it is no more) that the business

---

[1] Afterwards second Earl of Liverpool, and Prime Minister from 1812 to 1827. At this time Secretary of State for Home Affairs under Pitt.

regarding his dear granddaughter may be amicably arranged, that he went for that purpose to Blackheath, and has left her in the most perfect state of acquiescence to whatever he may judge right; but her conduct in the whole transaction is as becoming as it has been otherways in another quarter. . . .

v. To the Lord Chancellor

January 5, 1805.

The King authorizes the Lord Chancellor to inform the Prince of Wales that he has received with satisfaction the answer to the paper which the Lord Chancellor sent to the Prince of Wales from His Majesty, and will in consequence proceed with as little delay as the due consideration of so serious a concern requires, to state to the Prince, through the same channel, for the Prince's consideration, the names of the persons that shall occur to His Majesty as most likely to suit the situations necessary for the care and instruction of his granddaughter, the Princess Charlotte, who has every gift from nature to render her capable of profiting by that care and attention which may render her in future an honour to her family, and a blessing to those, if it pleases the Almighty to preserve her life, who must on a future day acknowledge her as their sovereign.

The matter of governesses was suitably arranged, and apartments fixed: there was some slight difficulty about the time she should spend with her father.

vi. To the Lord Chancellor

November, 1805.

The King has not thought it necessary previous to his return from Windsor to take any further steps for fixing the residence of his granddaughter, as the apartment is not yet entirely prepared for her reception. It has been His Majesty's earnest wish, from the beginning, in superintending and directing her education, to act in entire concurrence with the wishes of her father, and it was in full conformity to this principle that he directed a proper place to be prepared at Windsor for her residence, except at such times as she might occasionally visit either of her parents. Having since learnt that the Prince is desirous that she should remain under his roof during the time of his usual residence in Town, and that she should remain with His Majesty in the summer, except during the time of occasional visits, His Majesty is disposed to concur in that proposal; and is desirous to fix the period of her residence at Windsor from June to January, and is willing that she should reside at Carlton House the remaining months of the year. And His Majesty would not be desirous of making any alteration in this arrangement, which admits the absence of the Princess for so long a period of the year from his own roof, unless it should appear to him to become detrimental to the execution of the plan prepared for the education of the Princess, in which His Majesty can never cease to take the strongest interest, both from personal affection, and from what he feels to be due to the future welfare of his subjects.

The Princess, it need hardly be said, never came to the throne. She married Leopold, the future King of the Belgians, but died in childbirth of a still-born child.

On matters of more general concern the King continued to show an active, but more detached interest. Soon after the formation of the Addington ministry he wrote to his new Secretary of State for Foreign Affairs on receipt of the news of Nelson's victory at Copenhagen:

VII. To Lord Hawkesbury

Kew, 22 min. past 3 p.m., April 30, 1801.

Lord Hawkesbury may easily conceive what a balm to my heart so essential a piece of news as that he has just sent me must prove; I feel most fully the honour that must accrue to the British arms, but give me credit for saying that I more weigh on the manifest interposition of Divine Providence in a just cause, and for the destruction of the enemies of His Holy Word and of all civil and domestic happiness.

Yet he was happy to write advice to his new Irish Viceroy, which he did all the more readily as a previous letter, expressing his pleasure at once more having the Yorkes serving him, had been met with the response he was always eager to receive.

VIII. To the Earl of Hardwicke

Kew, May 10, 1801.

The Earl of Hardwicke's soon departure for Ireland inclines the King to write again as he finds his confidential hints have been taken as meant. The situation of the Lord Lieutenants of Ireland has been rendered more difficult from their not acting on one steady plan, but by degrees becoming the tools of some one of the parties who unfortunately by that conduct have been constantly fostered in that uncivilized island. The King is certain that the good private character of the Earl of Hardwicke and his having seen the rocks on which his predecessors have split, will be the best guide for his taking the right path; Ireland must be with temper taught to feel that till a better mode of education is established and that obedience to law which alone can render men advantageously industrious or their property secure, the solid good to be obtained from the union with this country cannot be effected. Another most necessary measure is the encouraging the residence of the clergy of the established Church and the attending to the calling on the Bishops by their examples as well as precepts enforcing it. The obliging them to keep their Cathedrals in good repair and having the choir service performed with great punctuality and decorum, that will certainly by degrees draw some of the Roman Catholics to our Church. His Majesty will not add more than his sincere wishes that the Earl of Hardwicke and all his family may enjoy good health and find Ireland a pleasant abode.

The letter would seem to indicate a certain lack of realism in politics; on the other hand his view of the Peace of Amiens, which was signed shortly afterwards, as ' an experimental peace ', was not without perspicuity. He still clung pertinaciously to the idea that the monarchic principle must be maintained at all costs, even in smaller issues.

IX. To the Princess of Orange

Weymouth, August 30, 1802.

My very dear Cousin,

I have received the letter you wrote at the moment of your leaving this country. No day goes by without our speaking of

T

you, and we really are very much attached to you. I am extremely pleased with your choice of trustees. Liston, who goes from here as Minister in Holland, has very express orders from me to sustain any claim that the Prince of Orange may make against the Republic for his lands or other goods, in accordance with the Treaty of Amiens, not with that which the King of Prussia made with the French Republic.

For the rest, I am, and shall always be,

My dear Cousin,

Your very affectionate cousin,

GEORGE.

It would appear that in his old age, the King inclined to political methods which in earlier days he would have stigmatized as ' Italian '. His scheme for the solution of the Irish problem is not without that fantastic charm which seems to appeal to some politicians of the present day, who wish to cure unemployment and in so doing cement the Empire.

x. TO LORD HAWKESBURY

Windsor, June 15, 1803.

The King is much pleased with the draft of the dispatch prepared by Lord Hawkesbury in answer to the one from Monsieur Talleyrand; but it has occurred to him, that as the Convention has been made without his knowledge and indeed that he has no authentic notice of it from his Electoral Regency, that he cannot in justice be called upon to ratify it. With this view the King has altered the last paragraph by omitting any promise of ratifying the Convention, and he thinks acquiescence is as much as can be expected from him.

xi. TO LORD MELVILLE[1]

Kew, 15 min. past 7 a.m., July 16, 1804.

The King sees much fair reasoning in the suggestions of Lord Melville to Admiral Cornwallis, and thinks them highly deserving of the most watchful attention. His Majesty has ever looked

[1] Which Henry Dundas had now become: he was at this time First Lord of the Admiralty.

upon the Cape of Good Hope as the key to our possessions in the East Indies, and therefore on the late peace ever feared the evils that might arise from giving that most essential position. Perhaps there never was a time when it might with more advantage be again in our hands; the Irish seem desirous of getting rid of their militia, and indeed it is composed of so bad a description of subjects, that many would be better employed against the enemy by retaking the Cape than remaining either in Ireland or what would be worse in Great Britain; a little bounty money would make them come forward in flocks for foreign service.

The last letter has taken us beyond the crisis which brought Pitt back into power. For some time after the fresh declaration of war, Pitt, though he was evidently the man destined to lead the country, played the amateur gardener and amateur soldier at Walmer Castle, while Addington floundered in the sea of politics he was not constituted to sail. The King was reluctant to part with Addington, who had stepped into the breach in 1801, and in whom he saw, perhaps, another North. In April 1804, however, Pitt approached the King, beginning by telling him that he could no longer even pretend to support Addington. He followed this up in May by a letter to Eldon, to be laid before the King, in which he suggested coming into the ministry, and promised not to agitate the Catholic question: he would, however, have to consult Grenville and Fox.

XII. To William Pitt

Queen's Palace, May 5, 1804.

The King has through the channel of the Chancellor expressed to Mr. Pitt his approbation of that gentleman's sentiments of personal attachment to His Majesty, and his ardent desire to support any measure that may be conducive to the real interest of the King or of his Royal Family; but at the same time it cannot but be lamented that Mr. Pitt should have taken so rooted a dislike to a gentleman[1] who has the greatest claim to approbation from his King and country for his most diligent and able discharge of the duties of Speaker of the House of Commons for

---

[1] Addington.

twelve years; and of his still more handsomely coming forward (when Mr. Pitt and some of his colleagues resigned their employments) to support his King and country when the most ill-digested and dangerous proposition was brought forward by the enemies of the Established Church. His Majesty has too good an opinion of Mr. Pitt to think he could have given his countenance to such a measure, had he weighed its tendency with that attention which a man of his judgement should call forth when the subject under consideration is of so serious a nature; but the King knows how strongly the two then Secretaries of State who resigned at that period had allied themselves to the Roman Catholics: the former by his private correspondence with a former Lord Lieutenant of Ireland,[1] showed he was become the follower of all the wild ideas of Mr. Burke; and the other,[2] from obstinacy, his usual director.

The King can never forget the wound that was intended at the Palladium of our Church Establishment, the Test Act, and the indelicacy, not to call it worse, of wanting His Majesty to forgo his solemn Coronation Oath. He therefore avows that he shall not be satisfied unless Mr. Pitt makes as strong assurances of his determination to support that wise law, as Mr. Pitt in so clear a manner stated in 1796 in the House of Commons, viz., that the smallest alteration of that law would be the death wound to the British Constitution.

The whole tenor of Mr. Fox's conduct since he quitted his seat at the Board of Treasury, when under age, and more particularly at the Whig Club and other factious meetings, rendered his expulsion from the Privy Council indispensable, and obliges the King to express his astonishment that Mr. Pitt should one moment harbour the thought of bringing such a man before his Royal notice. To prevent the repetition of it, the King declares that if Mr. Pitt persists in such an idea, or in proposing to consult Lord Grenville, His Majesty will have to deplore that he cannot avail himself of the ability of Mr. Pitt with necessary restrictions. These points being understood, His Majesty does not object to Mr. Pitt forming such a plan for conducting the public business as

[1] Dundas.
[2] Grenville.

may under all circumstances appear to be eligible; but should Mr. Pitt, unfortunately, find himself unable to undertake what is here proposed, the King will in that case call for the assistance of such men as are truly attached to our happy Constitution, and not seekers of improvements which to all dispassionate men must appear to tend to the destruction of that noble fabric which is the pride of all thinking minds, and the envy of all foreign nations.

The King thinks it but just to his present servants to express his trust that as far as the public service will permit, he may have the benefit of their further services.

It was not a promising beginning: this was to clip the eagle's wings with a vengeance: but on Pitt promising not to employ Fox, he was allowed to consult the Grenville faction. Fox nobly said they were not to regard him; but they refused to come in on King's terms, a decision arrived at at Carlton House. This increased the King's suspicions of Pitt: his friends considered Carlton House their centre!

xiii. To William Pitt

Queen's Palace, 50 min. past 11 a.m., May 9, 1804.

The King has this instant received Mr. Pitt's note. He shall with great pleasure see Mr. Pitt at half an hour past three, which will enable him to prolong his airing. It is not without *astonishment* he sees by the Times that the Opposition meeting was held at Carlton House.

It became certain then, that Pitt would form his truncated ministry: but it was with infinite regret that the King parted from Addington's safe mediocrity. 'The King's friendship for Mr. Addington is too deeply graven on his heart to be in the least diminished by any change of situation,' he wrote to him on the evening of the same day, offering to load him with titles and pensions. Nevertheless his sentiments towards Pitt grew more genial.

xiv. To William Pitt

Queen's Palace, 50 min. past 8 a.m., May 13, 1804.

The King's nature makes him decisive and active when he thinks the public service or the honour of his friends call for exertion. He knows those sentiments are most congenial to the disposition and character of his friend, and now most pleasing Chancellor of the Exchequer.[1] His Majesty therefore wishes Mr. Pitt would come here as soon as possible, as he will promise not to detain him above a quarter of an hour, or at most half an hour. . . .

There is a certain mental instability about that letter, especially when it goes on to explain that all this decision and action, this prating of honour, has to do with whether the feelings of Lord Hobart can be spared in the ministerial re-shuffle. The King was still upset about Addington: he wrote to Eldon that Addington was extremely sore at Pitt's contemptuous treatment of him, and ended, rather comically, by saying, 'This makes the King resolved to keep them for some time asunder.' To Addington himself he wrote in almost maudlin tones.

xv. To Henry Addington

Queen's Palace, 3 min. past 7 p.m., May 23, 1804.

The King is ever glad to mark the high esteem and friendship he has for so excellent a man as Mr. Addington, and will be truly gratified in seeing him this morning at ten o'clock in his usual morning dress—the King trusts in boots—as he should be glad to think Mr. Addington does not abstain from an exercise that is so conducive to his health, and [which] will keep him in readiness with his Woodley yeomen to join His Majesty should Buonaparte or any of his savage followers dare to cross the Channel.

When in the autumn the two ancient friends were reconciled, and Addington was brought into the government once more, the King was overjoyed: he had kept the friends apart long enough.

xvi. To Lord Hawkesbury

Windsor Castle, December 25, 1804.

Lord Hawkesbury is too well acquainted with the King's sentiments not to feel the gratification that has arisen in His Majesty's mind on the account of the two meetings of Messrs.

[1] Pitt had been gazetted to his old posts the day before.

Pitt and Addington having proved perfectly satisfactory; this gives the more pleasure as attachment to their King and country are the real ground on which these interviews have been founded. The King will with great pleasure see Lord Hawkesbury who has been the happy instrument of effecting the reconciliation of two men who ought ever to have been friends, and may now easily remain so, either of the days he has proposed. To secure if anything is wanting the continuation of the cordial intercourse now effected, His Majesty has prepared letters for each of the parties going no further than his thanks to both for having reunited for the good of his service, and indeed that it is one of the greatest eases to his mind that in a political view could have been effected. . . .

But in reality the King had lost his grip on political movements: he could not distinguish the new groups forming round Canning, Grey, or Castlereagh. These things made no impact upon his mind, which was more easily aroused by the pretensions of foreign potentates.

XVII. To Lord Harrowby[1]

King's Lodge, October 18, 1804.

It is [from] pure sentiments of compassion that one stifles the natural contempt which must arise in the breast of those who reflect on the extreme folly of the Emperor of Germany stooping in his station of Archduke of Austria to accept the title of Hereditary Emperor of Austria in imitation of the Usurper who has taken that title in France. . . .

When Napoleon was impertinent enough to write to him as a brother monarch, he made no attempt to stifle his natural contempt, and wrote to Pitt, ' The King is rather astonished that the French usurper has addressed himself to him, and if he judged it necessary, that he could not find a less objectionable manner.' As a symptom of his losing his energy we may note his quiet acquiescence during the invasion scare of 1805, that he should, if the enemy landed, withdraw to a place of safety.

[1] Secretary of State for Foreign Affairs.

XVIII. To THE BISHOP OF WORCESTER

1805.

MY DEAR GOOD BISHOP,

It has been thought by some of my friends, that it will be necessary for me to remove my family: should I be under so painful a necessity, I know not where I could place them with so much security as with yourself and my friends at Worcester. It does not appear to me probable that there will be any occasion for it, for I do not think that unhappy man who threatens us will dare to venture himself among us: but I thought it right to give you this intimation.

I remain, my dear good Bishop,

GEORGE.

That is very different in tone from a letter he had written to Hurd on a similar occasion two years previously.

XIX. To THE BISHOP OF WORCESTER

Windsor, November 30, 1803.

MY GOOD LORD,

. . . We are here in daily expectation that Buonaparte will attempt his threatened invasion, but the chances against his success seem so many that it is wonderful he persists in it. I own I place that thorough dependence on the protection of Divine Providence, that I cannot help thinking the usurper is encouraged to make the trial that his ill-success may put an end to his wicked purposes. Should his troops effect a landing, I shall certainly put myself at the head of mine, and my other armed subjects to repel them; but as it is impossible to foresee the events of such a conflict, should the enemy approach too near to Windsor, I shall think it right the Queen and my daughters should cross the Severn, and shall send them to your episcopal palace at Worcester. By this hint I do not in the least mean they shall be any inconvenience to you, and shall send a proper servant and furniture for their accommodation. Should such an event arise, I certainly would rather that what I value most in life should remain during the conflict in your diocese and under your roof, than in any other place in the island.

Believe me ever, my good Lord,

Most affectionately yours,

GEORGE R.

The King never had an opportunity of pitting his strategy against that of Napoleon, and the victory of Trafalgar finally disposed of any likelihood of such a combat. The only available note of the King's on this event is disappointing.

xx. To WILLIAM PITT

Windsor Castle, November 11, 1805.

The King cannot refrain from just expressing to Mr. Pitt the joy he feels at the good news now forwarded to him of the capture of four of the line-of-battle ships that had escaped on the 21st of last month. His Majesty has just received from Lord Hawkesbury an extract of Lord Nelson's will concerning his funeral, which has enabled directions to be given for his being buried at St. Paul's with military honours, which the brilliancy of the victory seems to call for.

The only event during Pitt's second administration which roused him at all was the attack made on Melville for malversation of funds. The charge was not altogether valid, but Melville, as Dundas, had been guilty of gross carelessness. He had to resign his seat at the Admiralty, and was struck off the Privy Council. What most affected the King, however, was a sense that some quality had gone out of Englishmen.

xxi. To WILLIAM PITT

Windsor, May 5, 1805.

Though the King is much hurt at the virulence against Lord Melville, which is unbecoming the character of Englishmen, who naturally when a man is fallen are too noble to pursue their blows, he must feel the prudence of Mr. Pitt's proposing his being struck out of the Privy Council, and it is hoped after that the subject will be buried in oblivion. . . .

He was becoming laudator temporis acti: *had he forgotten how Englishmen had pursued Bute with kicks long after he was down?*

He was frankly contemptuous at this time of attempts to revive the Catholic question.

XXII. To WILLIAM PITT

Windsor, May 14, 1805.

The King is not surprised, considering the enormous length to which gentlemen permit themselves to spin out their speeches, that it should have been necessary to adjourn the debate on the Catholic question from two this morning to the usual hour of meeting this day: it seems wonderful that the fatigue does incline gentlemen to compress their ideas in a shorter space, which must ever be more agreeable and useful to the auditors, and not less advantageous to the dispatch of business.

The political details of the rest of the reign up to the King's final lunacy can be briefly hurried over. In July 1805 the party of Addington, now Lord Sidmouth, retired, and in January 1806 Pitt died. He was succeeded by Grenville, at the head of the Ministry of All the Talents, with Fox as Secretary of State, a government which must have seemed to the King as humiliating as the old North-Fox coalition. Grenville proscribed the Pittites, which was another reason for the King's dislike of his Prime Minister, with whom he was extremely short, always on the look out for infringements of his prerogative.

XXIII. To LORD GRENVILLE

Queen's Palace, February 3, 1806.

The King has considered that part of the paper delivered to him by Lord Grenville which relates to the defence of the country, and the administration of military service.

The King regrets that the paragraph to which he refers together with any explanation he has been able to procure, should be of so general a nature as to render it impossible to pass it by without notice, or to answer it with any precision. His Majesty has no desire to restrain his confidential servants from the most thorough investigation into the various and extensive branches of the military service, and he will be favourably disposed to consider any measures relating to this important subject, which upon a full examination may be laid before him.

The King therefore desires that Lord Grenville will, with as little delay as possible, after conferring with those persons with whom he acts, convey to him specially on paper, for his consideration, the explanation which His Majesty requires; and the King must be understood as reserving to himself at all times the undoubted right of deciding on the measures which may be proposed to him respecting the military service, or the administration of it, both with reference to the prerogatives of the Crown, and the nature and expediency of the measures themselves.

Fox's death in September caused a certain re-shuffling of posts, but no major change. In the autumn, however, Grenville seems to have wanted to try the hazard of a general election —without consulting the King, who felt his dignity wounded.

xxiv. To Lord Grenville

Windsor Castle, October 13, 1806.

Although the King must lament that a proposal should be made to him for the dissolution of this Parliament which has sat so short a time, if it is considered by Lord Grenville a measure of urgent necessity, His Majesty will not withhold his acquiescence. At the same time the King cannot abstain from expressing his surprise that, although the report of such an intention on the part of his government had been so long prevalent, nothing should ever have been said to His Majesty on the subject which could induce him to give the least credit to public rumour.

xxv. To Lord Grenville

Windsor Castle, October 14, 1806.

The King has received Lord Grenville's letter of yesterday, and desires he will be assured that the explanation which it contains has been perfectly satisfactory to His Majesty. The King is, however, convinced that Lord Grenville will admit that, without such an explanation, the circumstances apparently connected with the proposal for a dissolution of Parliament would strike him in an awkward light.

The election did not take place until the following spring, when the Grenville ministry fell on the Catholic question, as has already been seen. Many considered the King's action a precarious gamble, but once more he triumphed: the Pittites came back into power, and remained there a great many years. Portland was head of the administration, but it was his Chancellor of the Exchequer, Perceval, and his Secretaries of State, Castlereagh and Canning, who fought for the leadership of the party.

The year 1809 was an anxious one for the King, and events plunged him into a gloom which no doubt hastened his final illness. The first of these was the scandal attaching to the Duke of York, who was accused of allowing one of his many mistresses to make money out of the sale of commissions, and of sharing the proceeds. The Parliamentary investigation, the revelation of the turpitude of the Duke's amours, made his resignation inevitable. The King was anxious that a man of good private character should succeed him.

XXVI. TO THE DUKE OF PORTLAND

Windsor Castle, March 18, 1809.

The King acquaints the Duke of Portland that he has this day reluctantly accepted the resignation of the Duke of York, which has been conveyed to His Majesty in a letter of which he has sent the copy to Mr. Perceval, and which he will, of course, communicate to his colleagues.

Under these painful circumstances, His Majesty's attention has been directed to the necessary arrangements for the future administration of the army, and after consulting the Army List, the King has satisfied himself that General Sir David Dundas is, of all those whose names have occurred to him, the fittest person to be entrusted with the chief temporary command, both from habits of business, respectability of character, and from the disposition which His Majesty is convinced he will feel to attend strictly to the maintenance of that system and those regulations which under the direction of the Duke of York have proved so beneficial to the Service. . . .

That was a severe blow; then followed the disastrous Walcheren expedition, combined with the last illness of the Duke of Portland, which seemed likely to bring about a change in the system of administration. To the King's horror, advances had once more to be made to the Grenville-Grey faction, which, however, refused to come in on the Catholic question being definitely barred. Perceval formed a ministry, but Canning refused to serve under him, having previously quarrelled with Castlereagh. He had told Portland that Castlereagh was unfit for his post; and when this came to Castlereagh's ears, he also resigned and fought a duel with Canning. The King was not left out of this quarrel, and the last long letter to be quoted here shows how he still took the keenest interest in all military matters. It is amusing to note that he approved of Wellington having been sent to the Peninsula solely because he thought such an appointment would ensure the campaign being an unimportant one.

XXVII. TO LORD CASTLEREAGH

Windsor Castle, October 3, 1809.

The King has received Lord Castlereagh's letter of the 1st instant, and, before His Majesty enters into transactions of which he must ever lament the occurrence and the consequences, he thinks it necessary to assure Lord Castlereagh that he readily admits that situated as he is, he could not with propriety have made his representation to the King in any other than the mode he has adopted.

The King does not recollect any communication to him of Mr. Canning's letter of the 24th March last to which Lord Castlereagh refers, nor has want of zeal, or of efficiency on the part of Lord Castlereagh in the execution of the duties of his department ever been urged to His Majesty as a ground for the arrangement which was suggested.

The Duke of Portland stated verbally to the King in May last that difficulties had arisen from Mr. Canning's representation that the duties of the Foreign and Colonial department clashed, and that unless some arrangement could be made for the removal of Lord Castlereagh, he had reason to believe that Mr. Canning would resign his situation in the government.

This was the reason assigned to His Majesty, and in June Lord

Wellesley's name was first submitted to him as the eventual successor to Lord Castlereagh,[1] the continuance of whose services as a member of the government it was hoped would be secured by some further agreement. It was not intended that the. communication to Lord Castlereagh of what was in agitation should have been subject to the delay which progressively took place from circumstances into which the King does not think it necessary to enter.

The King has no hesitation in assuring Lord Castlereagh that he has at all times been satisfied with the zeal and assiduity with which he has discharged the duties of the various situations which he has filled, and with the exertions which under every difficulty, he has made for the support of His Majesty's and the country's interests.

His Majesty must ever approve the principle which shall secure the support and protection of government to officers exposing their reputation as well as their lives in his service, when their characters and conduct are attacked and aspersed upon loose and insufficient grounds, without adverting to embarrassments and local difficulties on which those on the spot can alone form an adequate judgement. His Majesty has never been inclined to admit that Lord Castlereagh was wanting in zeal or exertion in providing for the reinforcement of the army in Portugal; on the contrary, Lord Castlereagh must remember that the King was not disposed to question the correctness of the representations made by the late Sir John Moore,[2] which subsequent experience has too fully confirmed; and although he was induced to yield to the advice of his confidential servants, he never could look with satisfaction to the prospect of another British army being committed in Spain under the possible recurrence of the same difficulties.

It was also this impression which prompted the King to acquiesce in the appointment of so young a Lieut.-General as Lord Wellington to the command of the troops in Portugal, as he hoped that this consideration would operate against any considerable augmentation of that army, although that augmentation

---

[1] Wellesley became Foreign Secretary under Perceval.
[2] Moore had been killed at Corunna on January 16th.

has been since gradually produced by events not then foreseen. In making this observation the King is far from meaning to reflect upon Lord Wellington, of whose zealous services and abilities he had the most favourable opinion, and whose subsequent conduct has proved him deserving of the confidence reposed in him. But as Lord Castlereagh has laid so much stress on this point, His Majesty has considered it due to himself and to Lord Castlereagh to show clearly that he had never entertained an idea that there had been any neglect on his part in providing for that service.

The occasion of the last letter to be quoted here must have given the King much gratification. Perhaps a monarch should not enter into such detail, but the King's pleasure in the extinction of at least one Bonaparte is understandable.

XXVIII. To Lord Liverpool[1]

Windsor Castle, October 16, 1810.

The King approves of the instruction which Lord Liverpool has prepared on the subject of Lucien Buonaparte, for Lieut.-General Oakes, whose proceedings appear to His Majesty to have been extremely proper and sensible. In the event of Lucien Buonaparte's arrival in this country, the King trusts that in the choice of a residence for him, the convenience of the individual will not be alone consulted, but that care will be taken to place him and his attendants where their presence cannot in any respect be prejudicial to the interests of this country; and with this view His Majesty concurs that an inland town would be most eligible. It equally occurs to him that the Transport Board should not be suffered to leave him in charge of one of their inferior agents, but that a man whose vigilance and distinction can be relied upon should be named to reside constantly in the same place and quietly watch the proceedings of Lucien Buonaparte. That a proper person named by the police should also be directed to attend to the conduct and proceedings of the numerous suite of servants and other persons.

[1] Second Earl; at this time Secretary for War and the Colonies.

It was at the end of this month that the King once more became deranged, but with normal intervals. During January a Regency Bill was introduced into Parliament, of which the King was cognizant. Though in possession of his faculties, he felt that his retirement was inevitable, and on February 5th, 1811, he gave his assent to the Bill, and the next day the Regency began. From that time his condition grew rapidly worse; he was blind, he was increasingly deaf, he had very few lucid periods. Into the details of his madness it is unnecessary to go: it is a pleasing thought that he was able to solace some of his happier intervals by performing music on various instruments. It seems that towards the end of his life he was able to gather something of what had happened in his blank decade: he learnt of the triumph of English arms, of Waterloo: he learnt of the collapse of the Napoleonic system, of the defeat of those terrible monsters who aimed at the destruction of family virtue, of all religion, and worst of all, of the monarchic idea. These things will have satisfied him if he was able to grasp their import; but his profoundest satisfaction would have been to learn that his eldest son on stepping into his father's shoes had also stepped into his political ideas, and to the disgust of his followers, had left the government exactly as it was. King George III died at midnight on the 29th January, 1820.

APPENDICES

APPENDIX I

AUTHORITIES

Explanation of References

Add. MSS.	Additional Manuscripts, British Museum.
Bedford Corr.	*Correspondence of John, Fourth Duke of Bedford*, edited by Lord John Russell. 3 vols. 1842.
Chatham Corr. . .	*Correspondence of William Pitt, Earl of Chatham.* 4 vols. 1839.
Donne	*Correspondence of George III with Lord North*, edited by W. Bodham Donne. 2 vols. 1867.
Egerton MSS. . . .	British Museum Manuscripts.
Fortescue	*Correspondence of King George III*, edited by Sir John Fortescue. 6 vols. 1927.
Grenville Papers . .	*The Grenville Papers*, edited by Smith. 4 vols. 1853.
H.M.C.	Historical Manuscripts Commission Reports.
Jesse	*Memoirs of the Life and Reign of George III*, by J. Heneage Jesse. 3 vols. 1867.
Mahon	*History of England, from the Peace of Utrecht to the Peace of Versailles*, by Lord Mahon. 7 vols. 1839.
Namier	*England in the Age of the American Revolution*, by L. B. Namier. 1930.
P.R.O.	Public Record Office.
Rockingham Memoirs	*Memoirs of the Marquis of Rockingham*, by the Earl of Albemarle.
Roxburghe	*Letters of George III, 1781-1783*, edited by Sir John Fortescue. Roxburghe Club. 2 vols. 1927.
Stanhope	*Life of the Rt. Hon. William Pitt*, by Philip Henry, fifth Earl Stanhope. 4 vols. 1861.
Spencer Papers . .	*Private Papers of Earl Spencer.* Navy Records Society. 2 vols. 1914.
Young's Annals . .	*Annals of Agriculture*; periodical edited by Arthur Young, *c.* 1786.

CHAPTER I

i. Add. MSS. 32684, f. 78.
ii. Add. MSS. 32684, f. 80.
iii. Namier, 96.
iv. Add. MSS. 32684, f. 92.
v. Namier, 98.

VI. Add. MSS. 32684, f. 96.
VII. Namier, 100.
VIII. Namier, 100.
IX. Namier, 101.
X. Namier, 103.
XI. Namier, 104.
XII. Add. MSS. 32893, f. 154.
XIII. Namier, 116.

CHAPTER II

I. Add. MSS. 32684, f. 121.
II. Add. MSS. 32930, f. 429.
III. Add. MSS. 35434, f. 214.
IV. Namier, 368.
V. Namier, 373.
VI. Bedford Corr., III, 139.
VII. Namier, 435.
VIII. Namier, 435.
IX. Namier, 435.
X. Namier, 483.
XI. Namier, 408.
XII. Grenville Papers, II, 161.
XIII. Grenville Papers, II, 166.
XIV. Grenville Papers, II, 267.
XV. Add. MSS. 32966, f. 445, and Fortescue, I, 106.
XVI. Add. MSS. 32966, f. 443, and Fortescue, I, 105.
XVII. Fortescue, I, 107.
XVIII. Grenville Papers, III, 40.
XIX. Fortescue, I, 118.
XX. Fortescue, I, 118.
XXI. Fortescue, I, 121.
XXII. Egerton MSS. 982, f. 6.
XXIII. Egerton MSS. 982, f. 11.
XXIV. Rockingham Memoirs, I, 256.
XXV. Fortescue, I, 252.
XXVI. Fortescue, I, 268.
XXVII. Fortescue, I, 273.
XXVIII. Fortescue, I, 212.
XXIX. Rockingham Memoirs, I, 266.
XXX. Fortescue, I, 218.
XXXI. Fortescue, I, 219.
XXXII. Fortescue, I, 220.
XXXIII. Rockingham Memoirs, I, 271.
XXXIV. Fortescue, I, 347.
XXXV. Chatham Corr., II, 436.
XXXVI. Chatham Corr., II, 443.
XXXVII. Chatham Corr., III, 21.

XXXVIII. Egerton MSS. 982, f. 20.
XXXIX. Egerton MSS. 982, f. 24.
XL. Chatham Corr., III, 134.
XLI. Chatham Corr., III, 135.
XLII. Chatham Corr., III, 137.
XLIII. Egerton MSS. 982, f. 26.
XLIV. Fortescue, I, 423.
XLV. Egerton MSS. 982, f. 28.
XLVI. Fortescue, I, 455.
XLVII. Chatham Corr., III, 229.
XLVIII. Fortescue, I, 477.
XLIX. Chatham Corr., III, 260.
L. Fortescue, I, 501.
LI. Jesse, I, 427.
LII. Donne, I, 2.
LIII. Jesse, I, 432.
LIV. Jesse, I, 434.
LV. Jesse, I, 435.
LVI. Jesse, I, 437.
LVII. Fortescue, II, 42.
LVIII. Fortescue, II, 44.
LIX. Chatham Corr., III, 343.
LX. Donne, I, 8.
LXI. Donne, I, 9.
LXII. Donne, I, 11.
LXIII. Fortescue, I, 414.
LXIV. Fortescue, I, 449.
LXV. Add. MSS. 35369, f. 119.
LXVI. Add. MSS. 35369, f. 119.

CHAPTER III

I. Donne, I, 12.
II. Donne, I, 13.
III. Donne, I, 17.
IV. Donne, I, 20.
V. Donne, I, 26.
VI. Donne, I, 27.
VII. Fortescue, II, 150.
VIII. Donne, I, 28.
IX. Donne, I, 39.
X. Donne, I, 39.
XI. Donne, I, 35.
XII. Donne, I, 40.
XIII. Donne, I, 41.
XIV. Fortescue, II, 175.
XV. Fortescue, II, 177.
XVI. Donne, I, 163.

XVII. Donne, I, 33.
XVIII. Donne, I, 34.
XIX. Donne, I, 57.
XX. Donne, I, 64.
XXI. Donne, I, 65.
XXII. Donne, I, 66.
XXIII. Donne, I, 68.
XXIV. Donne, I, 49.
XXV. Donne, I, 97.
XXVI. Donne, I, 91.
XXVII. Donne, I, 95.
XXVIII. Donne, I, 89.
XXIX. Fortescue, II, 341.
XXX. Donne, I, 101.
XXXI. Fortescue, II, 369.
XXXII. Donne, I, 59.
XXXIII. Donne, I, 105.
XXXIV. Fortescue, II, 384.
XXXV. Fortescue, II, 404.
XXXVI. Donne, I, 128.
XXXVII. Donne, I, 129.
XXXVIII. Donne, I, 134.
XXXIX. Fortescue, II, 428.
XL. Add. MSS. 35839, f. 307.
XLI. Donne, I, 78.
XLII. Donne, I, 158.
XLIII. Donne, I, 135.
XLIV. Donne, I, 141.
XLV. Fortescue, II, 475.
XLVI. Donne, I, 130.
XLVII. Donne, I, 154.
XLVIII. Fortescue, II, 465.
XLIX. Fortescue, III, 2.

CHAPTER IV

I. Donne, I, 164.
II. Donne, I, 173.
III. Donne, I, 174.
IV. Donne, I, 176.
V. Donne, I, 184.
VI. Donne, I, 169.
VII. Donne, I, 192.
VIII. Donne, I, 192.
IX. Donne, I, 194.
X. Donne, I, 201.
XI. Donne, I, 202.
XII. Donne, I, 214.

xiii. Donne, I, 216.
xiv. Donne, I, 219.
xv. H.M.C. Dartmouth Report, XI, v. 439.
xvi. Fortescue, III, 47.
xvii. Fortescue, III, 48.
xviii. Donne, I, 226.
xix. Donne, I, 241.
xx. H.M.C. Dartmouth Report, XI, v. 440.
xxi. Ibid.
xxii. Donne, I, 257.
xxiii. Donne, I, 265.
xxiv. Donne, I, 297.
xxv. Donne, I, 267.
xxvi. Donne, I, 275.
xxvii. Donne, I, 282.
xxviii. Donne, I, 301.
xxix. Add. MSS. 37833, f. 32.
xxx. Donne, II, 55.
xxxi. Add. MSS. 37833, f. 137.
xxxii. Donne, II, 70.
xxxiii. Donne, II, 92.
xxxiv. Donne, II, 125.
xxxv. Mahon, VI, Appendix lvii.
xxxvi. Donne, II, 149.
xxxvii. Donne, II, 151.
xxxviii. Donne, II, 153.
xxxix. Donne, II, 159.
xl. Donne, II, 207.
xli. Add. MSS. 37833, f. 236.
xlii. Donne, II, 212
xliii. Add. MSS. 37834, f. 39.
xliv. Donne, II, 214.
xlv. Donne, II, 224.
xlvi. Add. MSS. 37834, f. 72.
xlvii. Add. MSS. 37834, f. 93.
xlviii. Donne, II, 252.
xlix. Donne, II, 257.
l. Fortescue, IV, 473.
li. Add. MSS. 38564, f. 11.
lii. Donne, II, 298.
liii. Donne, II, 314.
liv. Donne, II, 321.
lv. Donne, II, 329.
lvi. Donne, II, 392.
lvii. Donne, I, 167.
lviii. Fortescue, III, 119.
lix. Jesse, II, 58.
lx. Donne, II, 233.

LXI. H.M.C. Dartmouth Report, XI, v. 441.
LXII. Donne, II, 382.
LXIII. Donne, II, 249.
LXIV. Add. MSS. 37833, f. 189.
LXV. Donne, II, 636.

CHAPTER V

I. Roxburghe, I, 19.
II. Roxburghe, I, 40.
III. Roxburghe, I, 79.
IV. Roxburghe, I, 81.
V. Add. MSS. 38564, f. 30.
VI. Roxburghe, I, 87.
VII. Roxburghe, I, 103.
VIII. Add. MSS. 38564, f. 33.
IX. Roxburghe, I, 119.
X. Roxburghe, I, 127.
XI. Roxburghe, I, 128.
XII. H.M.C. Dartmouth, Report XI, v. 442.
XIII. Roxburghe, I, 131.
XIV. Roxburghe, I, 152.
XV. Roxburghe, I, 186.
XVI. Roxburghe, I, 269.
XVII. Roxburghe, I, 280.
XVIII. Roxburghe, I, 291.
XIX. Roxburghe, I, 307.
XX. Roxburghe, I, 337.
XXI. Roxburghe, II, 365.
XXII. Roxburghe, II, 376.
XXIII. Mahon, VII, 300.
XXIV. Roxburghe, II, 437.
XXV. Roxburghe, II, 445.
XXVI. Roxburghe, II, 457.
XXVII. Roxburghe, II, 463.
XXVIII. Roxburghe, II, 468.
XXIX. Roxburghe, II, 487.
XXX. Roxburghe, II, 499.
XXXI. Roxburghe, II, 505.
XXXII. P.R.O., Chatham Papers, C. III.
XXXIII. Ibid.
XXXIV. Roxburghe, II, 510.
XXXV. P.R.O., Chatham Papers, C. III.
XXXVI. Roxburghe, II, 511.
XXXVII. Roxburghe, II, 513.
XXXVIII. Roxburghe, II, 524.
XXXIX. Roxburghe, II, 525.
XL. Roxburghe, II, 555.

XLI. Roxburghe, II, 612.
XLII. Roxburghe, II, 609.
XLIII. Roxburghe, II, 621.
XLIV. Roxburghe, II, 632.
XLV. Roxburghe, II, 590.
XLVI. Roxburghe, II, 593.
XLVII. Roxburghe, II, 594.
XLVIII. Roxburghe, II, 663.
XLIX. P.R.O., Chatham Papers, C. III.
L. Ibid.
LI. Ibid.
LII. Ibid.
LIII. Ibid.
LIV. Ibid.
LV. Ibid.
LVI. Ibid.
LVII. Ibid.
LVIII. Ibid.
LIX. Mahon, VII, App. xxxv.
LX. Mahon, VII, App. xxxvi.
LXI. Mahon, VII, App. xxxiv.

CHAPTER VI

I. P.R.O., Chatham Papers, C. III.
II. Ibid.
III. Ibid.
IV. Ibid.
V. H.M.C., Duke of Beaufort, 350.
VI. P.R.O., Chatham Papers, C. III.
VII. Ibid.
VIII. Ibid.
IX. Ibid.
X. Ibid.
XI. Ibid.
XII. Ibid.
XIII. Ibid.
XIV. Ibid.
XV. Ibid.
XVI. Ibid.
XVII. Ibid.
XVIII. Ibid.
XIX. H.M.C., Dropmore, I, 587.
XX. H.M.C., Duke of Beaufort, Report XII, ix, 368
XXI. Egerton MSS. 2159, f. 57.
XXII. P.R.O., Chatham Papers, C. III.
XXIII. Egerton MSS. 2159, f. 61.
XXIV. Young's Annals, VII, 65.

CHAPTER VII

I. H.M.C., Dropmore, II, 107.
II. H.M.C., Dropmore, II, 109.
III. H.M.C., Dropmore, II, 110.
IV. Add. MSS. 40100, f. 3.
V. Add. MSS. 40100, f. 11.
VI. Add. MSS. 34439, f. 132.
VII. H.M.C., Dropmore, II, 267.
VIII. Ibid.
IX. H.M.C., Dropmore, II, 282.
X. H.M.C., Dropmore, II, 308.
XI. H.M.C., Dropmore, II, 309.
XII. H.M.C., Dropmore, II, 372.
XIII. H.M.C., Dropmore, II, 378.
XIV. P.R.O., Chatham Papers, C. III.
XV. Add. MSS. 40100, f. 88.
XVI. P.R.O., Chatham Papers, C. III.
XVII. Ibid.
XVIII. H.M.C., Dropmore, II, 609.
XIX. P.R.O., Chatham Papers, C. III.
XX. Ibid.
XXI. Ibid.
XXII. P.R.O., Chatham Papers, C. IV.
XXIII. Spencer Papers, I, 30.
XXIV. Add. MSS. 40100, f. 169.
XXV. H.M.C., Dropmore, III, 174.
XXVI. H.M.C., Dropmore, III, 186.
XXVII. H.M.C., Dropmore, III, 227.
XXVIII. H.M.C., Dropmore, III, 255.
XXIX. H.M.C., Dropmore, III, 256.
XXX. H.M.C., Dropmore, III, 265.
XXXI. P.R.O., Chatham Papers, C. III.
XXXII. Ibid.
XXXIII. Ibid.
XXXIV. Ibid.
XXXV. Ibid.
XXXVI. Ibid.
XXXVII. Ibid. C. IV.
XXXVIII. Add. MSS. 40100, f. 190.
XXXIX. Spencer Papers, II, 124.
XL. Spencer Papers, II, 144.
XLI. Spencer Papers, II, 155.
XLII. P.R.O., Chatham Papers, C. IV.
XLIII. H.M.C., Dropmore, III, 327.
XLIV. Add. MSS. 40100, f. 235.
XLV. Spencer Papers, III, 182.
XLVI. P.R.O., Chatham Papers, C. III.

xlvii. H.M.C. Report XIV, App. iv, 542.
xlviii. P.R.O., Chatham Papers, C. IV.
xlix. Ibid.
l. Ibid.
li. Ibid.
lii. Add. MSS. 40100, f. 300.
liii. P.R.O., Chatham Papers, C. IV.
liv. Ibid.
lv. H.M.C., Dropmore, IX, 107; Add. MSS. 38103, f. 27b.
lvi. Jesse, III, 228.
lvii. Jesse, III, 231.

CHAPTER VIII

i. P.R.O., Chatham Papers, C. III.
ii. P.R.O., Chatham Papers, C. IV.
iii. *Correspondence between His Majesty, the Prince of Wales, the Duke of York and Mr. Addington, on the Offer of Military Service made by His Royal Highness the Prince of Wales.* 1808. p. 11.
iv. Add. MSS. 38190, f. 8.
v. H.M.C., Dropmore, VII, 359.
vi. H.M.C., Dropmore, VII, 364.
vii. Add. MSS. 38564, f. 41.
viii. Add. MSS. 35349, f. 75.
ix. Add. MSS. 44445, f. 518.
x. Add. MSS. 38564, f. 68.
xi. Add. MSS. 40100, f. 321.
xii. P.R.O., Chatham Papers, C. IV.
xiii. Ibid.
xiv. Ibid.
xv. Jesse, III, 373.
xvi. Add. MSS. 38190, f. 7.
xvii. H.M.C., Various, V, 181. Edmonstone.
xviii. Add. MSS. 33544, f. 157.
xix. Jesse, III, 330.
xx. P.R.O., Chatham Papers, C. IV.
xxi. Ibid.
xxii. Ibid.
xxiii. H.M.C., Dropmore, VIII, 8.
xxiv. H.M.C., Dropmore, VIII, 382.
xxv. H.M.C., Dropmore, VIII, 384.
xxvi. Jesse, III, 532.
xxvii. Add. MSS. 38243, f. 168.
xxviii. Add. MSS. 38190, f. 22.

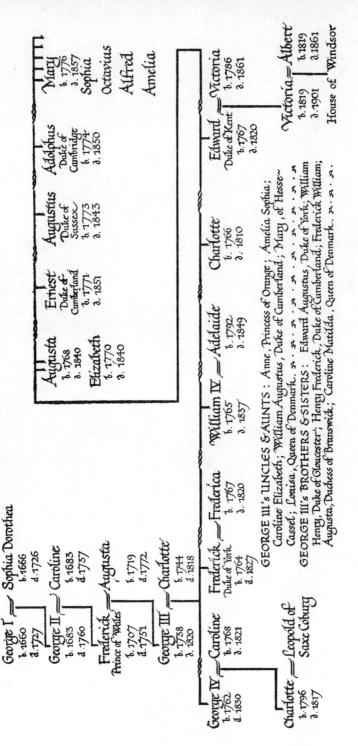

GEORGE III's UNCLES & AUNTS : Anne, Princess of Orange; Amelia Sophia;
Caroline Elizabeth; William Augustus, Duke of Cumberland; Mary, of Hesse-
Cassel; Louisa, Queen of Denmark. ʌ ʌ ʌ ʌ ʌ ʌ ʌ ʌ ʌ ʌ ʌ ʌ ʌ ʌ ʌ ʌ ʌ

GEORGE III's BROTHERS & SISTERS: Edward Augustus, Duke of York; William
Henry, Duke of Gloucester; Henry Frederick, Duke of Cumberland; Frederick William;
Augusta, Duchess of Brunswick; Caroline Matilda, Queen of Denmark. ʌ ʌ ʌ ʌ ʌ

INDEX

ABDICATION, George III's messages of, 154, 169

Abercromby, Sir Ralph (1734-1801), 238

Addington, Henry, later 1st Viscount Sidmouth (1757-1844), 244, 254, 259, 261, 262, 263, 266
letter to, 262

Adolphus Frederick, Prince, later Duke of Cambridge (1774-1850), son of George III, 251

Adolphus Frederick II, King of Sweden (1710-1771), 85

Aiguillon, Armand Vignerot Duplessis Richelieu, Duc d' (1720-1798), French Minister, 86 and *n*., 88, 89

Albemarle, George Keppel, 3rd Earl of (1724-1772), 28, 36, 37

Alfred, Prince (1780-1782), son of George III, 186

Allen, Mr., 91

America, General, 148, 149
Boston Massacre, 66
Boston Port Bill, 100, 101, 104, 120
Boston Tea-Party, 100, 101
Brandywine, battle of, 118
Bunker's Hill, battle of, 114
Camden, battle of, 137
Carolina, N., operations in, 114
Carolina, S., operations in, 116
Charleston, battle of, 137
Conciliatory Bills, 120
Congress, 105, 107
Corresponding Committees, 99
Declaration of Independence, 116
Duties, 46, 58, 66
Jerseys, the, operations in, 125
Lexington (Concord), battle of, 109, 110
Maryland, 105
Massachusetts, 106, 107
Massachusetts Bill, 101, 120
New York, operations at, 116
Ohio, 83
Philadelphia, operations around, 118, 125
Quebec, operations at, 116
Quebec Bill, 102, 103
Saratoga, battle of, 118
Stamp Act, 25, 33
Trenton, action at, 116, 117
Yorktown, surrender at, 137

Amherst, Sir Jeffrey, later Baron (1717-1797), 55, 99, 119 and *n*.

Amiens, Peace of, 257, 258

Anne, Queen (1665-1714), 147

Apsley, Henry Bathurst, Baron; later 2nd Earl Bathurst (1714-1794), Lord Chancellor, 76 and *n*.

Armed Neutrality, 137

Artois, Charles Philippe, Comte d'; later Charles X (1757-1836), 218, 219

Ashburnham, John Ashburnham, 2nd Earl of (1724-1812), 153, 156

Assassination Plot, 120

Augustus, Frederick, Prince. *See* Duke of Sussex

Avonmore, Barry Yelverton, 1st Viscount (1736-1805), 238 and *n*.

Aylesbury (Ailesbury), Thomas Brudenell, 1st Earl of (1729-1814), 153 and *n*.

BAKER, SIR GEORGE (1722-1809), specialist in colic, 198

Bank of England, suspension of cash payments, 227-9

Barré, Isaac, Colonel (1726-1802), 121, 123

Barrington, William Wildman Shute, 2nd Viscount (1717-1793), 111, 128

Barry, Marie Jeanne Bécu du, Comtesse (1746-1793), 86*n*.

Barthélémy, François, Marquis de (1747-1830), French Secretary in London; later Director, 197

Barwell, Richard (1741-1804), 142 and *n*.

Bath, William Pulteney, 1st Earl of (1684-1764), 65

Baudoin (de Champagne), Seigneur de Bazoges, French agent in Brandenburg, 33

Beckford, William (1709-1770), Alderman and Mayor, 45, 68, 69 and *n*.

Bedford, John Russell, 4th Duke of (1710-1771), xi, 22, 26, 27, 29, 30, 34, 43, 50, 65
letter to, 22

Behr, Baron von, Foreign Minister in Hanover, 60

Belgium, 216

Bergen-op-Zoom, 217

Bernstorff, Andreas Peter, Count von (1735-1797), 199 and *n*.

Billington, Mrs. Elizabeth (1768?-1818), opera singer, 206

Birmingham, riots at, 212

Bonaparte, Lucien, Prince of Cannino (1775-1840), 271

Bonaparte, Napoleon (1769-1821), 262, 263, 264, 265

287

Braun, Major-General, 60
Bristol, George William Hervey, 2nd Earl of (1721-1775), letters to, 82, 95
Brunswick, Carl Wilhelm Ferdinand, Duke of (1735-1806), 219
Brunswick, Caroline Amelia Augusta, Princess of. See Caroline, Queen
Buccarelli, Governor of Buenos Ayres, 72
Buckinghamshire, John Hobart, 2nd Earl of (1723-1793), Viceroy of Ireland, 101
Burgoyne, John, General (1722-1792), 114, 116, 118
Burke, Edmund (1729-1797), 65, 79, 81, 108, 134, 135, 152, 157, 159, 192, 193, 194, 225, 226, 235
Bute, John Stuart, 2nd Earl of (1713-1792), 5, 6, 8, 19, 20 and n., 22, 23, 25, 27, 30, 68, 69, 247, 266
  letters to, 6, 9, 10, 11, 12, 13, 15, 20, 21, 23, 24, 25

CAMELFORD, THOMAS PITT, 1st Baron (1737-1793), 172, 173, 186
Camden, Charles Pratt, 1st Earl (1714-1794), 25, 41, 42, 48, 54, 56, 58, 65, 108, 152, 159, 160
  letters to, 50
Camden, John Jeffreys Pratt, 2nd Earl, later 1st Marquess (1759-1840), 236, 238
Canning, George (1770-1827), 263, 268, 269
Cape of Good Hope, 148
Carleton, General Guy, later Baron Dorchester (1724-1808), 148
Carlisle, Frederick Howard, 5th Earl of (1748-1825), 163, 172
Carmarthen, Francis Osborne, Marquess of, later 5th Duke of Leeds (1757-1799), appointed Ambassador to France, but did not go, 195
  letters to, 206, 207
Caroline, Queen (1768-1821), wife of George IV, 252, 254
Caroline Matilda, H.R.H. Princess, Queen of Denmark (1751-1755), sister to George III, 79
Castlereagh, Robert Stewart, Viscount, later 2nd Marquess of Londonderry (1769-1822), 239, 240, 241, 263, 268, 269
  letter to, 269
Castries, Maréchal, Charles Eugène Gabriel, de la Croix, Marquis de (1727-1801), 218
Catherine II, Tsarina (1729-1796), 20n., 115, 157, 195, 196

Catholic Emancipation, 186, 233-46
Cavendish, Lord George, Controller of the Household, 23, 31
Cavendish, Lord John (1732-1796), 152, 159, 172. See also Devonshire, Duke of
Charlotte Augusta, Princess (1796-1817), daughter of George IV, 254, 255, 256
Charlotte Sophia, of Mecklenburg Strelitz (1744-1818), wife of George III, 80, 186, 200, 202, 251, 264
Chatham, Lady Hester (1721-1803), wife of 1st Earl of, 56
Chatham, John Pitt, 2nd Earl of (1756-1835), 201 and n., 221n.
Chatham, William Pitt, 1st Earl of (1708-1778), ix, 5, 19, 20, 25, 27, 30 and n., 31, 35, 36, 37, 38, 39, 41, 42, 45, 47, 48, 49, 50, 54, 56, 58, 65, 79, 108, 118, 119n., 120, 121, 122, 123, 124
  letters to, 31, 39, 40, 43, 47, 48, 56
Chauvelin, Bernard François, Marquis de (1766-1832), 213, 214, 215, 216
Chesterfield, Philip Dormer Stanhope, 4th Earl of (1694-1773), 5, 10, 45
Choiseul, Etienne François de Choiseul-Stainville, Duc de (1719-1785), French Foreign Minister, 22, 55 and n., 70, 86n.
Christian, Captain, later Admiral Sir Hugh Cloberry (1747-1798), 204
City, Remonstrances, etc., 68, 69, 70, 81, 102, 108; and America, 113n.
Clarence, Duke of. See William IV
Clinton, General Sir Henry (1739-1812), 114, 118
Clive, Robert Clive, Baron (1725-1774), 92, 93
Coburg-Saalfeld, Frederick Josias, Prince of Saxe (1737-1815), 217 and n.
Coke of Norfolk. See Leicester
Colpoys, Rear-Admiral Sir John (1742?-1821), 221
Conway, Henry Seymour (1721-1795), 26, 27, 31, 35, 37, 39, 41, 45 and n., 48, 50, 65, 66, 148, 149, 152, 160
  letters to, 32, 33, 41, 42, 44, 46
Copenhagen, battle of, 256
Corn Laws, 42
Cornwallis, Charles Cornwallis, 1st Marquess (1738-1805), General, 117, 137, 218, 238, 239
Cornwallis, Frederick (1713-1783), Archbishop of Canterbury, 139n.
  letter to, 139
Cornwallis, Sir William (1744-1815), brother of Marquess, 258
Corsica, 55
Coventry, George William, 6th Earl of

(1732-1809), Ranger of St. James's Park, 23

Cowper, George Nassau Cowper, 3rd Earl (1738-1789), 95
letter to, 95

Creutz, Gustav Philip, Count (1726-1785), 88

Crosby, Brass (1725-1793), Lord Mayor, 75, 76, 77, 88

Cumberland, H.R.H. Ernest Augustus, Duke of, later King of Hanover (1771-1851), son of George III, 218

Cumberland, H.R.H. Henry Frederick, Duke of (1745-1790), brother to George III, 74, 80

Cumberland, H.R.H. William Augustus, Duke of (1721-1765), uncle to George III, 5, 11, 15, 27, 28*n*., 29, 65
letters to, 28, 30

DARTMOUTH, William Legge, 2nd Earl of (1731-1801), 100, 104, 109, 138
letters to, 107, 109, 110, 140, 153

Deane, Silas (1737-1789), 116, 117

De Grey, William, later 1st Baron Walsingham (1718-1781), Attorney-General, 42, 51, 52

Denmark, 199

Devonshire, William Cavendish, 4th Duke of (1720-1764), 23*n*.

Devonshire, William Cavendish, 5th Duke of (1748-1811), 31

Diede, Baron D. von Fürstenstein, Wilhelm Christian, Danish Minister in England, 87

Dodington, George Bubb, later 1st Baron Melcombe (1691-1762), 4

Duckett, cultivator, 207, 208

Dundas, General Sir David (1735-1820), 268

Dundas, Henry. See Melville

Dunkirk, 217

Dunning, John, later 1st Baron Ashburton (1731-1783), 123, 134

ECONOMIC REFORM, Burke's Bill for, 135

Eden, William, later 1st Baron Auckland (1744-1814), 122, 128, 130 and *n*., 139, 196, 197

Edward, Prince. See Duke of York

Egmont, John Perceval, 2nd Earl of (1711-1770), 27, 29, 37
letters to, 29, 37, 38

Eldon, John Scott, 1st Earl of (1751-1838), 236 and *n*., 252, 253, 254, 259, 262
letters to, 255

Elizabeth (Petrovna), Tsarina (1709-1762), 20*n*.

Elliot, Hugh (1752-1830), 199 and *n*., 206

Ellis, Welbore, later 1st Baron Mendip (1713-1802), 148

Elphinstone, Captain George Keith, later Admiral Viscount Keith (1746-1823), 203

Emperor. See Joseph II and Francis II

Erskine, Thomas Erskine, 1st Baron (1750-1823), 253 and *n*.

FALKLAND ISLANDS, 70, 78

Family Compact, 205

Farmer George, 208

Faucitt (or Fawcett), Colonel Sir William (1728-1804), 111 and *n*., 112, 197 and *n*.

Ferrol, 233

Fifth son. See Cumberland, Dukes of

Fisher, John, later Bishop of Salisbury (1748-1825), tutor to Prince Edward, Duke of Kent, 187

Fitzherbert, Alleyne, later 1st Baron St. Helen's (1753-1839), 174

Fitzherbert, William (d. 1772), Lord of the Board of Trade, 26 and *n*.

Fitzherbert, Mary Ann (Maria), Mrs. (1756-1837), 194, 251, 252, 254

Fitzpatrick, Lieut.-Col. Richard (1747-1813), 158

Fitzwilliam, William Wentworth Fitzwilliam, 2nd Earl (1748-1833), 234, 235, 238, 241

Fox, Charles James (1749-1806), 78, 80, 81, 82, 102, 108, 116, 148, 152, 157, 158, 159, 160, 163, 172, 176, 179, 180, 181, 182, 184, 191, 192, 205, 212, 214, 226, 231, 246, 251, 259, 260, 261, 267
letters to, 157, 174, 175

Fox, Henry, 1st Baron Holland (1705-1774), 5, 9, 11 and *n*., 23, 24, 25

France, 22, 85 *seq.*, 119, 132, 137, 158, 161, 176, 196, 198, 205, Chap. VII *ubique*, 253, 257, 258, 264

Francès, Mons. de, French Chargé d'Affaires in London, 72 and *n*., 73

Francis II, last Emperor (1768-1835), 221, 263

Francis, Sir Philip (1740-1818), 141. See also possibly ' Junius '

Franklin, Benjamin (1706-1790), 116, 117, 130 and *n*.

Frazer, Mr., 180

Frederick William II, King of Prussia (1744-1797), 196, 197, 224

Frederick William III, King of Prussia (1770-1840), 258

Freytag, Major-General von, 60

GAGE, LIEUT.-GEN. THOMAS (1721-1787), 99, 100, 106, 109, 114, 116

General Warrants, 25, 26

George II, King (1683-1760), 3, 5, 7, 9, 10, 13*n.*, 15, 16, 65, 147, 203, 253
letters to, 3, 8, 9, 14

Germain, Lord George, later 1st Baron Sackville (1716-1785), 115, 120, 148

Germany (German Empire), 195, 205, 221, 222, 223, 263

Gibraltar, 137, 161, 162

Gloucester, H.R.H. William Henry, Duke of (1743-1805), brother to George III, 80

Goodrich, Sir John (1708-1789), 87 and *n.*

Gordon, Lord George (1751-1793), 143

Gordon riots, 143

Gower, Granville Leveson-Gower, 2nd Earl, later 1st Marquess of Stafford (1721-1803), xii, 43, 44 and *n.*, 50, 83, 84, 122, 132, 150, 164, 165, 169, 181, 212, 215

Grafton, Augustus Henry Fitzroy, 3rd Duke of (1735-1811), xi, 30, 31, 33, 34, 35, 36, 37, 38, 39, 41, 47, 48, 49 and *n.*, 50, 56, 58, 65, 79, 124, 127, 132, 152, 160
letters to, 45, 46, 54, 55, 60

Granby, John Manners, Marquess of (1721-1770), 28*n.*

Grantham, Thomas Robinson, 2nd Baron (1738-1786), 159
letters to, 162, 165

Granville, John Carteret, Earl (1690-1763), 65

Grasse, François Joseph Paul, Marquis de Grassetilly, Comte de (1722-1788), French Admiral, 157

Grattan, Henry (1746-1820), 141, 157

Grenville, George (1712-1770), xi, 22, 23, 25, 27, 29, 30*n.*, 44, 45, 47, 56, 65, 78
letter to, 26

Grenville, William Wyndham Grenville, 1st Baron (1759-1834), 173 and *n.*, 198 and *n.*, 213, 216, 241, 244, 245, 259, 260, 261, 266, 267, 268, 269
letters to, 205, 211, 212, 214, 215, 216, 222, 223, 224, 225, 232, 266, 267

Grey, Charles Grey, 2nd Earl (1764-1845), 226 and *n.*, 263, 269

Grimaldi, Dominic Geronimo, Marquis de Grimaldo (1720-1786), 72 and *n.*

Grosvenor, Richard, 1st Earl (1731-1802), 74

Grosvenor, Countess of (d. 1820), 74

Gunning, Robert (1731-1816), minister at St. Petersburg, 87

Gustavus III, King of Sweden (1746-1792), 85, 198, 199

Halifax, George Montagu Dunk, 1st Earl of (1716-1771), 28*n.*
letter to, 28

Hanover, 5, 59, 60, 188, 220, 221, 223

Harcourt, Simon Harcourt, 1st Earl (1714-1806), 141, 202

Hardwicke, Philip Yorke, 1st Earl of (1690-1764), xi, 5, 65

Hardwicke, Philip Yorke, 3rd Earl of (1757-1834), 257
letter to, 257

Harley, Thomas (1730-1804), Lord Mayor, 142 and *n.*

Harris, James. *See* Malmesbury

Harrowby, Dudley Ryder, 2nd Baron, later 1st Earl of (1762-1847), 263*n.*
letter to, 263

Hastings, Warren (1732-1818), 141, 175, 193, 207

Hawkesbury. *See* 2nd Earl of Liverpool

Heyne, Professor at Göttingen, 188

Hicks, Augusta, laundress, 95

Hobart, Robert, Lord, later 4th Earl of Buckinghamshire (1760-1816), Secretary for War, 262

Holland, 137, 196, 197, 198, 216, 217, 219, 233, 257

Horne. *See* Tooke

Howe, Richard Howe, Earl (1726-1799), Admiral, 116, 117, 120, 128, 181, 230

Howe, William, afterwards 5th Viscount (1729-1814), General, 114, 116, 117, 118, 120

Howe, Lady Mary, dau. of Earl Howe, 246

Howe, Mrs. (courtesy title), sister to Earl Howe, 246

Howe, Countess, wife of Earl Howe, 246

Howe, Sophia Charlotte, Baroness (1762-1835), dau. and heiress of Earl Howe, to whom the Barony passed, 246

Hume, David (1711-1776), 32 and *n.*

Hurd, Richard (1720-1808), Bishop, finally of Worcester, 186, 188
letters to, 186, 187, 188, 264

Hutchinson, Thomas (1711-1780), Governor of Massachusetts, 104, 110

Hynson, American agent, 117

India, 44, 45, 73, 91, 99, 141, 161, 193
East India Bills, 93, 179, 182, 192
Madras Council, 142-3
Wargaum, 141

Ireland, 91, 92, 115, 141, 193, 257, 258
Rebellion of 1798, 238
Union with, 233 *seq.*

Irwin, General Sir John (1728-1788), 27

INDEX

JENKINSON. *See* Liverpool
John the Painter, 116
Jordan, Dorothea, Mrs. (1762-1816), actress, 205
'Junius', 50, 58, 65, 79. *See also* Francis, Sir Philip

KEMPENFELDT, RICHARD (1718-1782), Admiral, 148
Kenyon, Lloyd Kenyon, 1st Baron (1732-1802), 236
letter to, 236
Keppel, Augustus Keppel, 1st Viscount (1725-1786), 126, 128, 157, 161, 163, 172

LAMBETH PALACE, routs at, 139
Leeds, Duke of. *See* Carmarthen
Legge, Henry (1765-1844), 140. *See also* Dartmouth and Lewisham
Legrand, Edward, 75 and *n.*
Leicester, Thomas William Coke, 1st Earl of (1729-1808), 168, 182
Leopold I, King of the Belgians (1790-1865), 256
Lewisham, George Legge, Viscount, later 3rd Earl of Dartmouth (1755-1810), 138
Liston, Sir Robert (1742-1836), 258
Liverpool, Charles Jenkinson, 1st Earl of (1729-1808), 76, 128, 151, 160
letters to, 133, 150, 151
Liverpool, Robert Banks Jenkinson, Lord Hawkesbury, and later 2nd Earl of Liverpool (1770-1828), afterwards Prime Minister, 254*n.*, 265
letters to, 251, 254, 256, 258, 262, 271
Lodge, Sir Richard, xiii
Loughborough, Alexander Wedderburn, 1st Baron; later 1st Earl of Rosslyn (1733-1805), 78, 94, 121, 123, 129, 130, 225, 241
Louis XV of France (1710-1774), 86
Louis XVI of France (1754-1793), 104*n.*, 211, 212, 215
letter to, 213
Louis, Prince of Brunswick-Wolfenbüttel (1718-1788), 60
Luttrell, Henry Lawes, Colonel, later 2nd Earl of Carhampton (1743-1821), 56, 57, 80

MACKENZIE, JAMES STUART (d. 1799), brother to Lord Bute, 27, 31
Maclean, Lieut.-Col. Allan (1725-1784), 114
Malden, George Capel, Viscount, later 5th Earl of Essex (1757-1839), 141
Malmesbury, James Harris, 1st Earl of (1746-1820), 70, 72, 73, 157 and *n.*, 196, 197, 224, 225
Mann, Sir Horace (1701-1786), 55 and *n.*
Mansfield, William Murray, 1st Earl of (1705-1793), 70, 71, 76, 143
Marie Antoinette, Queen of France (1755-1793), 211, 215
Marriage Act, Royal, 80, 81
Masserano, Ferrero de Fiesque, D. Felipe-Victorio-Amadeo, Prince de, Spanish Ambassador, 71
Melville, Henry Dundas, 1st Viscount (1742-1811), 148, 212*n.*, 233, 241, 243, 244, 258*n.*, 260, 265
letters to, 212, 213, 217, 220, 221, 222, 229, 232, 241, 258
Meredith, Sir William, Bt. (1724?-1790), 130
Ministry of All the Talents, 246
Minorca, 137, 148
Mirabeau, Honoré Gabriel Riqueti, Comte de (1749-1791), 199*n.*, 206
Moira, Francis Rawdon Hastings, 2nd Earl, later 1st Marquess Hastings (1754-1826), 252
Montagu, George Brudenell, 4th Earl of Cadogan, 1st Duke of (1712-1790), 153
letter to, 153
Montmorin St. Hérem, Armand Marc, Comte de (1745-1792), French Foreign Minister, 196, 197
Moore, General Sir John (1761-1809), 270 and *n.*
Mortanges, M. de, 89
Münchausen, Baron von, Hanoverian Resident in London, later Minister in Hanover, 4*n.*, 59
letters to, 4, 59
Murray, Lady Augusta, wife of Prince Augustus, 252
Murray, Sir James Pulteney, 7th Bt. (c. 1751-1811), Adjutant Gen. of the forces on the Continent, 217
Music, George III and, 206, 207
Mutinies, Naval, at Spithead and the Nore, 227, 229, 230

NAMIER, PROFESSOR L. B., xiii, 14, 19*n.*, 65
Nelson, Horatio Nelson, Viscount (1758-1805), 256, 266
Nepean, Evan (1751-1822), Secretary to the Admiralty, 180
Newcastle, Thomas Pelham Holles, Duke of (1693-1768), xi, 5, 9, 20, 21, 23, 30, 31, 35, 36, 65, 116
Newfoundland fisheries, 32, 161
Nootka Sound, 205

North, Frederick Lord, later 2nd Earl of Guilford (1732-1792), 50, 57, 58, 59, 65, 66, 75, 76, 83, 84, 102, 116, 117, 118, 119, 120, 122, 123, 124, 125, 126, 128, 129, 130, 132, 133, 135, 136, 137, 147, 149, 150, 151, 153, 156, 160, 163, 164, 168, 172, 173, 259, 266
letters to, 51, 57, 58, 66, 67, 68, 69, 70, 71, 73, 75, 76, 77, 78, 79, 80, 81, 82, 83, 85, 88, 89, 91, 92, 93, 94, 99, 100, 101, 102, 103, 104, 105, 106, 108, 109, 110, 111, 112, 113, 114, 115, 117, 118, 119, 121, 123, 124, 125, 126, 127, 128, 130, 132, 135, 137, 139, 140, 141, 143, 147, 148, 149, 150, 151, 152, 156, 160, 165, 166, 175, 176, 178, 180
Northington, Robert Henley, 1st Earl of (1708-1772), Lord Chancellor, 33n., 39, 40, 41, 42, 48, 50
letters to, 33, 35, 37
Northumberland, Hugh Smithson (Percy), 1st Duke of (1714-1786), Master of the Horse, 123
Nuthall, Thomas (d. 1775), Solicitor to the Treasury, confidential friend of Pitt, Earl of Chatham, 50

Oakes, Lieut.-Gen. Sir Hildebrand, Bt. (1754-1822), 271
Octavius, Prince (1779-1783), 187
Oliver, Richard (1734?-1784), Alderman, 75, 76, 78
Orange, William V, Prince of (1748-1806), 60, 61, 196, 258
Orange, Frederica Sophia, Princess of (b. 1751), 196
letter to, 257

Palliser, Captain, later Vice-Admiral Sir Hugh (1723-1796), 32, 128
Paoli, Pasquali (1725-1807), Corsican hero, 55
Paris, Peace of, 23
Parker, Richard (1767-1797), Naval mutineer, 231
Parliament and Press, 75-8
Parliamentary reform, 192, 226 and n., 231
Pelham, Thomas, later 2nd Earl of Chichester (1756-1826), Irish Chief Secretary, 238, 239, 240
Peninsular War, 270
Perceval, Spencer (1762-1812), Prime Minister, 268, 269, 270n.
Peter III, Tsar (1728-1762), 20n.
Pigot, George, Baron (1719-1777), 142, 143
Pitt, Thomas. See Camelford
Pitt, William, the elder. See Chatham

Pitt, William, the younger (1759-1806), xii, 29, 147, 152, 157, 158, 159, 160, 163, 164, 167, 168, 169, 180, 181, 182, 183, 184,. 186, 191, 192, 194, 195, 196, 198, 200, 201, 205, 212, 213, 214, 218, 219, 222, 224, 225, 226, 233, 241, 242, 243, 244, 246, 259, 261, 263, 266
letters to, 167, 168, 169, 180, 181, 183, 184, 185, 191, 192, 193, 194, 195, 196, 198, 200, 201, 202, 204, 206, 216, 218, 219, 220, 225, 226, 227, 228, 229, 231, 234, 238, 239, 240, 242, 244, 252, 259, 261, 265, 266
Pole, Captain, R.N., later Admiral Sir Charles Morice (1757-1830), Groom of the Bedchamber to Prince William, 204
Portland, William Henry Cavendish-Bentinck, 3rd Duke of (1738-1809), 159, 164, 165, 166, 168, 172, 178, 179, 180, 182, 184, 225, 234, 239, 268, 269
letters to, 166, 177, 179
Pownall, Thomas (1722-1805), Governor of Massachusetts, 66, 110
Powys, M.P., 182, 184
Priestley, Joseph (1733-1804), 139 and n., 140, 212
Prussia, 32, 33, 196, 197, 198, 219, 220, 221, 223, 224, 258, 263
Prussia, Kings of. See Frederick William II and III

Queen Caroline, Queen Charlotte, etc. See under names
Quiberon Bay, 220

Regency, 27, 200, 251, 272
Richmond, Charles, 3rd Duke of Richmond and Lennox (1735-1806), Master Gen. of the Ordnance, 163, 180, 181
Robinson, John (1727-1802), 116, 117, 118, 126, 129, 130, 132, 133, 135, 141, 151
letters to, 116, 117, 125, 126, 129, 130, 142
Robinson, Mary, Mrs. ' Perdita ' (1758-1800), actress, 140, 176
Robinson, Ralph, pseudonym for George III, as farmer, 208
Rochford, William Henry Zuylesten, 4th Earl of (1717-1781), 54, 72n., 73, 79, 82, 83, 84, 88
letters to, 72, 73, 74
Rockingham, Charles Watson Wentworth, 2nd Marquess of (1730-1782), xi, 23, 30, 31, 33, 34, 35, 36, 37, 38n., 39, 58, 65, 79, 120, 136, 151, 152, 155, 157, 159
letters to, 36, 37, 38, 155

Rodney, George Brydges Rodney, 1st Baron (1718-1792), 137, 157, 158
Römer, Mr., German agent, 112
Roveray, du, M., 214
Rumbold, Sir Thomas (1736-1791), 143
Russia, 20 and n., 87, 88, 115, 157, 195, 196
Russia, Tsars of. See Peter and Catherine
Rutland, John Manners, 3rd Duke of (1696-1779), Master of the Horse, 23

SACKVILLE. See Germain
Sailors' strike, 52
Saints, battle of the, 157, 158
Sandwich, John Montagu, 4th Earl of (1718-1792), xii, 78, 79, 89, 122, 128
Savile, Sir George, Bt. (1726-1784), 159
Saxony, Frederick Augustus, Elector, later King of (1750-1827), 195
Scheither, Lieut.-Col. George Heinrich Albrecht, later General (1731-1789), 112
Scott, Sir John. See Eldon
Sedition Bill, 226
Shelburne, William Petty Fitzmaurice, Earl of, later 1st Marquess Lansdowne (1737-1805), 48 and n., 49 and n., 54, 56, 108, 121, 123, 140, 150, 151, 152, 155, 156, 157, 158, 159, 160, 161, 163, 164
letters to, 152, 155, 156, 158, 159, 161, 163
Sheridan, Richard Brinsley Butler (1751-1816), 157, 159, 214
Silk-weavers, 27, 28, 93
Sinking fund, 191
Smith, Mary, laundress, 95
Southampton, Charles Fitzroy, 1st Baron (1737-1797), Lieut.-Gen., 194 and n., 195
Spain, 20, 70 seq., 88, 132, 205
Spencer, George John Spencer, 2nd Earl (1758-1834), 221n., 229, 241, 244, 245n.
letters to, 221, 230, 231, 233, 245
Spörcken, Field-Marshal August Friederich, Baron von (1698-1776), 112
letter to, 59
Stanislas Augustus Poniatowsky, King of Poland (1732-1798), 90
letter to, 91
Stone, Andrew (1703-1773), Secretary to the Duke of Newcastle, 116
Stormont, David Murray, 7th Viscount, later 2nd Earl of Mansfield (1727-1796), 86 and n., 87, 88, 89, 132, 172, 178
Stratton, 142
Stroud, collieries at, 206

Stuart, Lieut.-Gen. Sir Charles (1753-1801), son of the Earl of Bute, 247n.
Stuart, William (1755-1822), Bishop of St. David's, later Archbishop of Armagh, son of the Earl of Bute, 247n.
letter to, 247
Stuart. See also Bute
Suffolk, Henry Howard, 12th Earl of, xii, 78, 79, 88
letters to, 83, 87, 94, 121, 122, 126
Sussex, Ernest Augustus, Duke of (1773-1843), son of George III, 252, 253
Sweden, 84 seq., 198, 199, 200
Sweden, Kings of. See Augustus Frederick and Gustavus
Sydney, Thomas Townshend, 1st Viscount (1733-1800), 159, 195
letters to, 162, 164, 181

TALLEYRAND-PÉRIGORD, CHARLES MAURICE DE, Bishop of Autun, Prince of Benevento (1754-1838), 214, 258
Temple, George Nugent-Temple Grenville, 2nd Earl, later 1st Marquis of Buckingham (1753-1813), 159, 173, 179, 180, 201
letter to, 173
Temple, Richard Grenville-Temple, 1st Earl (1711-1779), xi, 5, 27, 29, 30n., 31, 35, 40
Test Act, 81. See also Catholic Emancipation
Texel, the, 233
Thurlow, Edward Thurlow, 1st Baron (1731-1806), 78, 94, 104, 121, 123, 129, 133, 150, 151, 152, 153, 155, 156, 157, 164, 167, 168, 181, 194, 195, 200, 225, 253
letters to, 133, 164, 165, 167, 169
Tooke, John Horne (1736-1812), 102, 137, 138
Toulon, 218
Townshend, Charles (1725-1767), Chancellor of the Exchequer, 45 and n., 46, 47, 48, 49, 50, 66, 111
Townshend, George Townshend, 4th Viscount, later 1st Marquess (1724-1807), Viceroy of Ireland, 92
Townshend, Thomas, senior (1701-1780), Teller of the Exchequer, 35, 36
Townshend, Thomas, junior. See Sydney
Triple Alliance, 198

UNIVERSITY monopoly of almanacs, 129
University of Göttingen, 188

VENDÉENS, 220

Vergennes, Charles Gravier, Comte de (1717-1787), French Secretary of State for Foreign Affairs, 196

Viry, Count de, Sardinian envoy in London, 22

WALCHEREN expedition, 269

Waldegrave, James, 2nd Earl (1715-1763), 4, 6, 8

Waldegrave, Maria, Countess of (d. 1807), 80

Wales, Augusta of Saxe-Gotha, Princess of (1719-1772), mother of George III, 4, 5, 9, 27, 68, 79

Wales, Frederick Louis, Prince of (1707-1751), father of George III, 3, 4

Wales, George Augustus Frederick, Prince of, later Prince Regent and George IV (1762-1830), 27, 154, 171, 176, 177, 178, 179, 194, 198, 200, 251, 252, 253, 254, 255, 256, 272
letter to, 254

Walpole, Sir Edward (d. 1784), brother of Sir Robert, 1st Earl of Orford, 80

Walpole, Horace, later 4th Earl of Orford (1717-1797), 5, 154

Ward, John, 51

Waterloo, 272

Wedderburn. See Loughborough

Wellesley, Richard Colley Wesley, 1st Marquess (1760-1842), 270 and n.

Wellington, Arthur Wellesley, 1st Duke of (1769-1852), 169, 270, 271

West Indies, 148

Westmorland, John Fane, 10th Earl of (1759-1841), 241

Weymouth, Thomas Thynne, 3rd Viscount (1734-1796), 50, 71, 72, 78, 115, 118, 121, 122, 126, 132, 150, 169
letters to, 51, 52, 53, 133, 168

Whitbread, Samuel (1758-1815), 214, 231

Wilberforce, William (1759-1833), 215, 226

Wilkes, John (1727-1797), 23, 25, 50, 51, 52, 53, 58, 66, 67, 70, 75, 76, 77, 81, 105, 121

William, Prince, Duke of Clarence, later William IV (1765-1837), 147, 201, 202, 204, 205
letters to, 203, 204

Windham, William (1750-1810), 241, 243, 244

Woodford, Sir Robert, 211

Woronzow, Count, Russian Ambassador, 195

YARMOUTH, Amalie Sophie Marianne Walmoden, Countess of (1704-1765), 13n.

Yelverton. See Avonmore

York, H.R.H. Edward Augustus, Duke of (1739-1767), brother to George III, 4, 6, 34
letter to, 34

York, H.R.H. Frederick Augustus, Duke of (1763-1827), son of George III, 198, 200, 202, 204, 216, 217, 218, 219, 232, 233 and n., 254

Yorke, Charles (1722-1770), Solicitor and Attorney-General, xi, 58

Yorke, Sir Joseph, later 1st Baron Dover (1724-1792), letters to, 60, 61

Yorke. See also under Hardwicke

Young, Arthur (1741-1820), traveller and agriculturist, letter to, 207